Advance Praise for

JFK

THE LAST SPEECH

"*JFK: The Last Speech* is a project that could not have come to a boil at a more appropriate time in our nation's history nor been presented in so compelling a way. At its heart it is a call to arms in the battle to preserve and enhance civic life, a challenge the project meets in film, on its website and—most ambitiously—as a book. Essayists from academia, journalism, the arts, and from a distinguished array of the country's deepest thinkers offer thoughts provoked by John F. Kennedy's last speech. The speech reminds us what an inspiration a president can be and each of these essays proves it. It is a volume to be read, reread, and then read yet again."

DOUG CLIFTON, *Pulitzer Prize-winning journalist, former executive editor of the* Miami Herald, *and editor of the* Cleveland Plain Dealer

---

"Over a half a century later, John F. Kennedy's October 1963 visit to Amherst College still resonates. The many legacies of Kennedy's soaring speech and brief appearance are captured wonderfully in these fascinating pages."

ELLEN FITZPATRICK, *Historian specializing in modern American political and intellectual history; author of nine books, including* Letters to Jackie *and* The Highest Glass Ceiling

---

"When President Kennedy headed to Amherst College for a dedication ceremony, he might have expected to be a big voice in national affairs for decades to come. Instead, we got an unexpected valedictory, a statement of values at the end of a man's life. In this book you'll travel to a small town in Massachusetts in 1963 and see how this speech from JFK echoed through the lives of the young men there to hear it. Sometimes small events end up being big ones."

RAY SUAREZ, *Journalist, author, visiting professor at Amherst College*

"The arrival of this documentary film, book, and website could not be more timely. Our deeply divided nation needs more humanistic reflection, not less; more art, not less; more attempts to understand ourselves and each other, as we try to reach some agreement about what truly matters. That is what is championed in this outstanding collection of essays."

DAVID TEBALDI, *Ph.D., executive director of Mass Humanities since 1985; editor of* Reflecting on Values, The Unity and Diversity of the Humanities; *2017 recipient of the Commonwealth Award for Leadership in improving civic life in Massachusetts*

"A month before he died, President Kennedy gave a stirring speech to the students at Amherst College as he dedicated a library named for Robert Frost. JFK called that generation to lives of civic action that would be guided by the insights of liberal arts education and would challenge entrenched power appropriately. *JFK: The Last Speech* reissues his challenge to a nation that sorely needs it. The book is a rich, diverse, and moving collection of original materials from the dedication (and then memorial) events of the fall of 1963 at Amherst, stories of how the speech galvanized students in the audience to lead lives of civic commitment, and reflections on these themes by a set of distinguished commentators. The book is a civics course in a nutshell."

HAROLD BRUFF, *J.D., former dean of the University of Colorado Law School; former senior attorney and advisor for the Office of Legal Counsel, U.S. Dept. of Justice; author of* Untrodden Ground: How Presidents Interpret the Constitution

---

"In a time when the value of contributing to the common good must return to the political foreground, this book and the man it details serve as reminders of the power of service. JFK, the builder of the Peace Corps and the inspiration of a generation, is set as a model and challenger for current and future generations, posing the timeless and urgent question: 'for what do we use our powers, or does power use us?'"

ROSANNE HAGGERTY, *Founder and CEO of Community Solutions; a leader in solving problems that create and sustain homelessness; MacArthur Foundation Fellow; Ashoka Senior Fellow; recipient of Jane Jacobs Medal for New Ideas and Activism*

"Required reading for anyone who wants to learn about the power of words in providing political and civic leadership. President Kennedy mastered the art of language in conveying a timeless message about our nation and its highest principles. Like Lincoln and Franklin Roosevelt, he used language to reinforce our loftiest ideals."

KENNETH FEINBERG, *Former administrator of the 9/11 Victims Compensation Fund; former chairman of the board of directors for the John F. Kennedy Library Foundation; author of* What Is Life Worth? *and* Who Gets What: Fair Compensation after Tragedy and Financial Upheaval

offers an opportunit'
I might add, by pol
was one of the uno
arved his poetry
ngland Indian summe
mpshire hills.   He w
erican.   As we refle
ect on the abiding value
A nation reveals itsel
en it honors.   "A soci
e of heroes.   In A
f large and drama
ds, magnates, invent
ble enterprise in p
honor a man whose c
not to our ideology
r self-comprehension.
o the deepest source

JFK
THE LAST SPEECH

Edited by Neil Bicknell, Roger Mills, and Jan Worth-Nelson

www.mascotbooks.com

JFK: The Last Speech

For more information, please contact:
Mascot Books
620 Herndon Parkway #320
Herndon, VA 20170
info@mascotbooks.com

Library of Congress Control Number: 2018906179

CPSIA Code: PBANG0718A
ISBN-13: 978-1-64307-074-2

Printed in the United States

CONTENTS

CHAPTER 4
Kennedy on Campus   **67**

JFK'S HANDWRITTEN EDITS
to the Speech Drafted by Arthur Schlesinger, Jr.   **91**

CHAPTER 5
Annotated Timeline—Rip Sparks, '64   **97**

PART 2
Doing the Work He Couldn't Complete   **113**

CHAPTER 6
The Life of an Activist—Ted Nelson, '64   **115**

A golden age of poetry and power
Of which this noonday's the beginning hour.
—Robert Frost, "Dedication"

The people of this countryside, may forget in ordinary human course what anyone says on this occasion, but they will remember for many, many years that a young and gallant president of the United States, with the weight of history heavy upon his shoulders, somehow found time to come to our small corner of the world to talk of books and men and learning.
—Archibald MacLeish
"FROST AND STONE" address at the
Robert Frost Library Convocation

An essential quality of the learned then is generosity of the soul, for without it, knowledge becomes a tool for control and even oppression.
—Farzam Arbab, BA (physics) magna cum laude, *Amherst, 1964; PhD (elementary particle physics) University of California, Berkeley, 1968: DSc (hon), Amherst, 1989. "Knowledge and Civilization"*

NOTE FROM CULLEN MURPHY
Chair of the Board of Trustees of Amherst College

———

BY THE TIME I was an undergraduate, John F. Kennedy's visit to the campus was a decade in the past. And that decade had seemed like a century. But the visit itself remained fresh in many minds. And the message can never be dimmed by age. Has any president spoken more eloquently about the critical role of literature and the arts in the life of our republic? Or about the critical responsibilities that go with privilege? I use the word "critical" in all senses of that term. To deliver this message at Amherst was especially appropriate—a college with a long tradition of service, one that would be revitalized by many of the students who heard Kennedy speak. To hear Kennedy's words—and to see the copy of the speech he revised by hand, which shows him to have been a superb literary craftsman—is to connect with a moment that transcends the conventional unfurling of time. Amherst College is proud to congratulate all who played a part in creating *JFK: The Last Speech*.

FOREWORD
Poetry and Politics

Biddy Martin, President of Amherst College

Our national strength matters, but the spirit which informs and controls our strength matters just as much.
—John Fitzgerald Kennedy

ON OCTOBER 26, 1963, just a few weeks before he was assassinated, President Kennedy traveled to Amherst College to speak at the groundbreaking of Robert Frost Library and to honor the poet Robert Frost, who taught for years at Amherst and whom Kennedy admired. In his speech, Kennedy paid tribute to Frost's particular achievement, but also hailed the critical role that artists play in society, reminding his audience that "if sometimes our great artists have been the most critical of our society, it is because their sensitivity and their concern for justice, which must motivate any true artist, makes them aware that our Nation falls short of its highest potential."

Kennedy emphasized the importance of art, artists, and poetry in helping a nation define its values, expose its failings, and hold its leaders accountable. His voice was clear and emphatic, and his rhetorical gifts fully evident. Looking at the original typescript of his address, it is bracing to see the scrawl of his pen clearing away swaths of words and crossing through high-flown language, honing the power and impact of his statement to match the significance of his thoughts. The following frequently cited lines, with their repetition, rhythm, and economy, instantiate what they assert: the irreplaceable role of poetic language in leading us to important truths:

> When power leads man toward arrogance, poetry reminds him of his limitations. When power narrows the area of man's concerns, poetry reminds him of the richness and diversity of his existence. When power corrupts, poetry cleanses, for art establishes the basic human truth which must serve as the touchstone of our judgment.

Basic human truth as the touchstone of judgment; art as the source of human truth. Good art, as Kennedy points out, does not aim to indoctrinate, but to question, enlarge our sense of the possible, and remind us of our limits. Art and poetry are humbling in their power to make us bigger people.

In October 2017, Amherst celebrated Kennedy's centennial birthday with a series of talks by students, faculty members, and alumni who shared their thoughts about his 1963 speech at the College. The day was capped by a speech that Congressman Joseph Kennedy III gave at the spot where JFK had stood over fifty years earlier. It was a speech that called us to our capacity for empathy, imagination, and civic responsibility.

I was asked to open the symposium with reflections of my own, and I responded by talking about Kennedy's impact on the child I was in 1960 when he was elected president and in 1963 when he was assassinated. The poetry and the politics in his speeches were a source of wonder for me as a child. I grew up in a part of the world, then still a rural part of Virginia, some twelve miles outside of the Lynchburg city limits. In my family the designation "Kennedy-lover" came to serve as a substitute for a vile and frequently-heard slur hurled at white people who supported civil rights or merely failed actively to oppose those rights. Kennedy-lovers were those who did not follow the behavioral, attitudinal, or emotional rules that governed relations between the races in the Jim Crow South. I became known as a Kennedy-lover. I did, in fact, revere John Fitzgerald Kennedy, and it was related, in part, to race and racism that was and is so destructive of "human truths." I loved to say his name in my head over and over. I idolized him in the way that only a child can idolize a person so remote from her own experience, so virtual in his presence. His words offered hope of something other than the fear and anger I experienced in the people around me. His intelligence, education, eloquence, and wit were sources of pleasure; the secrecy I was forced to keep about their appeal surely intensified their allure. Kennedy's speeches and debate performances provided a counterpoint to the disdain for education I experienced around me.

I was in the fourth grade when Kennedy ran for president, and I have memories of watching the Democratic Convention on TV with my father. It was the summer of 1960. At the time, my father still had a job as a distributor of FFV—Famous Foods of Virginia—cookies. On special occasions he would allow us to get in the red and white van and choose the box of cookies we wanted. For some reason I remember eating vanilla sandwich cookies during the coverage of the convention. My father was furious about the outcome. He must have already been wavering in his identity as a Democrat, but Lyndon Johnson's defeat to a "damned Yankee" shook him, not only because of that Yankee's elite education, powerful family, Northern roots, and politics, but also because of his Catholicism. It is not easy to explain why, but I can easily recall the confusion I felt then about the targets of my family's prejudice and rage. I could not make sense of them and seemed to the family to be a traitor as a result.

When Mrs. Rainey required her fourth-grade class to write a paper about the differences between the Republican and Democratic parties during the fall of 1960, I sought my father's help and remember that he said, "the Democratic Party cares about the little people like us, and the Republican Party is for the rich and powerful." Those little people "like us" clearly included only white people. It must have been in the months that followed that my father, who voted for Nixon, officially made the shift that so many white Southerners made at that time—from the Democratic to the Republican Party.

I watched Kennedy's inauguration in awe. I memorized the entire speech, reciting it to myself at night alone in my room. I remember being frustrated that I couldn't replicate the particular way Kennedy placed his emphasis on the word "not" in those famous lines that begin, "ask not." I collected everything I could find about him; every magazine and newspaper article, every photograph, and I filled more than one cardboard box with print coverage of his presidency and assassination, which later my father burned along with family photographs.

When, in 1963, Kennedy federalized the Alabama National Guard to force the desegregation of the University of Alabama, he committed what many white Southerners considered an unforgiveable outrage. I was only dimly aware of what was occurring in the world beyond the narrow confines of family and region. The news reached me through my father's outbursts and palpable rage.

Kennedy's use of language, his appeal to fundamental democratic ideals, his emphasis on the responsibility that comes with freedom, and his opposition to hate were, for me, a kind of poetry that countered hatred's destruction of language and thought. Idealizing Kennedy and, in particular, the Kennedy of his speeches, became a sign and a means of differentiation from my family. For whatever series of reasons, his use of language helped enlarge my sense of the possible and fed my love of school, despite the mockery in our home of the educated and educators at higher levels, those "eggheads" who, in my father's eyes, were invariably "sissy men" and "horsey women."

Like millions of other people who were alive when Kennedy was assassinated, I remember the moment vividly. I remember exactly where I was. Now in the seventh grade, I was in the girl's bathroom of Leesville Road Elementary School, washing my hands, when one of my classmates ran into the bathroom and screamed, "The president was shot!" I have no memory of how we got home from school, only that we went home early and sat in front of a black-and-white TV, glued to the screen that my father feared because of the radiation he believed it emitted. I remember hearing Walter Cronkite say that President Kennedy was dead, remember watching Jack Ruby kill Lee Harvey Oswald on live TV, sitting spellbound watching the rituals that followed orchestrated by Jacqueline Kennedy. I can also easily call up the sense of shock, dread, and disbelief I felt as the world seemed to spin out of control. Convinced, as I was early on, that the assassination must have been a plot that involved more than one shooter, I recall the seemingly endless number of times I watched the footage that was used to prove and disprove the finding that Oswald had acted alone.

It was my first experience of grief over a death—a grief shared by millions of people across the country and the world. Because of my age, where I grew up, and the isolation I felt, this was also the personal loss of a figure in whom I had invested my capacity for idealism, my fantasy of other ways of thinking, and my attraction to "grace and beauty."

Poetry and its relationship to power, the theme of Kennedy's speech in Amherst, is a theme to which I return over and over. One writer to whom I often turn is the French Algerian Jewish writer and poet Hélène Cixous, who in 1979 presented a piece (at a conference I attended in New York City celebrating the thirtieth anniversary of the publication of Simone de Beauvoir's *The Second Sex*). In her talk, "Poetry is/and the Political" ("La Poésie e(s)t la politique"), Cixous uses her definition of the poetic to expose and lament how rigidly ideological and divisive feminist politics had become by the end of the seventies. She defines "the poetic" as an approach to people and to things of this world that is characterized by openness and the capacity to "let things in" in their strangeness without trying immediately to grasp them in ready-made categories or on the basis of what we think we already know— and, moreover, to allow their complexity to change the grasp and shape of those ready-made categories themselves. As her title suggests, Cixous sees an intimate connection between poetry and politics: the poetic holds open the space that ideological extremes and power grabs would close. But poetry that is closed to the world, poetry that denies the political can also do damage. For Cixous, a poetic approach holds open a space that is not immediately engulfed by the political but that may help to reshape it productively. At the heart of poetic practice is a use of language that reveals, rather than erasing, the Other.

At Amherst in October 1963, Kennedy praised Robert Frost for proposing poetry as the means to save power from itself. Kennedy promoted the importance of art and poetry as forms of critique. He did this while president. Citing Robert Frost's hired man, he urged us to see that "the nation which disdains the mission of art invites the fate…of having nothing to look backward to with pride and nothing to look forward to with hope." However complex his legacy, his words inspire. They helped give me a way out of the many forms of loyalty white supremacy demanded in the Jim Crow South.

I am pleased and proud to be president of the college where Kennedy gave one of his most powerful and important speeches, a speech now appropriately celebrated in these pages. Here, love of knowledge, poetry, independent thought, and human truth lives on.

INTRODUCTION

Ted Nelson, '64; Roger Mills, '64; and Reunion '64

SOME YEARS AGO, a group of aging men planning their fiftieth college reunion decided to do something more than drink beer and share old stories. They had heard President John F. Kennedy deliver his last public address less than a month before a shot fired in Dallas, now almost fifty-five years ago, suddenly ended his life. He had delivered a direct, personal call to civic engagement, linked to an appeal for the liberal arts and their role in questioning and humanizing the use of power. The president's words, and the events that followed, changed their lives.

The documentary *JFK: The Last Speech* and this supplemental volume emerged from the fiftieth reunion project of the Amherst College Class of 1964. The film and the book describe the background of Kennedy's relationship with Robert Frost, the challenge President Kennedy presented to students at Amherst College, how some of those students responded over the following half-century, and the relevance and haunting irony that JFK's words bring to the problems of now. When civic culture is fractured and the value of the liberal arts is questioned, this message from 1963 has particular resonance.

In 1961, for the first time in America's history, John F. Kennedy invited a poet, Robert Frost, to read a poem at a presidential inauguration. Their relationship continued through most of JFK's term, until a schism in the fall of 1962. Nonetheless, President Kennedy accepted an invitation to speak at a convocation at Amherst College for the groundbreaking of the Robert Frost Library.[1] That speech, little noticed at the time, has since been recognized as Kennedy's finest. We heard that speech firsthand; we wanted a new generation to hear those words. Our classmates' stories show the impact that speech—and Calvin Plimpton's eulogy—had on our lives and demonstrate how to put ideas into action. Finally, and more important, we wanted to show that Kennedy's message is more relevant now than ever before.

The first section of this book introduces contemporary readers to Robert Frost and John F. Kennedy and provides critical source documents: the text of Kennedy's speech, his remarks at the library's groundbreaking, and Amherst president Calvin Plimpton's brief eulogy for the fallen president on November 22, 1963. First-person accounts of the president's visit from a variety of perspectives round out the section, and an annotated timeline adds the context of national and world events at the time.

In the second section, the four individuals featured in the documentary—Ted Nelson, Steve Downs, Gene Palumbo, and George Wanlass—tell their remarkably different stories in greater depth. Nelson, a lifelong activist, describes his experiences with the Peace Corps in rural Turkey; Downs, an attorney, recounts his efforts to bring justice to wrongly accused immigrants; Palumbo, who reports for the *New York Times*, witnesses the ravages of war on life in El Salvador; Wanlass, a rancher, tells of collecting the art of the American West for the University of Utah. Nine additional classmates tell their stories as well, stories that illustrate the lasting impact of Kennedy's speech and Plimpton's eulogy.

---

1   Several authors in this volume reference JFK's travel to Amherst "to dedicate the Robert Frost Library." The occasion was actually the library groundbreaking. The formal dedication occurred two years later on October 24, 1985, but, in the annals of history, JFK's Convocation Address may ultimately be remembered as a dedication of the library to Robert Frost

In the final section, more than a dozen distinguished individuals—historians, writers, artists, political and religious leaders—have contributed their thoughts on the role of education and the liberal arts in our world today. All of the authors have been in the forefront of the effort to clarify our values. Congressman Joseph P. Kennedy III, Robert Redford, and Fareed Zakaria have graciously allowed us to reprint their work. Two noted biographers, Jay Parini and Jon Meacham, have shared their knowledge of Frost and Kennedy with us. Nobel prize-winning economist Joe Stiglitz, '64, offers his thoughts on education. Steven Olikara, president of the Millennial Action Project and Dakota Foster, Marshall Scholar Amherst '18, address issues of leadership in the coming years.

The collection of stories found in these pages, from various perspectives, all recall or revisit a towering speech. Also included is the background of the Frost-Kennedy relationship and the words the audience heard, words that produced over five decades of action and lessons for us today. If these stories—the memories of a presidential speech one fall day, the lives our classmates lived, and the reflections of historians and scholars—stimulate well-informed, civil, serious discussions and renewed civic engagement, then we have done what we set out to do.

On April 9, 1963, President Kennedy issued a presidential proclamation that made Winston Churchill an honorary citizen of the United States. In that proclamation, Kennedy stated that Churchill "...mobilized the English Language and sent it into battle." In the spirit of John F. Kennedy and Winston Churchill, in our own modest efforts to bring light to darkness, we send our words into the breach.

PART 1
Fall 1963 on Campus

[Lighting the Torch]

1

ONE FALL DAY[1]
Frost and Kennedy

Roger Mills, '64

EARLY SATURDAY MORNING, October 26, 1963, a thick ground fog obscured the Connecticut Valley, but directly overhead the sky was clear. By about 9 a.m. the fog burned off.

At 9:20 a.m. that morning, President John F. Kennedy and his party departed the White House for Andrews Air Force base. There, they boarded Air Force One and flew to Westover Air Force base in western Massachusetts; at 11:30 a.m., they transferred to three waiting Marine helicopters. Secretary of the Interior Stewart Udall rode with the president.[2] Minutes later, the trio of helicopters thundered over the still-green practice fields just downhill from the Amherst College gymnasium and touched down.

Kennedy had come to participate in the groundbreaking for the Robert Frost Library at Amherst. His formal speech at the college convocation began just before midday. A few minutes after 1 p.m., he followed with

---

1   Portions of this essay were previously published as "The President and The Poet" in *The Massachusetts Review,* Volume 59, Number 2 (Summer 2018).

2   John F. Kennedy's Appointment Books, October 1963, from the President's Appointment Books collection, https://jfklibrary.libguides.com/ld.php?content_id=26059831.

brief remarks at the groundbreaking ceremony for the library construction site where the gargoyle-studded neo-Gothic Walker Hall had recently been demolished. At 2:05 p.m., he departed.[3]

Three weeks later, he was dead.

Lee Harvey Oswald brought Kennedy's life to an untimely end, fixing the forty-six-year-old president's convocation message in time as firmly as if it had been encased in amber.

———

THE OCCASION THAT DAY, the groundbreaking for the Robert Frost Library at Amherst, had no obvious political significance, yet it was important enough to draw Kennedy away from Washington despite high international tensions and the early stirrings of his reelection campaign.

The president's address received remarkably modest press coverage. The following day, an article in the Sunday *New York Times* emphasized Kennedy's friendship with Frost and described the event as "without any overt political tones."[4] The *Times* article included a few quotes from the convocation speech, and gave a modest nod to Archibald MacLeish, a three-time Pulitzer Prize winner and former librarian of Congress who, along with the president, also spoke and received an honorary doctorate. In contrast, the front page of the newspaper had three above-the-fold Cold War headlines featuring Russia: "Soviet bars race with U.S. to land men on the moon," "Moscow says it may balk at wheat sale conditions," and "Khrushchev asks easing of rancor in China dispute." And, on page E3 a young reporter named David Halberstam had a foreboding feature under the headline "View in Saigon."

Assessed by column inches in the news of that week, the president's speech at a small college in the hills of New England had very little impact.

———

3   JFK's Appointment Books, October 1963.

4   Warren Weaver, Jr., October 27, 1963. "Kennedy, honoring Frost, bids US heed its artists." Page 1, of the Late City Edition, https://timesmachine.nytimes.com/timesmachine/1963/10/27/89562393.html?pageNumber=1.

History judged differently.

Kennedy's speech at Amherst has been described as, "One of the remarkable speeches of his presidency…a recognition of the vital role the artist plays in a free society."[5] Stewart Udall described it as, "the most noble speech of his [Kennedy's] career. It was more than a personal tribute to Frost. He used Frost's inaugural theme as his text and delivered a soaring, powerful paean to poetry and power."[6]

Without a working understanding of who Frost and Kennedy were and what their relationship had included, at worst one is bound to interpret the speech out of context, and, at best, without context. Without further ado, let us look at the Frost and Kennedy relationship. Then, we will briefly meet the audience, the Amherst students, and review the critical points of the speech.

FROST

Robert Frost, like many other successful modern writers, managed to contrive his own public image. In the words of biographer Jay Parini, "He liked to mythologize himself, and had a vested interest in putting forward certain views of himself."[7]

Frost was a San Francisco native, where his father had been a newspaper editor, but he relentlessly promoted himself as a crusty New England farmer whose ambition was "a quiet job in a small college where I would be allowed to teach something a little new…and where I should have some honor for what I suppose myself to have done in poetry."[8]

His thirty-four-year-old father died when Robert was eleven. The newly impoverished Frosts abandoned San Francisco to move in with family in Lawrence, Massachusetts. Later, they went on their own to Salem, New Hamp-

---

5   Bob Seay, "Remembering JFK's Speech at Robert Frost Library Dedication," WGBH News, November 25, 2013, https://news.wgbh.org/post/remembering-jfks-speech-robert-frost-library-dedication.

6   Stewart L. Udall, *Robert Frost's Last Adventure, New York Times Books*, June 11, 1972, https://archive.nytimes.com/www.nytimes.com/books/99/04/25/specials/frost-last.html.

7   Jay Parini, *Robert Frost: A Life* (New York: Henry Holt and Co., 1999), 75.

8   Parini, *Robert Frost: A Life*, 156.

shire. After achieving both academic and athletic success in high school, young Rob (as he was known) began to experience recurrent bouts of depression. He dropped out of Dartmouth, and later out of Harvard as well, and tried to support himself and his family by teaching and journalism. To settle the family, his grandfather purchased a Derry, New Hampshire, farm ("the Magoon place"). There, from the fall of 1900 until September 1909, Frost and his family supported themselves marginally, by haphazard farming and with the income from a small annuity, while Rob worked on his poetry. "Frost was, himself, a very learned man. He just wore his learning very, very lightly. He was trained in Latin. He read *The Aeneid*, Catullus, the great Latin poets in the original, right to the end of his life."[9] When Rob began teaching again to supplement his income, he had more success.

When his grandfather died, the terms of the will permitted Frost to sell the Derry farm in November 1911, which he did. Although he had continued to write while working the farm, Frost's breakthrough as a poet would not come in New England, but during the next two years—September 1912 through February 1915—he spent living and writing in England, funded by the proceeds of the sale.

What did Frost have in mind for his travel abroad? It would not have been like him to lay out a clear statement of purpose. Perhaps he realized that his work was so different technically from the American poetry of the time that he might be accepted more readily outside the country.

Late in 1912, not long after the Frosts arrived in England, the small English publishing house of David Nutt accepted Frost's first collection, *A Boy's Will*. Nutt was "a small but well-established firm" headed by Mrs. M. L. Nutt, widow of the founder's son.[10] Mrs. Nutt may well be one of the least-known and most important figures in American poetry.

As a newly published American poet in England, Frost worked the literary scene to develop contacts with Ezra Pound, William Butler Yeats, T. E. Hulme, and Edward Thomas. Over the following eight months, he com-

---

9   Jay Parini interviewed by Brian Lamb September 12, 1999, CSPAN *Booknotes*, http://booknotes.org/FullPage.aspx?SID=151354-1.

10   Parini, *Robert Frost: A Life*, 122.

pleted "nearly a dozen finished poems…including 'Mending Wall,' 'Home Burial,' 'After Apple-Picking,' and 'Birches'—four of the best-known poems in the whole of American literature"—for his second book, *North of Boston,* also published by Nutt.[11]

As the threat of war in Europe grew, Frost continued to work and to expand his literary contacts. Finally, with increasing concern about German submarine attacks on merchant shipping, the Frosts left England in February 1915.[12] His plan, as he said in a letter, was to find "a farm in New England where I could live cheap and get Yankier and Yankier."[13] He had developed a unique and marketable vision of his public image. F.D. Reeve, a Wesleyan professor who knew Frost well, commented that "He remembered his two years in England with special affection. It was there…that he passed from obscurity to recognition, that he became the sort of man he wanted to be, that he was first called 'a poet'."[14]

Back in the States, Frost found a few good reviews and a publisher— Henry Holt and Company—for his first two books (and so many more to come over his next forty-seven years). He undertook a lecture tour, and "… was rapidly building a stage presence and perfecting a mode of public address that satisfied him…"[15] "Frost put himself forward boldly and cleverly. Although he continued to play the role of the Yankee farmer-poet, especially when reading his poems in public, he did not want to be mistaken for a rube, especially by critics of poetry."[16] Commenting on an interview published during the first year after his return, Parini stated, "Frost was busily at work creating a self-myth that would accommodate and facilitate his writing life… He was intensely ambitious, artistically."[17]

---

11   Ibid, 123.

12   The Cunard liner, *RMS Lusitania,* would go down on May 7, 1915. (*Lusitania* sunk by a submarine; probably 1000 dead, 1915.)

13   Parini, *Robert Frost: A Life,* 158.

14   F. D. Reeve, *Robert Frost in Russia* (Brookline: Zyphr Press, 2001), 32.

15   Parini, *Robert Frost: A Life,* 174.

16   Ibid, 189.

17   Ibid, 173.

On the return leg of his tour, in response to an invitation from a student group, he spent two days at Amherst College. "It occurred to him that here was the kind of small college where he might like to teach one day."[18] A few months later, Alexander Meiklejohn, then Amherst's president, offered Frost a faculty position for the spring semester of 1917. Frost's association with Amherst would endure despite interruptions for forty-six years and culminate in the Robert Frost Library.

By 1920, Frost's growing prominence brought two important appointments. He joined the Middlebury College summer English program at Bread Loaf Mountain, and he agreed to spend a year at the University of Michigan as a visiting fellow and recipient of an honorary degree. By this point, Parini noted, "the mask and the man were closely bound. From this point on Frost would rarely distance himself from the mask and would wear it freely—even defiantly—in public."[19]

His new collection, *New Hampshire*, brought Frost his first Pulitzer Prize for Poetry in 1924, followed by honorary degrees from Middlebury, Yale, and Bowdoin. Frost turned fifty in 1925. In the fall of that year he returned to Ann Arbor as "permanent fellow in letters," a sort of poet-in-residence. The following spring, he accepted an offer from Amherst to rejoin the faculty there. Parini aptly described Frost's literary development in this period, saying "he did not, like most poets, grow and shift; rather, like a tree, he added rings."[20] The second Pulitzer Prize came for *Collected Poems* in 1931, and Frost was elected to the American Academy of Arts and Letters. The third Pulitzer followed in 1937 for *A Further Range*.

Frost's growing public recognition occurred on the background of recurring episodes of illness and personal tragedy. In May of 1934, his daughter Marjorie died shortly after childbirth. In March of 1938, Elinor, his wife of forty-two years, died from a heart attack complicating major cancer surgery. Elinor's death was a "curtain that fell in the play of Frost's life, signaling the

---

18   Ibid, 175.

19   Ibid, 198.

20   Ibid, 262.

final act."[21] Two and a half years later, in October of 1940, Frost's son, Carol, committed suicide, and in 1947, Frost had to commit his daughter Irma to an insane asylum.

During the later decades of his life, Frost continued his "barding about," with visits to college campuses. Whenever he gave recitations or readings, he insisted that the personal performances were "saying" his poems. His fourth Pulitzer came in 1943 for *A Witness Tree*, and his honors continued to accumulate thereafter.

———————

AS EARLY AS 1941, Frost had started to eye a role in public affairs. In connection with a presentation at the Library of Congress, he gave a lecture titled "The Role of a Poet in a Democracy,"[22] in which he stated that "Democracy would always mean refraining from power beyond a certain point."

He was appointed Consultant in Poetry to the Library of Congress (the position now known as the Poet Laureate Consultant in Poetry to the Library of Congress) for the 1958-1959 term. With obvious delight, he remarked, "The inclination I had towards affairs of state will be amply and handsomely satisfied by the small token job I am to have down there. I promise."[23] With this Washington appointment, he developed the friendship with then-Congressman Stewart Udall[24] that would shape his future public life.[25] Signaling his interest in continuing his Washington activities, in 1959 Frost accepted a three-year appointment as honorary consultant in the humanities at the Library of Congress.

Politically, Frost inclined toward the conservative but, "Party affiliations

———————

21   Ibid, 314.

22   Henry Hart, *The Life of Robert Frost* (Hoboken: Wiley-Blackwell, 2017), 319.

23   Mark Richardson (ed), *The Collected Prose of Robert Frost* (Cambridge: Belknap Press of Harvard University Press, 2007), 192.

24   Udall later served as secretary of the interior from 1961 to 1969 under Presidents John F. Kennedy and Lyndon B. Johnson.

25   L. Boyd Finch, *Legacies of Camelot: Stewart and Lee Udall, American Culture, and the Arts* (Norman: University of Oklahoma Press, 2008).

just do not apply to Frost, who was neither a Republican nor a Democrat in any consistent or recognizable way."[26] In addition to their friendship, Frost and Udall shared their political enthusiasm for Senator John F. Kennedy. In the course of his congressional campaigns in Massachusetts, Kennedy had acquired a staunch supporter in Frost, forty-six years his senior.

At Frost's eighty-fifth birthday celebration, he spoke out in support of Kennedy. "Before Jack Kennedy had even declared himself as running, Robert Frost announced that the young man from Boston would be the next president. On March 26, 1959, prior to a gala to celebrate his eighty-fifth birthday, Frost gave a press conference at the Waldorf-Astoria Hotel in New York City. Among the questions was one concerning the alleged decline of New England, to which Frost responded: 'The next president of the United States will be from Boston. Does that sound as if New England is decaying?' Pressed to name who he meant, Frost replied: 'He's a Puritan named Kennedy. The only Puritans left these days are the Roman Catholics. There. I guess I wear my politics on my sleeve.'"[27]

Afterward, "as he traveled across the country to read and lecture, he seemed almost to be campaigning for Kennedy."[28]

For his part, Kennedy had developed a set campaign speech that concluded with the closing lines of Frost's "Stopping by Woods,"

"But I have promises to keep, / And miles to go before I sleep, / And miles to go before I sleep."

After Kennedy's election victory, Udall successfully urged JFK to invite Frost to "say" a poem at the new president's inauguration. Once Frost accepted, Kennedy called the poet to ask whether he wanted to write a new poem for the occasion. When Frost said he couldn't be counted on to do that, the president asked him to read "The Gift Outright," but to change the last line so that it presaged an even brighter future, and the poet readily agreed.

---

26   Parini, *Robert Frost: A Life*, 264.

27   L. Wolfe, "Power and Poetry: The President, the Poet and the American Cultural Mission," October 25, 2013, The Schiller Institute, http://www.schillerinstitute.org/poetry/2014/wolfe-jfk_poetry.html.

28   Parini, *Robert Frost: A Life*, 412-413.

Just days before the inauguration, however, Frost decided to write a new poem to serve as a "preface" for saying "The Gift Outright." In the concluding two lines of his seventy-seven-line poem "Dedication," Frost foresaw "A golden age of poetry and power / Of which this noonday's the beginning hour." But fresh snow and blinding sunshine made it impossible for him to read "Dedication" at the inauguration, and the eighty-five-year-old poet stumbled badly for more than two embarrassing minutes as he tried to decipher it. Summoning all the stagecraft of his years, the old poet explained his plight and said "The Gift Outright" from memory, including the promised change in the final line. Frost's performance in Washington, the first poet to speak at a presidential inauguration "stole the hearts of the inaugural crowd."[29]

Before returning home, Frost called on the new President and First Lady at the White House to receive Kennedy's thanks for participating in the event. The poet presented Kennedy with a copy of his "Dedication" poem, on which he had written, "Amended copy. And now let us mend our ways." He also gave the president some typically blunt advice: "Be more Irish than Harvard. Poetry and power is the formula for another Augustan Age. Don't be afraid of power."

A few days later, the White House staff presented a typed thank-you letter for Frost to the president for his signature. Kennedy read the letter and wrote diagonally across the page in pen, "It's poetry and power all the way" (Academy of American Poets, 2014).

KENNEDY

Who was John Fitzgerald Kennedy, the president who spoke at Amherst in October of 1963?

JFK was seven years older than George H. W. Bush, but he remains forty-six years old forever in our communal memory. His grandfathers, P. J. Kennedy and John J. "Honey Fitz" Fitzgerald, were well-known Boston-Irish politicians. His father, Joseph P. Kennedy ("Joe Sr.") graduated from Harvard, married Rose Fitzgerald, and set about making money, which he did

---

29   L. Boyd Finch, *Legacies of Camelot* (Norman, OK: University of Oklahoma Press, 2008).

with questionable methods and great success. When their second child, Jack, was ten, Joe Sr., Rose, and the Kennedy clan moved to Riverdale, New York.[30]

Jack Kennedy grew up as a member of a rich and famous family with homes in New York and Palm Beach and a summer compound on Cape Cod. His schooling included Choate and then Harvard. A thin and chronically ill young man, he became something of a WWII hero following the sinking of his torpedo boat, *PT-109*, in the Pacific.

The eldest of the Kennedy siblings, Joe Jr., had been the senior Kennedy's choice to run for public office. Then Joe Jr., a Navy pilot, died flying a combat mission in 1944, one of a long series of tragedies that battered the Kennedys. For Joe Sr., Jack was the natural next-in-line.

As Kennedy biographers Robert Dallek and David Nasaw have documented, Joseph P. Kennedy, the head of the Kennedy clan, provided the motivation, direction, and financing for JFK's political career. Joe Sr. recognized that, "High public office, which FDR's administration opened to Catholics and Jews, had replaced accumulating money as the greater social good and a worthy aspiration for second- and third-generation immigrants reaching for higher social status." Despite business practices that had made him "almost a pariah on Wall Street,"[31] Joe Sr.'s wealth had brought him appointments as the first chairman of the Securities and Exchange Commission, the first chairman of the Maritime Commission, and U.S. Ambassador to the United Kingdom. Joe Sr. wanted a president in the family.

Mixed with all his very real flaws, Joseph P. Kennedy Sr. had a streak of genius. He foresaw trends developing in public life and understood how to profit from them. He had successfully invested in Hollywood, where he learned to make the magical seem real. He grasped the emerging importance of the media and public relations in national politics. And Joe Sr. directed the show.

After WWII, Jack returned to Boston to launch his career in politics. A

---

30   David Nasaw, *The Patriarch: The Remarkable Life and Turbulent Times of Joseph P. Kennedy* (New York: Penguin Press, 2012), 106.

31   Kai Bird, *The Chairman: John J. McCloy and the Making of the American Establishment* (New York: Simon & Schuster, 1992), 495.

bachelor with no property of his own in Boston, he initially resided at the Hotel Bellevue.[32] Privately, in addition to Jack's lifelong health issues, his behavior had sometimes been problematic. In their early biography, the Blairs quoted a Kennedy friend, Betty Spalding, describing him: "'He was nice to people, but heedless of people.'"[33] Udall made a similar observation: "Reserved men are often thoughtless men, and John Kennedy for all his public charisma was essentially a very private person."[34] Jack also had a temper. As Richard Goodwin observed, "'There was an inner hardness, often volatile anger, beneath the outwardly amiable, thoughtful, carefully controlled demeanor of John Kennedy.'"[35]

With Joe Sr.'s financial and strategic backing, Jack won election to three successive terms as a Massachusetts congressman in 1946, 1948, and 1950, and then to the U.S. Senate in 1952 and 1958.

By the time Senator John F. Kennedy embarked on his campaign for the presidency, the Kennedy political organization had worked tirelessly for years to create his public image: the tanned, fit WWII hero of PT-109, a Harvard-educated writer with two books and a Pulitzer Prize (for *Profiles in Courage*) to his credit, a foreign-policy expert in the U.S. Senate, and a loving husband and father with a beautiful wife and baby daughter.

Jack won the 1960 presidential election over Richard Nixon by only 112,827 (0.17 percent) votes nationwide to become the nation's first Catholic president.

"John Kennedy was essentially a much more cautious and conservative politician than either his supporters or his detractors thought."[36] After the elec-

---

32   Robert Dallek, *An Unfinished Life: John F. Kennedy 1917–1963* (Boston: Little, Brown and Company, 2003), 126.

33   Joan and Clay Blair Jr., *The Search for J.F.K.* (New York: Berkley Publishing Corporation, 1976).

34   Stewart L. Udall, recorded interview by W.W. Moss, John F. Kennedy Library Oral History Program, September 17, 1970, 39, https://docs.google.com/viewerng/viewer?url=https://archive1.jfklibrary.org/JFKOH/Udall,+Stewart+L/JFKOH-SLU-08/JFKOH-SLU-08-TR.pdf.

35   Op. cit. Dallek, 2003, 370.

36   Op. cit. Bird, 1992, 495.

tion, when he began to fill the top positions in his administration, he wanted to bring aboard men who had established their credentials, particularly those who had been close to the noted public servant, Henry Stimson.[37] One of his prize recruits was John J. McCloy, who accepted a position as Kennedy's disarmament adviser. Apparently, "part of his attraction to these men stemmed from the fact that they came from an elite slice of society from which the Irish Catholic Kennedys had always been excluded."[38]

A successful New York lawyer, McCloy's public service had included appointments as assistant secretary of war for much of WWII, as president of the World Bank from 1947 to 1949, and as high commissioner for Germany from 1949 to 1952. In the private sector, he had been chairman of the Chase Manhattan Bank from 1953 to 1960, chairman of the Ford Foundation from 1958 to 1965, and since 1954, he had chaired the prestigious Council on Foreign Relations in New York. McCloy's unofficial title was the "chairman of the Establishment."

Free of Joe Sr.'s influence and faced with a series of crises between 1960 and 1963, the young president learned a new approach to the exercise of political power from his advisors, not just Robert McNamara and Dean Rusk, but also from McCloy and men like him who worked behind the scenes.

Theodore Sorensen, Kennedy's friend and speechwriter, observed and documented this maturing process: "Unlike many who attain high public office, John F. Kennedy continued to grow in mind and spirit throughout his service in Washington. His concern for his country…his judgement… expanded in each of his seventeen years in office."[39]

Kennedy had always been interested in power. In conversations with people like McCloy and Frost, and working with Sorenson, he began to explore and articulate his own thoughts about the exercise of power in a series

---

37 Stimson served as secretary of war (1911–1913) under William Howard Taft, secretary of state (1929–1933) under Herbert Hoover, and secretary of war (1940–1945) under Franklin D. Roosevelt and Harry S. Truman.

38 Op. cit. Bird, 1992, 495-96.

39 Theodore Sorensen, *Let the Word Go Forth: The speeches, statements, and writings of John F. Kennedy 1947-1963* (New York: Bantam Doubleday Dell, 1988), 79

of speeches beginning in 1961.

At the University of Washington, November 16, 1961, he said:

— "We must face the fact that the United States is neither omnipotent nor omniscient—that we are only six percent of the world's population…and that therefore there cannot be an American solution to every world problem."

— "At a time when a single clash could escalate overnight into a holocaust of mushroom clouds, a great power does not prove its firmness by leaving the task of exploring the other's intentions to sentries…"

— "[I]t is a test of our national maturity to accept the fact that negotiations are not a contest spelling victory or defeat."

Two days later, on November 18, 1961, at the California State Democratic Party dinner he continued on similar themes:

— "Now we are face-to-face…with a period of heightened peril… And under the strains and frustrations…the discordant voices of extremism are once again heard in the land."

— "But you and I—most Americans, soldiers and civilians—take a different view of our peril. We know it comes from without, not within. It must be met by quiet preparedness, not provocative speeches."

At the UN General Assembly, September 20, 1963, shortly before the Amherst speech, he was even more succinct:

— "We have the power to make this the best generation of mankind in the history of the world—or to make it the last."

KENNEDY AND FROST: THE FINAL ACT

As he grew older, Frost "came to see himself as a cultural activist."[40] At a Washington dinner party, he had met warmly with Anatoly Dobrynin, the Russian ambassador. Dobrynin proposed a cultural exchange in which Frost would visit Russia, and Alexander Tvardovsky, the leading Russian poet and writer, would subsequently visit the United States. (Tvardovsky's visit never materialized.) Udall, who had become Kennedy's secretary of the interior, helped with the arrangements. Frost and F. D. Reeve (Wesleyan University professor of letters and Frost's Russian translator) accompanied Udall on a visit to Moscow in August.

While Frost and Udall visited Russia, the first inklings of the Cuban missile crisis began to unfold.[41]

As Udall would later recall, when he and Frost arrived home from Russia on September 9:

> [Frost] had been awake 18 hours…and was bone-tired. I should have stopped any further press interviews, but the reporters were out in force and anxious to persuade him to expand on his impressions of Khrushchev. As he was beginning to repeat himself near the end of his New York press conference, Frost astonished me by suddenly blurting out, "Khrushchev said he feared for us because of our lot of liberals. He thought that we're too liberal to fight—he thinks we will sit on one hand and then the other." This was the fresh news the reporters were waiting for, and the next day the *Washington Post* carried a banner headline: Frost Says Khrushchev Sees U.S. as "Too Liberal" to Defend Itself.

---

40   Quoted from F.D. Reeve, *Robert Frost in Russia*. Zephyr Press, 2001, 10.

41   Sen. Keating had first said the Russians were moving missiles in August of '62. On August 17, 1962, CIA Director John McCone stated that circumstantial evidence suggested that the U.S.S.R. was constructing offensive missile installations in Cuba. Dean Rusk and Robert McNamara disagreed with McCone's, arguing that the build-up was purely defensive. (Chronology of John McCone 's Suspicions on the Military Build-up in Cuba Prior to Kennedy's October 22 Speech, 11/30/62).

Reeve later observed, "In the fall of 1962 the controversy around the 'too liberal to fight' phrase exceeded reasonable proportions. Few people understood what Frost had said or what his position was." Udall wrote, "Frost himself many times used the expression 'Too liberal to fight' prior to his Soviet trip. It was his gibe at professor-types who, he felt, had the Hamlet curse. One of Frost's Washington friends, Scotty Reston,[42] sensed immediately that the expression was probably a Frost conclusion rather than a Khrushchev quote."[43]

Nonetheless, "JFK felt betrayed by Frost, and there was nothing he disliked more than being crossed. When he thought himself wronged, he did not seek revenge; instead, he ignored the offending individual. For the rest of his life, Frost felt Kennedy's 'cold shoulder.'"[44]

By the fall of 1962, faced with a series of crises at home and abroad, Kennedy had soon developed into a mature and powerful president, while Frost, an eighty-eight-year-old man, had slipped badly due to his significant health problems.

"Old age had finally caught up with Frost, who now stumbled from crisis to crisis." His prostate problems became more severe, and "his doctor in Cam-

---

42   James Reston, columnist and executive editor of the *New York Times,* was "perhaps the most influential journalist of his generation." (Apple, 1995)

43   Understanding the relevance of Frost in Russia is difficult, but it is very important to unraveling the Frost-ian concept of poetry and power. Frost's vision for the U.S.-Soviet relationship was that the two global superpowers, while stalemated by their nuclear weapons in mutually assured destruction, would engage in a decades-long non-military contest to determine which could build a more successful political system (power) and a richer, more sophisticated, culture (poetry). The concept of the stalemate was critical to Frost's hopes; the Russians had to believe that the U.S. would not initiate a conflict, but they also had to know that the U.S. response to Soviet aggression would be immediate and overwhelming. (This mirrors McCloy's pragmatic view of how to engineer eventual disarmament. Each side would agree to incremental nuclear de-escalation with verification.) Therefore, in Frost's view, this would only work if Khrushchev knew the U.S. was NOT "too liberal to fight." Frost may well have wanted JFK to say, "no, we're not 'too liberal'." The old poet was subtle. Remember how in "The Road Not Taken" he manages to convince the reader that the road he took was less-traveled, even "Though as for that the passing there / Had worn them really about the same." The Frost-in-Russia episode shows how personally dedicated Frost was to his vision of the poetry/power relationship. He was old. He was sick. But this trip was the culmination, the high point, of his Washington career.

44   (Udall, Stewart L. Udall Oral History Interview - JKF #8, 9/17/1970, 1970)

bridge explained that surgery loomed in the not-too-distant future."[45] One bright spot in that fall came when the president of Amherst College, Calvin Plimpton,[46] announced a gift of $3.5 million would be used to fund a major new building, the Robert Frost Library.

On December10, Frost at last underwent surgery at the Peter Bent Brigham Hospital in Boston.[47] His prostate was cancerous, and the disease had spread. Post-operatively, he experienced recurrent pulmonary emboli. He died January 29, 1963.

———

DESPITE HIS MISSTEP a few months earlier, Frost had supported Kennedy from the beginning, had "said" a poem at Kennedy's inauguration, and with his personal conversation, correspondence, and the "Dedication" poem had explored his concepts of power and poetry with the president. The task of inviting John F. Kennedy, the President of the United States, to speak at the groundbreaking for the Robert Frost Library, called for someone with influence at the very highest levels. It fell to the distinguished Amherst alumnus, John J. McCloy, Class of 1916.

Kennedy acknowledged McCloy's role in bringing him to Amherst by beginning his address, "Mr. McCloy, President Plimpton, Mr. MacLeish, distinguished guests, ladies and gentlemen: ..." He went on. "I was privileged to accept the invitation [from Mr. McCloy] somewhat rendered to me in the same way that Franklin Roosevelt rendered his invitation to Mr. MacLeish.[48] The powers of the presidency are often described. Its limitations

———

45   Ibid, 435.

46   Calvin H. Plimpton, MD was the younger half-brother of Francis T.P. Plimpton, another New York "establishment" lawyer, who served as deputy United States Representative to the United Nations under John F. Kennedy. (Margolick, 1983) Francis was a longtime friend of John J. McCloy. (Bird, 1992)

47   Now Brigham and Women's Hospital.

48   As MacLeish put it, "The President [Roosevelt] decided I wanted to be Librarian of Congress." MacLeish, William H. (2001). *Uphill with Archie: a son's journey.* New York, NY [u.a.]: Simon & Schuster. p. 141. ISBN 0-684-82495-7.

should occasionally be remembered. And therefore, when the chairman of our Disarmament Advisory Committee, who has labored so long and hard, Governor Stevenson's assistant during the very difficult days at the United Nations during the Cuban crisis, a public servant of so many years, asks or invites the President of the United States, there is only one response. So I am glad to be here."

IN THE AUDIENCE, THE CLASS OF 1964

In the fall of 1960, Amherst students, some wearing freshman "beanies," had crowded the white-painted, incredibly uncomfortable pews of Johnson Chapel to hear Amherst's best-known faculty member, Robert Frost, "say" a selection of his poems. By fall of 1963, the freshman of that gathering had turned into seniors, and they would crowd into the dirt-floored echoing indoor practice area of the gym, "the cage," to hear President Kennedy honor Frost.

In his convocation speech President Kennedy described his listeners by saying, "Privilege is here." Rhetorically, the description worked. The data, however, suggest that "lucky" would have been more accurate.

The Class of 1964 represented the last of a generation that the demographer Elwood Carlson labeled "The Lucky Few" and described in detail in his book of the same name (Carlson, 2008). Born between 1929 and 1945, they fell in between the WWII heroes of "the greatest generation" and the coming baby-boomers. Because of low birth rates during the Great Depression, they were the first generation of Americans who numbered fewer than the preceding generation.

In their book, *Crafting a Class*, Elizabeth Duffy and Idana Goldberg examined liberal arts college admission processes between1955 and 1994. They focused on data from Amherst and Williams as representative of the most selective formerly men's colleges, along with Smith, Wellesley, and Mt. Holyoke representing competitive women's colleges. They frequently quoted Amherst's former dean of admissions, Eugene Wilson.

In 1959, the year that the Class of '64 applied to Amherst, Wilson stated

"For generations prior to the last war the central problem of admissions at Amherst and similar institutions had been one of *recruitment*—finding enough qualified candidates to fill each entering class. Since 1946, however, the central problem…has increasingly been one of *selection*—picking the 'best' candidates from a great excess of qualified applicants."[49] The Class of 1964 had six applicants for each place.

As the number of applicants increased, their mean SAT scores also increased, so that "for all but three of the twelve colleges for which we have data in the earliest years [of this study], their 1965 mean SAT scores were the highest that have ever been reported." A late 1950s admissions summary at Amherst reported, "By 1965, an Amherst class as a whole will compare with the upper half of any class in the thirties."[50] This prompted Dean Wilson to reformulate his policy of selection, "No longer do we pick students largely by marks and test scores. Instead we look among our qualified applicants for [those] who will give us a class of broad diversification."[51]

Diversity by present standards was still limited. The 283 members of the all-male Amherst Class of '64 were overwhelmingly white.[52] These numbers, however, were consistent with other similar schools. As Duffy observed, "minority recruitment policies operated within the framework of selective college admissions," with limited success. Duffy continued, "A 1965 article by S.A. Kendrick, executive associate of the College Board, reported that in 1965/66, there were only 2,216 black students enrolled at New England colleges and that at the private, four-year colleges such as those represented in our study, blacks generally represented about 1 percent of total enrollment."[53]

Culturally, the Amherst Class of 1964 remained firmly grounded in the late 1950s, the second term of the Eisenhower administration. At Amherst, as Gillett described at Yale, "as the era receded, references to 'the sixties' as-

---

49   Elizabeth A. Duffy and Idana Goldberg, *Crafting a Class: College Admissions and Financial Aid, 1955-1994* (Princeton: Princeton University Press, 1998), 37.

50   Ibid, 83.

51   Ibid, 246.

52   Six (2 percent) of the entering Class of 1964 were African or African-American.

53   Op. cit. Duffy and Goldberg, 1998, 139.

sumed…a set of connotations associated with the latter part of the decade [and on] into the early 1970s." The social, cultural, and political excesses of the "long 1960s" are more accurately associated with the years from 1963 to 1974.[54]

Or, simply stated, the Class of '64 was a class of making out, beer, and Chuck Berry, not sex, drugs, and the Rolling Stones.

The Amherst seniors who listened to Kennedy's speech that October were lucky: they had performed well in high school, scored very well on standardized tests, and gained admission to a highly competitive college. On the downside, they were almost uniformly white males whose college years had cloistered them in an idealized environment; their college experience had left them unprepared for the cultural changes that were already beginning to engulf their country.

KENNEDY'S SPEECH

In his speech at the Amherst Convocation, Kennedy bluntly challenged his audience by stating, "In return for the great opportunity which society gives the graduates of this and related schools, it seems to me incumbent upon this and other schools' graduates to recognize their responsibility to the public interest."

"Privilege is here, and with privilege goes responsibility."

He continued, "There is inherited wealth in this country and also inherited poverty. And unless the graduates of this college and other colleges like it who are given a running start in life—unless they are willing to put back into our society those talents, the broad sympathy, the understanding, the compassion—unless they're willing to put those qualities back into the service of the Great Republic, then obviously the presuppositions upon which our democracy are based are bound to be fallible."

"The problems which this country now faces are staggering, both at home and abroad. We need the service, in the great sense, of every educated man or woman…"

---

54   Howard Gillette Jr., *Class Divide. Yale '64 and the Conflicted Legacy of the Sixties* (Ithaca: Cornell University Press, 2015), xvii.

The president did not pull his punches; with his opening remarks, he meant to forcefully engage the undergraduates.

He could have concluded these remarks with a brief eulogy for Frost. But the president had not come to bury the poet. Instead, he came to the poet's academic home to praise Frost as no one else could, by exploring in depth what Kennedy had come to believe were the ideal roles for poetry and power in American life, thought and democracy. "Today this college and country honor a man whose contribution was not to our size but to our spirit...not to our self-esteem but to our self-comprehension." Frost had fulfilled the poet's true role in public life. "The men who question power make a contribution... especially when that questioning is disinterested. For they determine whether we use power or power uses us."

The president continued, "If art is to nourish the roots of our culture, society must set the artist free to follow his vision wherever it takes him." He continued, "...in democratic society, the highest duty of the writer, the composer, the artist, is to remain true to himself and to let the chips fall where they may."

Kennedy articulated a vision of the engaged, liberally educated electorate that was actively taking shape and maturing during his presidency; his privileged audience had a moral responsibility to serve the public good, to live their lives with personal integrity, and to promote the role of the liberal arts in questioning and humanizing the exercise of political power, "the men who question power...determine whether we use power or power uses us."

He gave a succinct description of the relevance of Frost's poetry, and by extension, the liberal arts, to government:

> At bottom, he [Frost] held a deep faith in the spirit of man, and it is hardly an accident that Robert Frost coupled poetry and power, for he saw poetry as the means of saving power from itself. When power leads men towards arrogance, poetry reminds him of his limitations. When power narrows the areas of man's concern, poetry reminds him of the richness and diversity of his existence. When power corrupts, poetry cleanses. *For art estab-*

lishes the basic human truth which must serve as the touchstone of
our judgment.

"And the nation which disdains the mission of art invites the fate of Robert Frost's hired man, the fate of having 'nothing to look backward to with pride, and nothing to look forward to with hope.'"[55]

THE MESSAGE FOR TODAY

Kennedy's speech at Amherst went far beyond a "farewell, Godspeed" for Robert Frost. It was a message of the importance of civic engagement, of fidelity to the hard search for facts and the truth. Speaking directly to the students, he took the opportunity to challenge talented young people to become involved in public life. As we shall see in the following essays, many of the young men in the audience found meaningful ways to serve the public interest. They lived out in practice the concept that, whatever one's career choice, being engaged, informed, honest, and active in the civic life of the community should be part of one's life, particularly for those who have been advantaged in our society.

Kennedy addressed the critical role of the arts, and by extension the liberal arts, in questioning, moderating, and humanizing political power. He told his audience "that men who question power make a contribution." He did not say he liked, or enjoyed, the questioning. But he realized how important the process was in determining "whether we use power or power uses us." In the view that Kennedy had grown to share with Frost, the arts continually remind us of the richness and diversity of our existence. The arts engender empathy and convey the wisdom distilled from our shared experience. The arts provide a "touchstone of our judgment."

For our "Great Republic" at large, the importance of the liberal arts for broadly educating citizens to think, write, and speak clearly and for their humanizing influence, has now come into question. Much of this questioning arises from the debater's clever artifice of framing the question as "should one

---

55   Kennedy, National Endowment for the Arts, 1963 (italics added).

choose to study the liberal arts *or* a science-technology-engineering-math (STEM) program?"

Yet, under pressure from the concept of the modern research university as an institution that exists primarily for the creation of new knowledge, from the pragmatic need for new technical skills, and from an increasingly divided society, we must answer the question: "Why does liberal education matter today?"

Many widely acclaimed authorities have addressed this question in books and academic papers. I favor Fareed Zakaria's simple and straightforward answer: "The central virtue of a liberal education is that it teaches you how to write, and writing makes you think. Whatever you do in life, the ability to write clearly, cleanly, and reasonably quickly will prove to be an invaluable skill."[56]

---

56   Fareed Zakaria, *In Defense of a Liberal Education* (New York: W.W. Norton & Company, Inc., 2015), 72.

2

ROBERT FROST
The Poet as Educator

Paul Dimond, '66; and Roger Mills, '64

UNCOVERING ROBERT FROST'S educational philosophy requires some literary heavy work akin to archeology, going back to his early writing. As Frost grew fond of saying in later interviews, "Three things have followed me, writing, teaching a little, and farming."[1] We will explore how Frost came to speak of each in explaining his "philosophy of education" and his poetry.

After dropping out of Dartmouth and Harvard with little advance and less interest in a college degree, Frost became an autodidact. He studied Latin and then turned to Greek; he read the English writers and poets of the past and of his day. He was as well read as any literature professor. He also explored the learning and scientific theories of James, Dewey, Bohr, Einstein, and Planck, to name only a few of the many he studied and remarked on.

One of the first hints that Frost would also expect his students to read widely came in his concise description of the English curriculum at Pinkerton Academy in 1910: "The general aim of the course in English is twofold: to bring our students under the influence of the great books, and to teach them the satisfaction

---

1   Natalie S. Bober, *A Restless Spirit: The Story of Robert Frost* (New York: Henry Holt and Co., 1998), 129.

of superior speech."[2] And he already had a healthy appreciation for, and skepticism of, the mind versus matter and spirit versus science debates of the day.

In 1912, at age thirty-eight, Frost and his wife, Elinor, sold the Derry, New Hampshire, farm where he had composed poems and toiled in obscurity for ten years. He uprooted his family of six to find his way in England. There he published his first two books of poems. Written in the voices of common New England rural folk and with the uncommon metaphor of his experience, *A Boy's Will* and *North of Boston* earned high praise across the pond. In 1915 he returned a budding celebrity determined to become the greatest American poet ever and the foremost poet writing in English of his day.

In order to support his family and his writing, however, he needed a steady, predictable income that he could only provide through teaching. He joined the faculty of Amherst College in 1917. In 1919, he wrote about his emerging philosophy of creating, writing, and learning, using a metaphor from his farming days:

A man who makes really good literature is like a fellow who goes into the fields to pull carrots. He keeps on pulling them patiently enough until he finds a carrot that suggests something else to him. It is not shaped like other carrots. He takes out his knife and notches it here and there, until the two pronged roots become legs and the carrot takes on something of the semblance of a man. The real genius takes hold of that bit of life which is suggestive to him and gives it form. But the man who is merely a realist, and not a genius, will leave the carrot just as he finds it.[3]

Frustrated by the "progressive" philosophy of education embraced by Amherst President Alexander Meiklejohn, Frost moved on. He found a kindred spirit in the University of Michigan's President, Leroy Burton, in 1921. Both were born in 1874, both had accomplished much, and both had greater ambitions. They also shared a common concept of creating and learning. As Burton wrote in 1921, "A real university should be a patron of art, litera-

---

2   Mark Richardson, ed., *The Collected Prose of Robert Frost* (Cambridge: The Belknap Press of Harvard University Press, 2007), 77.

3   Robert Frost, "Remarks on Form in Poetry," in Mark Richardson, ed., *The Collected Prose of Robert Frost* (Cambridge: The Belknap Press of Harvard University Press, 2007), 79.

ture and creative activity. We ought to have upon the campus persons of the rarest type of personality…who see visions and dream dreams…but [are] free of the fetters of academe."[4] Frost flourished under Burton's patronage; the poet, the artist and the inventor-in-residence could "always be about" creating "definite deeds to be growing."[5]

Frost led the monthly meetings at a fellow professor's home for the student writers of the literary magazine, *Whimsies*. Frost shared his poems, and the students shared theirs. He also welcomed students into his (larger) rental house to recite their poems and encouraged them "to keep it around for a while and deepen, deepen it."

After two years, Frost left Michigan to return to Amherst, now under a new president, and to his family. Back in New England, he acquired the first of a series of several Vermont homes. In 1924 Frost won his first of four Pulitzer Prizes for his fourth book of poems, *New Hampshire*, which he had dedicated to the University of Michigan. Meanwhile, Burton had reworked the Literary School's budget and wooed Frost back to Michigan as a permanent, i.e., tenured Fellow in Letters. Unfortunately, Burton died in February 1925 at age fifty. After the 1925-26 school year, the now-acknowledged great poet left Michigan for a similar position at Amherst, as a tenured professor of English, again without any regular classroom responsibilities.

The Michigan experience had been critical to shaping Frost's thinking about creating, teaching, and learning. Frost and Burton shared a vision for, in the poet's words, "keeping the creative and the erudite together in education where they belong; and [where the creative can also] make its demand on the young student."[6] Whatever campus activities he chose to join, Frost encouraged his students to learn by doing—going out, pulling carrots, looking harder, and imagining something new.

Frost often told a version of Mark Twain's most famous short story, "The Celebrated Jumping Frog of Calaveras County," to help his students and col-

---

4   Quoted in Robert Warner, *Frost-Bite Frost Bark: Robert Frost at Michigan*, (Ann Arbor: Bentley Historical Library, 1999), 9.

5   Ibid, 13.

6   Ibid, 13.

leagues understand the difference between *teaching* and *learning*:

The owner of an 'edercated' frog named 'Dan'l Webster' bet forty dollars his frog could jump farther than any other. A stranger took up the bet and managed to stuff quail shot down Dan'l's throat 'that filled him pretty near up to his chin.' Sure enough when the starter 'touched up the two frogs from behind, the stranger's frog 'hopped off' while Dan'l couldn't budge.'"

Frost would then ask the meaning of this parable. If no one guessed, the poet would pounce with his punchline: "There are two kinds of teachers: those who try to fill their students with so much quail shot they can't budge, and those who give them a little kick in the rear and the students fly much farther on their own."[7]

As Frost said in a 1931 talk at Amherst College, "Education by poetry is education by metaphor…We like to talk in parables and in hints and in indirections…[T]he literary [belief] in every work of art, not cunning and craft, mind you, but real art; that of believing a thing into existence. Saying as you go more than you even hoped you were going to be able to say and coming with surprise to an end that you foreknew only with some sort of emotion." [8]

As for grades, Frost admitted he could mark for many things and mark "hard." But the "hard part," what really matters, "is the part beyond [any mark,] the part where the *adventure* begins." This is the invention of metaphor, the seeing and creating—the believing and imagining—a poem, a short-story, other work of art or even a scientific theory into existence.

In 1938, at age sixty-four, Frost left Amherst for other, similar, faculty positions: first as the Ralph Waldo Emerson Fellow and Fellow in American Civilization at Harvard, and then as the George Ticknor Fellow in the Humanities at Dartmouth. He finally returned to Amherst in 1949 as the Simpson Lecturer in Literature and remained at Amherst until his death in 1963. In 1938, Frost also returned to the Middlebury College Bread Loaf School of English, the famous summer writing program, where he continued to inspire aspiring writers and teachers every summer, living on his new farm and old cabin with his final patron.

---

7   Paul Dimond, *The Belle of Two Arbors*. (Dexter: Cedar Forge Press, 2017).

8   "Education by Poetry," *Amherst Graduates Quarterly*, February 1931.

During the 1938-39 winter, he distilled his thoughts about creating, composing poetry and the surprise of learning by doing in his essay, "The Figure a Poem Makes."[9] First, he addressed sound and subject. "The sound is the gold in the ore…the object in writing poetry is to make all poems sound as different as possible from each other…We need the help of context—meaning—subject matter."

Then, he addressed "wildness," apparently substituting it for the quality he earlier called "genius" in the carrot-puller. "Just as the first mystery was how a poem could have a tune in such a straightness as meter, so the second mystery is how a poem can have wildness and at the same time a subject that shall be fulfilled…The figure a poem makes. It begins in delight and ends in wisdom."

Next came structure and emotion. "No tears in the writer, no tears in the reader. No surprise for the writer, no surprise for the reader."

And finally, Frost addressed creativity. "The artist must value himself as he snatches a thing from some previous order in time and space into a new order with not so much as a ligature clinging to it of the old place where it was organic…Like a piece of ice on a hot stove, the poem must ride on its own melting. A poem may be worked over once it is in being but may not be worried into being."

Like love, a poem "begins in delight, it inclines to the impulse, it assumes direction with the first line laid down, it runs a course of lucky events…It finds its own name as it goes and discovers the best waiting for it in some final phrase at once wise and sad…It will forever keep its freshness as a petal keeps its fragrance. It can never lose its sense of meaning that once unfolded by surprise as it went."

So, with some digging, Frost the erstwhile academic shows us the evolution of his teaching. As a young man, he began at Pinkerton Academy with a disciplined list of books to read, themes to write, and passages. In mid-life, at Michigan in a remarkable partnership with Burton, he helped to define a new role as an artist-in-residence, an example to students of learning by creating. Then, finally freed of the bonds of didactic teaching, he went on to explore the actual process of writing poetry: the how and the why of his art

---

9   Op. cit. Richardson, 2007, 131-133.

that he shared with generations of students by encouraging them to write but "deepen it, deepen it," in ways that can only be imagined and willed by belief and emotion into being.

At his eighty-fifth birthday party, Frost first spoke out for Jack Kennedy, the then forty-one-year-old junior Senator from Massachusetts for president of the United States. Later, after JFK won and invited the old poet to read the first poem ever at a presidential inauguration, Frost might even have dreamed that the new poem, "Dedication," that he had composed to serve as a preface to the old poem he'd agreed to read, "The Gift Outright," would influence the new president's thinking. The new composition foretold a "A golden age of poetry and power/Of which this noonday's the beginning hour." But the octogenarian's eyes failed him: the bright noonday sun reflecting off the snow blinded the old man so he couldn't read any of the seventy-seven lines he'd written. Never one to cry over spilt milk, Frost hand-delivered a copy to the president at the White House with his good wishes, "Be more Irish than Harvard. Poetry and power is the formula for another Augustan Age. Don't be afraid of power." A few days later, Kennedy scrawled across the typed thank-you note for Frost, "It's poetry and power all the way!" [10]

Frost chose for his epitaph the line that would mark his grave after his death in January 1963, "I have had a lover's quarrel with the world."

But Frost could never have dreamed how JFK would memorialize him. In his last speech, the forty-six-year-old Kennedy by an act of imagination and belief willed into his prose the power of Frost's best poems and his lifetime of "teaching a little":

> When power leads man towards arrogance, poetry reminds him of his limitations. When power narrows the areas of man's concern, poetry reminds him of the richness and diversity of his existence. When power corrupts, poetry cleanses. For art establishes the basic human truths which must serve as the touchstone of our judgment.

10   Robert Frost at the White House after JFK's inauguration, January 20, 1961, https://www.poets.org/poetsorg/text/poetry-and-power-robert-frosts-inaugural-reading.

3

THOSE WHO WERE THERE—
VIGNETTES

The young men who experienced President Kennedy's October visit to Amherst and his assassination the following month had widely differing perspectives. The seven stories in this chapter describe scenes that fit together as if they were an Escher drawing, with classmates moving in different planes in the same time and space.

Cheering Loudly, Fearing Quietly

———————————

James T. Giles, '64

AS PRESIDENT KENNEDY'S motorcade wound its way onto the Amherst campus on October 26, 1963, I watched with anticipation and cheered wildly with my small group of white fraternity brothers. But I wondered how many of my white classmates shared my apprehension that we might witness an assassination attempt on the president's life. Certainly, such a thing could not happen at bucolic Amherst; it was evident to everyone that the Secret Service agents and the Massachusetts State Police were taking no chances.

It had been a volatile year. On January 14, 1963, Alabama's Governor Wallace, in his inaugural address, had called for "segregation today, segregation tomorrow, segregation forever." On June 11, 1963, he stood in the doorway of Foster Auditorium at the University of Alabama, defying a federal court order requiring admission for enrollment of two qualified black Alabama citizens, and forcing Kennedy to nationalize the state's National Guard. Confronted with the possibility of an armed battle between Alabama federalized troops and Alabama state troopers, Wallace had backed down from the doorway, but not away from his political mantra.

That same day, JFK addressed the nation from the Oval Office. He had served notice to the white supremacist faction of the country that he was committed to breaking the strangling vise of state-sanctioned racial segregation. He asked Congress to enact legislation targeting segregation, discrimination, and intimidation in jobs, in public accommodations and in voting.

On June 12, within four hours of the president's equal rights speech, black civil rights leader Medgar Evers lay bleeding to death in the driveway of his Jackson, Mississippi, home. A member of the Ku Klux Klan had shot him in the back. The FBI agents assigned to protect him mysteriously had been no-shows. Was FBI Director J. Edgar Hoover in cahoots with the Klan and plotting an inside hit job on the president?

Most of the black people I knew feared that the president had now put a target on his own back.

On September 2, 1963, a month after the March on Washington for Freedom and Jobs and Rev. Dr. Martin Luther King, Jr.'s commanding "I Have a Dream" speech, Wallace had been at it again. He had ordered the Birmingham public schools closed rather than comply with a federal court desegregation order. Emboldened, on Sunday, September 15, Klan members had bombed the Sixteenth Street Baptist Church, killing four little girls in the basement Sunday school room and wounding many in attendance.

So there I was that October day, with so much turbulence in the nation, feeling the tension in the air. As I watched the motorcade, I wondered, had the FBI known about the plot and let it happen anyway? I cheered loudly. I feared quietly.

———

THE FRATERNITY BROTHERS standing with me were tuned in to the same American horror story that I watched daily on television. Police and mobs bombarded non-violent demonstrators and "sit-ins" with hatred, venom, and violence. As a group, those standing with me had refused the all-white fraternity's invitation to pledge unless I was included. By association, they had experienced a small, bitter taste of what it meant to be black at the hands of the established members who had voted to maintain the status quo. Unintentionally, my classmates had taken a big step in standing against racial discrimination, and the fraternity was the better for it.

They were not alone. Other Amherst students, attempting to rally the will of all around them to stand up and be counted for what was legally and morally right, stood holding signs that urged passage of the president's proposed civil rights legislation. Yet, they knew, we knew, and President Kennedy knew we knew, that there were "miles to go before we sleep."[1]

The long dark shadow of American racism, legalized by the U.S. Supreme Court in the 1896 *Plessy v. Ferguson* decision that upheld racial segregation under the "separate but equal" doctrine, was not going quietly into the night. That same year, my maternal grandfather, born into slavery in 1865, graduated from New York Law School. But in Virginia, I had seen no law diploma hanging on his living room wall. He had been an elementary school teacher in a rural one-room school, built with his own funds, that stood just a country hollow away from the former plantation of his hard memories. He was not uniquely shackled by *Plessy* and Jim Crow. He prayed that one day there would be no more racial segregation and left the need for any change of heart up to God.

In June 1960, I graduated from Virginia's segregated public-school system. At the time, Virginia, my home state, led the massive resistance movement in the southern states, where the state governments often successfully stagnated the implementation of *Brown v. Board of Education,* and kept intact the second-class citizenship wall against people of color that the Supreme Court had codified more than six decades before.

I assumed my fraternity brothers standing with me on October 26, 1963, had also come from schools that were racially segregated either by custom or law. Now, we stood together, friends, wondering what the president would say about an America where, increasingly, it looked like many were gearing up for a race war. And, we wondered whether our friendships would survive beyond the college walls, back home, despite likely future separate worlds.

On that October day, I hoped that President Kennedy would deliver some version of Dr. King's "Dream" speech, that he would vindicate us who at the time may have been regarded by some as "rabble rousers." Kennedy

---

1   Robert Frost, "Stopping by Woods on a Snowy Evening," from The Poetry of Robert Frost, edited by Edward Connery Lathem (New York: Henry Holt and Company, 1969).

spoke to our questions about a common future. He challenged us to recognize our responsibility to the "public interest" by giving the best of all of us "to make it possible for Americans of all races and creeds to live in harmony, to make it possible for a world to exist in diversity and freedom." He gave a "Dream" speech, after all.

I reflected on Robert Frost's "Mending Wall":

Something there is that doesn't love a wall,
That sends the frozen ground swell under it
And spills the upper boulders in the sun
And makes gaps even two can pass abreast.

We were, despite racial, religious, and regional differences, part of something that would chip away at the wall of racial prejudice in ways that we could not then foresee, simply because it divided us.

By February 1964, the proposed Civil Rights Act, which now included "sex discrimination," had been propelled forward in the House of Representatives by the force of President Kennedy's assassination. In the Senate it faced the Southern Bloc filibuster, a formidable force which had killed prior civil rights bills and promised to kill this one. But the labors of Charles Hamilton Houston, Amherst Class of 1915, and William H. Hastie, Amherst Class of 1925, the Howard Law School mentors of Thurgood Marshall, had laid the groundwork for the reversal of *Plessy* in *Brown vs. Board of Education*. And there was Dr. King's March 1963 "fierce urgency of now," and President Kennedy's admonition of that October, "Privilege is here and with privilege goes responsibility."

That was the context in which Dean C. Scott Porter, Class of 1919, my fraternity's faculty advisor and esteemed elder fraternity brother, called me to his office. He wanted to discuss my post-graduate plans. I had been accepted into Harvard's master of arts in teaching program and was focused on completing my major studies and writing assignments. He said, "The civil rights struggle is at a critical point and needs lawyers of color; the numbers are few and among your people the need is great." He told me to apply to law school and promised Harvard would understand my withdrawal from the teaching program. He was right on all scores.

I attended Yale Law School. After I had practiced law for twelve years, ever mindful of the "public interest," President Jimmy Carter honored me with his nomination to fill a district court judicial vacancy in Philadelphia, Pennsylvania. He had campaigned on a promise to change the face of the judiciary by nominating more minorities, women, and younger candidates for judicial vacancies, thereby making the federal judiciary more reflective of the face of the nation. In 1979, I was confirmed by the Senate, and I served as a district judge for nearly twenty-nine years, including seven as chief judge.

I was encouraged to accept and continue in this "public interest" endeavor by those who stood with me to cheer President Kennedy at Amherst College.

The Vigil Outside Kirby

———————————

Mitch Meisner, '64

ON OCTOBER 26, 1963, ground was broken for the Robert Frost Library at Amherst College. According to the *Amherst Student*, the school paper, then-Amherst President Calvin Plimpton described that moment as the "birth of a memory," saying, "We too will tell our grandchild of this day." At the time, Plimpton could not have known that the day that would actually live forever in our collective memory would be November 22, 1963, although some of us might later embellish our stories of where and when we learned of the tragic event in Dallas with the footnote that we had seen the president just weeks before at the Amherst convocation. For me, however, October 26, 1963, was never the "birth of memory." It was, instead, a more modest memory: the civil rights vigil that occurred outside the convocation and the contention within the college community leading up to it.

On the front page of that same convocation issue of the *Amherst Student* was a smaller article titled "Subdued Civil Rights Vigil Greets Kennedy On Arrival." The reporter noted that about sixty students and faculty took part in a demonstration outside Kirby Theater. The demonstrators had carried previously approved signs and had been instructed by the demonstration leadership that the vigil was to be "quiet and orderly." In retrospect, this reporting seems about right, although the attached photo clearly showed several women among the demonstrators—at that time, none of them could have been Amherst students or faculty (except for our newly arrived lone female faculty member). The photo also showed me—serious, dressed up, and holding one of the ultra-negotiated signs, "Mr. President, we support your civil rights program." But what I remember most vividly is not the actual event but rather the conflict against the official college opposition to holding the demonstration at all.

The demonstration organizers, Amherst College Students for Racial Equality (SRE), had been inspired by a wave of Southern civil rights protests, many of which were led by students from black colleges. Northern college students organized in groups like SRE to play supporting roles. In 1963, Amherst students had become an active part of this movement, which was still developing and gathering supporters.

For many of us, it was not the first time we had been involved in civil rights activities. I had been active since 1961. When I returned to campus in the fall of 1963, the event on my mind, and the event about which *I will tell my grandchildren,* was the famous August 28, 1963, March on Washington for Jobs and Freedom. I will tell them that I was there to hear live, for the first time, the words, "I have a dream." In fact, the March on Washington and the political context surrounding it likely gave the real impetus and meaning to the Amherst vigil.

The political context was clear. While a new civil rights bill had been introduced in Congress with nominal support from the Kennedy White House, the president had done little to support it effectively, for whatever personal or political reasons. The signs displayed at the vigil evidenced very tight "message control" (to use a contemporary term), but the subtext clearly was, "Mr. President, why aren't you supporting your own civil rights bill? How about some actual vigor?" This subtext was the message that the SRE organization and its allies set out to communicate, but the college administration was fearful of subverting "the lustre" of the day.

Amherst's President Plimpton had made it clear that he personally opposed any demonstration while Kennedy was on campus. The organizers felt the considerable pressure over the implied or overt threats of disciplinary action. Despite whatever pushback occurred from the administration, the students did not back down. There was a compromise designed to remove any outward hint of opposition or criticism, so as not to "embarrass" President Kennedy or the college or detract from the great day. Notwithstanding the decorous images of the vigil, we demonstrators were not particularly crazy about the diluted, buttoned-down slogans, the "quiet and orderly" protocol, and the awkward feeling of understatement. Even the term *vigil* was a compromise designed to put a more decorous label on things. Of course, that was consistent with the Amherst culture of the early 1960s, when worries about taste and decorum tended to mask deeper concern for maintaining hierarchies of power and control. (The recent reactions to the NFL "take a knee" demonstrations suggest these concerns still remain active today.) Nonetheless, I do remember with great satisfaction the fact that the demonstration occurred.

In his remarks that day, President Plimpton declared that the Amherst curriculum exemplified the "liberating arts." The *Amherst Student* paraphrased him, giving the College credit for "liberat[ing] its students to deal with problems both old and new." What nonsense! This claim did little justice to the actual history of student political engagement at Amherst during those years.

The college did offer our class a very high quality liberal education, but any *liberating* was done by the students themselves. The students' persistence in holding the civil rights vigil was but one instance of widespread Amherst student political activism during the first half of the 1960s, often with similarly motivated Smith, Mt. Holyoke, and UMass students. For example, busloads of students from the four colleges traveled to Washington for the major 1962 Turn Toward Peace demonstration. (Photos of Amherst students at this event appeared on the front page of the *New York Times*.) Silent vigils along the road to Andover Air Force Base, off-campus civil rights activities, and anti-apartheid demonstrations also took place.

Our engagement and protest focused more on what we now call "resistance" rather than "service," the watchword of Kennedy's address. Did it work? By early 1965, a major civil rights conference with speakers of national prominence convened, held principally at the college and organized by students from Amherst, UMass, Smith, and Mt. Holyoke.

Noises Off

Chatland Whitmore, '64

I REMEMBER KENNEDY'S visit to Amherst College, Saturday, October 26, 1963, very clearly. I was sure the squash courts would be empty. So, as I often did, I went to the courts to practice and get a workout.

As I was leaving the court, heading back to the locker room, who did I see but the very recognizable President Kennedy walking my way deep in thought with notes in his hand. He didn't even notice me until he was a few feet away and then said, "Hello!" Marveling at the fact that he was unaccompanied even by Secret Service agents, I belted out, "Hello to you, Mr. President," and continued on my way. His parting remarks were something to the effect that he was rehearsing his notes for the address he was to give.

That is the true version of events! I was in such a state of shock I scarcely remember what actually happened. Moreover, as the years have passed it's even more difficult to remember the details of the experience. The whole episode lasted at most about twenty seconds!

The President and the Poet

Mark J. Sandler, '64

WHEN I THINK of the president and the poet, my memories go from them and what they said to how the experience changed me, to what other things meeting them set in motion—springboard memories.

I was a senior at Amherst in 1963 when I received a note from Calvin Plimpton, the president of Amherst, announcing that President John F. Kennedy was coming to the college to speak at a convocation celebrating the groundbreaking of the new library dedicated to his friend and fellow New Englander, Robert Frost. Dr. Plimpton asked if I, along with seven others, could help out at the post-convocation reception for JFK. I could bring a date. For decades I have had the framed invitation and a picture of Presidents Plimpton and Kennedy hanging on my wall.

I am embarrassed to admit this, but my primary thought upon receiving the invitation was not of the honor and extraordinary experience I had in store. My primary thought was how I could leverage the invitation into a date with a Smith girl who thus far had been friendly but showed no interest in a relationship. So I called her up and asked if she were free that Saturday at midday. She asked what I had in mind. And I deftly played my card.

"How would you like to come over and meet the president of the United States, John F. Kennedy?" I asked.

There was an extended reflective pause on the line before she said, "No, I don't think so, but thanks."

It's the best card I've ever had to play.

When I finally did meet Kennedy, as he worked his way down the line greeting each of us, I was star struck. I had planned a sentence or two to say to him. When he got to me, he looked down at my name tag, then directly at me and said with his broad smile, "So, Maaak, you're from West Haaatfud," speaking Bostonian.

I think I responded with, "Havadahavadahav." I can't remember.

He moved on.

Since that day I have had the good fortune to meet quite a few celebrated people. None have made the impression that he did.

Then there's the poet. I saw him twice when he was in his late eighties, reflective, grizzled but clear-headed. The first time was during a small forum discussion with Archibald MacLeish. MacLeish was a much younger poet of great renown, widely traveled and urbane. He would become Amherst's poet after Frost died. They had a conversation more or less about their poetry, their lives, and what they had learned. I remember clearly my primary impression of that talk. MacLeish had traveled broadly and seemed to know everyone. Frost was New England. But whatever the topic, it seemed as if Frost plumbed a far greater depth. You just wanted to sit with Frost and have him share his perspective on the things that mattered in life. At nineteen, I thought he could save me a lot of time and effort if he shared what he had come to know.

The second time I was with Robert Frost was at a small dinner. I got to sit on his left side. I remember only one thing about that evening. The table was set for a number of courses. The salad was out and there was a low murmur as the group settled in. Everyone was waiting, a little impatiently, for Frost to begin. He finally turned to me and said quietly, "I can never remember which fork to start with." I told him I thought you always started with the one on the outside. That was my only one-on-one conversation with the great poet.

I've wondered what it was that made those two into friends, the old poet at the end of his life and the dashing young president at the height of his. For sure, they both had New England deep inside. But that can't be enough. The president asked Frost, a poet, to speak at his inauguration and to write a special poem for that day. He sent the old man to Russia to speak with Khrushchev. And Frost was comfortable telling Kennedy basically to keep the "Harvard" in him in check.

It may sound strange, but I have come to believe that the key to their relationship was a deep, broad exposure to, and respect for, the liberal arts. They could both speak lucidly about history and power, art, and poetry. They both understood responsibility in human relationships. Kennedy spoke easily and powerfully about the responsibility that privilege imposes: the privilege of good fortune and education that provides a perspective on an individual's life. Kennedy comfortably quoted Frost's line that "when power corrupts, poetry cleanses." Kennedy had great appreciation for the role of the arts in tempering power. Frost could easily look at the sweep of human history and write that, "The land was ours before we were the land's." They both understood the profound nature of taking "the road less traveled" and why that could make all the difference. They both understood friendship, and home, and the brevity of life.

What a quirk of fate that the poet and the president became friends. What a quirk of fate that their paths should cross at Amherst College. What a quirk of fate that death should take them both only months apart, one by old age and the other an assassin's bullet. What a quirk of fate that I was there.

Kennedy Has Been Shot

Robert Knox, '64

AS AN ORDINARY curious student bystander that day, I took no active role in the events of October 26, 1963. I observed such novelties as military helicopters landing on the practice fields and police and security personnel posted everywhere.

Standing back a bit in the crowd between the Alumni Gym and South Pleasant Street and watching the president's motorcade pass by, I thought, "Wow, he's actually right there, so near and so visible, a stone's throw away. If some nut actually wanted to get him, and didn't care about the consequences, it would be pretty easy." Why did that thought come at that time? I do not know. It has, of course, stayed with me ever since, fixed in memory by Kennedy's assassination just twenty-seven days later.

On November 22, I was walking into Fayerweather [the physics building in 1963] by the northern door. I passed by the door to the lab where my classmate Doug Reilly worked. He buttonholed me and said "Knox, come in here; listen to the radio. Kennedy has been shot." My first reaction was that Doug was playing some sort of weird prank. He persisted; I went into his lab where the radio was on, and there it was. Thunderstruck doesn't begin to describe me at that moment.

Shortly thereafter, I encountered the titanic physics professor Arnie Arons. His face and manner evidenced a major storm brewing. We knew his demeanor could be gruff, even in his lighter moments. Under storm conditions, it was memorably severe. We didn't talk long. He was visibly upset, at least as much as I was. But he did comment to the effect that it now seemed "they"—presumably some right-wing fanatic or group of fanatics—had finally managed to take down the president. Of course, he had no evidence as to who had done what; none of us did in that first hour or so. But as a gauge of Arons' emotional side, and of his high esteem for JFK, it was telling. In later years, I never drew him out on that remark, but there it was. I remember it still.

Neither Kennedy's speech nor the assassination had an immediate noticeable effect on my conscious choices about conducting my life. Like many of my friends, I pursued what I found interesting; for me, that was science. I did shift from physics into oceanography, work with a bit more bearing on the actual lives of earthlings than modern physics. Still, I have the incentive of research and discovery that gets scientists of all stripes to wake up in the morning, go the lab, or get the equipment out on deck.

In retrospect, there was a connection to Kennedy's exhortation to make good, not frivolous or selfish, use of the first-rate education we were receiving. Plimpton underscored that idea in his speech after the assassination when he called us to stand a moment in memory of JFK and then go and do the work he could not finish. While I cannot claim some "Road to Damascus" epiphany that stemmed from JFK's visit, such as signing up for the Peace Corps, I did have, like many of us, a sense that one could and should do something that was both personally rewarding and also meaningful in the wider setting of life and the world around us.

Communal Guilt?

David Pearle, '64

I VIVIDLY REMEMBER President Kennedy's October 1963 visit to Amherst. I attended the formal convocation speech and the remarks at the outdoor Frost Library groundbreaking. I briefly met and shook hands with the president. He was charismatic and strikingly handsome. I was particularly struck by his golden tan, which we now know was a consequence of his Addison's disease.

Three weeks later, I had an interview in Boston for Harvard Medical School. I was in the office of a distinguished physician at Massachusetts General Hospital. As we left his office, the staff had gathered around a radio listening to the first reports of the shooting in Dallas. My interviewer said, "Mr. Pearle here is from Dallas." Everyone looked at me as if I had pulled the trigger.

My high school girlfriend from Dallas was a student at Wellesley. I drove there and attended a memorial service at Wellesley that evening. Suzi told me that the news of the assassination had interrupted one of her classes. The professor made the announcement to gasps of horror and grief, then dismissed the class. As everyone got up to leave, the professor looked up and said "Suzi Flaxman, you're from Dallas. I can't stand to look at you."

I remember driving through the streets of Boston as the progressively pessimistic reports were unfolding. There was little traffic, and it was unusually quiet. Several people sat on the curb, feet in the street, heads in their hands, crying.

When I returned to Amherst the next day, multiple notes had been taped to my door or slipped under, mostly to the effect of "Dallas go home," "I hate you and your f—ing town," "How can you show your face?" and worse. I subsequently spoke to several of my Dallas high school friends who attended out-of-state schools; most described similar personal attacks based on their Dallas roots. I was only mildly bothered by the notes at the time. Like everyone else, I was in a state of shock about the assassination. As I thought about it subsequently, everyone was so emotionally overwhelmed that we wanted to blame someone for the catastrophe. But who? Lee Harvey Oswald was such a pathetic and preposterous figure.

For the Amherst community, the assassination had a special resonance because of JFK's magical visit just weeks before.

The impact was similarly amplified for those of us from Dallas. We knew that the city had many with extreme right wing political views and the potential for violence. Ironically, if the official history is to be believed, the assassin came from the left. My parents were liberal activists in Dallas and had been invited to meet with JFK the weekend of the assassination. I knew Jack Ruby a little. He liked to invite (underage) teenage boys from our synagogue to his strip club to show off. We were indeed impressed. Dallas, although predominantly right wing, had a vibrant political culture, a great sense of civic pride, and was a wonderful place to grow up. But many years passed before I was once again proud to be from Dallas.

Do the Work He Couldn't Complete

Rip Sparks, '64

DURING MY CAREER, I had conversations with university students I was considering for graduate research or an internship. They asked about the path I followed from undergraduate to my current position. When I mentioned that I joined the Peace Corps, some nodded knowingly. Remembering that I date from the sixties, they would comment that it was a good way to avoid the draft and the Vietnam War.

It wasn't that at all.

MY CLASSMATES AND I came of age during a series of major historical events that were by turns incredibly inspirational and heart-wrenchingly tragic. We experienced a liberal arts *and* science education that was daunting but sparked conversations that started back then and that resume at each reunion, as though we had just walked out of class.

In the fall of 1960, when we entered Amherst, then-presidential candidate John F. Kennedy spoke directly to our desire to do something significant with our young lives, although most of us weren't sure what that would be. On October 14, 1960, at a late-night rally at the University of Michigan following his third televised debate with Richard Nixon, candidate Kennedy first broached the idea of American college graduates serving people in developing countries.

The inspiring words of Kennedy's January 1961 inauguration as president came to all of us through live television: "...the torch has been passed to a new generation of Americans..." and "Ask not what your country can do for you—ask what you can do for your country." And this less familiar excerpt: *To those people in the huts and villages of half the globe struggling to break the bonds of mass misery, we pledge our best efforts to help them help themselves, for whatever period is required—not because the communists may be doing it, not because we seek their votes, but because it is right. If a free society cannot help the many who are poor, it cannot save the few who are rich.*

The day after the inauguration, the president asked his brother-in-law, Sargent Shriver, who had coordinated the Wisconsin and West Virginia primaries, to set up the Peace Corps as its first director.[2]

Still in our freshman year, we watched news reports of the debacle of the Bay of Pigs Cuban invasion. Although the previous president (Eisenhower) had directed the Central Intelligence Agency to plan the invasion, Kennedy had given the final approval. His administration was the one tarnished with the misjudgments, failures, and losses incurred during the failed attempt to overthrow Fidel Castro's Communist regime, closely allied with the Soviet Union.

The Cold War, Cuba, and Kennedy broke into our lives in an even bigger, more ominous way during our sophomore year. On October 22, 1962, I saw the president announce a naval blockade to turn back Russian ships bearing nuclear-capable missiles for Cuba. I remember my anxiety and despair at these words: *It shall be the policy of this Nation to regard any nuclear missile launched from Cuba against any nation in the Western Hemisphere as an attack by the Soviet Union on the United States, requiring a full retaliatory response upon the Soviet Union.*

My classmates and I tensely followed the approach of the Russian cargo ships to our warships. I remember thinking that many previous wars had started through miscalculations in situations like this, with the difference that an error now could bring a nuclear holocaust, the certain end of all our dreams, and perhaps of us. "I may never have a chance to decide my own future...

---

2   Mark K. Shriver, *A Good Man: Rediscovering My Father, Sargent Shriver* (New York: Henry Holt & Co., 2012), 58.

or to know the love of a good woman," I thought. Within a few days, the Russian ships had turned back. Premier Khrushchev had agreed to remove the missiles that were already on Cuba, and we could go back to our studies and our dreams.[3]

The first two years at Amherst combined boot camp and intellectual awakening. We were among the last students to experience the New Curriculum, which was new in 1947 and ended in 1967. Our freshman year courses, all required, were physics, mathematics, history, and English composition. Except for a few men in our class who were apparently holdovers from the Renaissance, most of us found at least one of the subjects to be extraordinarily difficult. There was no hope in employing approaches that might have worked in high school, such as brute memorization or anticipating what answer the teacher wanted. No, mastery of the language of the subjects (math and English) was necessary, but critical analysis and the cultivation of our own nascent ability to reason were what was demanded.

The boot camp aspect grew from the shared experience of overcoming difficulty, relying on buddies who helped each other, and the rigor of our instructors. There was no opting out of the core curriculum and no awards for trying hard or for most improvement.

We were also the last Amherst students to encounter Robert Frost. He would spend some time on campus in the fall and spring giving public readings, including Parent's Day, October 20, 1962. Frost's poetry was in the at-

---

3   Decades later we learned how dreadfully close we had come to nuclear war. The Soviets shot down a U-2 spy plane over Cuba on October 27, 1962, and Kennedy's military leaders urged him to launch airstrikes against Cuba's air defense. There were three Soviet submarines near the blockade line, each equipped with a nuclear-armed torpedo. The U.S. Navy was forcing each of them to identify themselves by continuously tracking and bombarding them with practice depth charges until the subs ran out of air for their crews and diesel-electric motors and had to surface. The first was "surfaced" the same day the U-2 was shot down, the second and third on October 30 and 31. If the subs had used their Hiroshima-sized nuclear warheads, the U.S. would have made a nuclear counter response. See William Burr and Thomas S. Blanton (eds.), *The Submarines of October: U.S. and Soviet Naval Encounters During the Cuban Missile Crisis*, National Security Archive Electronic Briefing Book No. 75, 2002. https://nsarchive2.gwu.edu/NSAEBB/NSAEBB75/ Also see the docu-drama about officer Vasili Arkhipov on Soviet Submarine B-59, The Man Who Saved the World, a Bedlam Production Ltd. for THIRTEEN in association with WNET (2012).

mosphere—you could not be at Amherst without breathing in some of the lines. What young man would not ponder his future in choosing between divergent roads, knowing that each choice inevitably leads to another farther down that road?

> And both that morning equally lay
> In leaves no step had trodden black.
> Oh, I kept the first for another day!
> Yet knowing how way leads on to way,
> I doubted if I should ever come back.
>
> I shall be telling this with a sigh
> Somewhere ages and ages hence:
> Two roads diverged in a wood, and I—
> I took the one less traveled by,
> And that has made all the difference.[4]

October 1963, our senior year, and the president was coming! At the time, it never occurred to me to wonder why the president, at the height of the Cold War and the civil rights movement and with the 1964 elections approaching, accepted an invitation to speak in our little corner of the world. In my naïve, overweening pride, Amherst, if not the intellectual capital of the U.S., was at least one of its centers, so why wouldn't he come?

The day began with fog that delayed the arrival of the president. The curtain lifted, and soon we could hear the three helicopters, and see them landing from the vantage point of the War Memorial that sits at the edge of the central quad and overlooks the athletic practice fields below and the Cage— the field house where Amherst President Calvin Plimpton awarded Honorary Doctor of Laws degrees to both Kennedy and Archibald MacLeish, poet, writer and the ninth Librarian of Congress (1939-1944).

The speech did not soar at the start. Kennedy opened with self-evident

---

4   Third and fourth stanzas from "The Road Not Taken," Robert Frost, *The Complete Poems of Robert Frost* (New York: Holt, Rinehart and Winston, Inc., 1968), 131.

geography: "This college is part of the United States. It belongs to it. So did Mr. Frost, in a large sense." The next few sentences, intended to be self-deprecatingly humorous, were lost on most of us. He noted that "The powers of the presidency are often described," but "Its limitations should occasionally be remembered." Then he deftly honored two people on the stage, comparing his invitation to speak at the event from the chairman of Amherst's Board of Trustees, John J. McCloy, '16, to MacLeish's invitation to be Librarian of Congress from President Franklin Roosevelt. Kennedy concluded that in each case "…there is only one response. So I am glad to be here."

What followed has been characterized as Kennedy's most magnificent speech. I now understood how we, and Amherst, were in the larger sense, part of the United States.

We were privileged and because of that privilege, obligated: "…what good is a private college or university unless it is serving a great national purpose?" National purpose included the cumulative contributions of artists, writers, and poets. We had heard about liberal arts before (speak truth to power, hold the mirror up to reality), but the idea was freshened and vastly reinforced in the speech of this sitting president at the height of his powers.

His speech soared to its conclusion, "I look forward to a great future for America—a future in which our country will match its military strength with our moral restraint, its wealth with our wisdom, its power with our purpose." Finally, the last sentence returned us to Amherst, and to Frost ending with a Frost-ian phrase: "Because of Mr. Frost's life and work, because of the life and work of this college, our hold on this planet has increased."

President Plimpton characterized the day as "the birth of memory." Little did we realize that in just four weeks there would be another memory, the kind where you remember exactly where you were when you first heard the terrible news.

I was crossing the campus when I heard a radio through an open window, "The president has been shot." Later, from the hospital came the confirmation that he had died. The scenes on television were nearly unbearable. Air Force One, which had borne a president eager to engage the people and political leaders in a state that was projected to be one of the most difficult for him in his campaign for a second term, was now about to bear his casket back to Washington. His wife still wore the blood-stained dress in which she had cradled him. Then, suddenly, we had a newly sworn-in president.

The Student Council asked President Plimpton to address us in Johnson Chapel. That evening, we quietly filed into the building. Only a few times in my life have I heard a speaker so perfectly attuned to an event and to what the audience was feeling. "Four weeks ago he was here. We saw him; we heard him; and we knew him. He was one of us, for he was our most recent alumnus." Plimpton described moments during that day with Kennedy and the people surrounding him. Little things that made it personal, such as taking their jackets off at Plimpton's house, but talking about big things. "But in the midst of life there is death. That is the problem; that is the question. What is the meaning? Where is the sense?" There is one response—rededication and resolve, in the metaphor of Kennedy's inaugural address, to pick up the torch. "Let us remember to advantage our late, great President's toughness in mind, body, and soul. Let us stand a moment in silence, to honor him; then let us go and do the work he couldn't complete."

As I stood that night, I knew I was going to join the Peace Corps.

———

I TURNED BACK to the student in my office, "Do you see how it was?"

4

KENNEDY ON CAMPUS

Many of the authors to this anthology refer to one or more of three important speeches given on October 26, 1963: President Kennedy's convocation address, the President's remarks at the library groundbreaking, and the convocation address by Archibald MacLeish. Others refer to President Plimpton's address of November 22, 1963, and to an essay by the former secretary of the interior Stewart L. Udall titled, "Poetry, Stalinism, and the Cuban Missile Crisis."

This chapter presents the source documents, not only for reference but also as noteworthy examples of excellence in public discourse.

President Kennedy delivered the convocation address in a space known as "the cage." Dank, dreary, and dirt-floored, but the largest enclosed area on campus at the time, the college dressed it for the occasion in flags, curtains, and bunting. Films of the event, however, clearly show its utilitarian architecture.

The Convocation Address

John F. Kennedy
October 26, 1963

MR. McCLOY, PRESIDENT PLIMPTON, Mr. MacLeish, distinguished guests, ladies and gentlemen:

I am very honored to be here with you on this occasion which means so much to this College and also means so much to art and the progress of the United States.

This college is part of the United States. It belongs to it. So did Mr. Frost, in a large sense. And, therefore, I was privileged to accept the invitation somewhat rendered to me in the same way that Franklin Roosevelt rendered his invitation to Mr. MacLeish, the invitation which I received from Mr. McCloy.

The powers of the Presidency are often described. Its limitations should occasionally be remembered, and, therefore, when the Chairman of our Disarmament Advisory Committee, who has labored so long and hard, Governor Stevenson's assistant during the very difficult days at the United Nations, during the Cuban crisis, a public servant of so many years, asks or invites the President of the United States, there is only one response. So I am glad to be here.

Amherst has had many soldiers of the king since its first one, and some of them are here today: Mr. McCloy, who has been a long public servant; Jim [James A.] Reed, who is the Assistant Secretary of the Treasury; President [Charles W.] Cole, who is now our Ambassador to Chile; Mr. [James T.] Ramey, who is a Commissioner of the Atomic Energy Commission; Dick [Richard W.] Reuter, who is head of the Food for Peace. These and scores of others down through the years have recognized the obligations of the advantages which the graduation from a college such as this places upon them: to serve not only their private interest but the public interest as well.

Many years ago, Woodrow Wilson said, "What good is a political party unless it's serving a great national purpose?" And what good is a private college or university unless it's serving a great national purpose? The library being constructed today—this College itself, all of this, of course, was not done merely to give this school's graduates an advantage, an economic advantage, in the life struggle. It does do that. But in return for that, in return for the great opportunity which society gives the graduates of this and related schools, it seems to me incumbent upon this and other schools' graduates to recognize their responsibility to the public interest.

Privilege is here, and with privilege goes responsibility. And I think, as your president said, that it must be a source of satisfaction to you that this school's graduates have recognized it. And I hope that the students who are here now will also recognize it in the future.

Although Amherst has been in the forefront of extending aid to needy and talented students, private colleges, taken as a whole, draw 50 percent of their students from the wealthiest 10 percent of our nation. And even state universities and other public institutions derive 25 percent of their students from this group. In March 1962, persons of 18 years or older who had not completed high school made up 46 percent of the total labor force, and such persons comprised 64 percent of those who were unemployed. And in 1958, the lowest fifth of the families in the United States had four and a half percent of the total personal income, and the highest fifth of the families had forty-five and a half percent.

There is inherited wealth in this country and also inherited poverty. And unless the graduates of this College and other colleges like it who are given a running start in life—unless they are willing to put back into our society those talents, the broad sympathy, the understanding, the compassion— unless they're willing to put those qualities back into the service of the Great Republic, then obviously the presuppositions upon which our democracy are based are bound to be fallible.

The problems which this country now faces are staggering, both at home and abroad. We need the service, in the great sense, of every educated man or woman, to find 10 million jobs in the next two and a half years, to govern our relations—a country which lived in isolation for 150 years, and is now suddenly the leader of the free world—to govern our relations with over 100 countries, to govern those relations with success so that the balance of power remains strong on the side of freedom, to make it possible for Americans of all different races and creeds to live together in harmony, to make it possible for a world to exist in diversity and freedom. All this requires the best of all of us.

And therefore, I am proud to come to this College whose graduates have recognized this obligation and to say to those who are now here that the need is endless, and I'm confident that you will respond.

Robert Frost said it:

Two roads diverged in a wood, and I—
I took the one less traveled by,
And that has made all the difference.

I hope that road will not be the less traveled by, and I hope your commitment to the great public interest in the years to come will be worthy of your long inheritance since your beginning.

This day devoted to the memory of Robert Frost offers an opportunity for reflection which is prized by politicians as well as by others, and even by poets, for Robert Frost was one of the granite figures of our time in America. He was supremely two things: an artist and an American. A nation reveals itself not only by the men it produces but also by the men it honors, the men it remembers.

In America, our heroes have customarily run to men of large accomplishments. But today this College and country honors a man whose contribution was not to our size but to our spirit, not to our political beliefs but to our insight, not to our self-esteem, but to our self-comprehension. In honoring Robert Frost, we therefore can pay honor to the deepest sources of our national strength. That strength takes many forms, and the most obvious forms are not always the most significant. The men who create power make an indispensable contribution to the nation's greatness, but the men who question power make a contribution just as indispensable, especially when that questioning is disinterested, for they determine whether we use power or power uses us.

Our national strength matters, but the spirit which informs and controls our strength matters just as much. This was the special significance of Robert Frost. He brought an unsparing instinct for reality to bear on the platitudes and pieties of society. His sense of the human tragedy fortified him against self-deception and easy consolation. "I have been," he wrote, "one acquainted with the night." And because he knew the midnight as well as the high noon, because he understood the ordeal as well as the triumph of the human spirit, he gave his age strength with which to overcome despair. At bottom, he held a deep faith in the spirit of man, and it's hardly an accident that Robert Frost coupled poetry and power, for he saw poetry as the means of saving power from itself. When power leads man towards arrogance, poetry reminds him of his limitations. When power narrows the areas of man's concern, poetry reminds him of the richness and diversity of his existence. When power corrupts, poetry cleanses. For art establishes the basic human truths which must serve as the touchstone of our judgment.

The artist, however faithful to his personal vision of reality, becomes the last champion of the individual mind and sensibility against an intrusive society and an officious state. The great artist is thus a solitary figure. He has, as Frost said, a lover's quarrel with the world. In pursuing his perceptions of reality, he must often sail against the currents of his time. This is not a popular role. If Robert Frost was much honored during his lifetime, it was because a good many preferred to ignore his darker truths. Yet in retrospect, we see how the artist's fidelity has strengthened the fiber of our national life.

If sometimes our great artists have been the most critical of our society, it is because their sensitivity and their concern for justice which must motivate any true artist, makes him aware that our nation falls short of its highest potential. I see little of more importance to the future of our country and our civilization than full recognition of the place of the artist.

If art is to nourish the roots of our culture, society must set the artist free to follow his vision wherever it takes him. We must never forget that art is not a form of propaganda; it is a form of truth. And as Mr. MacLeish once remarked of poets: "There is nothing worse for our trade than to be in style." In free society art is not a weapon and it does not belong to the sphere of polemics and ideology. Artists are not engineers of the soul. It may be different elsewhere. But democratic society—in it, the highest duty of the writer, the composer, the artist is to remain true to himself and to let the chips fall where they may. In serving his vision of the truth, the artist best serves his nation. And the nation which disdains the mission of art invites the fate of Robert Frost's hired man, the fate of having nothing to look backward to with pride and nothing to look forward to with hope.

I look forward to a great future for America, a future in which our country will match its military strength with our moral restraint, its wealth with our wisdom, its power with our purpose. I look forward to an America which will not be afraid of grace and beauty, which will protect the beauty of our natural environment, which will preserve the great old American houses and squares and parks of our national past, and which will build handsome and balanced cities for our future.

I look forward to an America which will reward achievement in the arts as we reward achievement in business or statecraft. I look forward to an America which will steadily raise the standards of artistic accomplishment and which will steadily enlarge cultural opportunities for all of our citizens. And I look forward to an America which commands respect throughout the world not only for its strength but for its civilization as well. And I look forward to a world which will be safe not only for democracy and diversity but also for personal distinction. Robert Frost was often skeptical about projects for human improvement, yet I do not think he would disdain this hope. As he wrote during the uncertain days of the Second War:

> *Take human nature altogether since time began,*
> *And it must be a little more in favor of man,*
> *Say a fraction of one per cent at the very least,*
> *Our hold on the planet wouldn't have so increased.*

Because of Mr. Frost's life and work, because of the life and work of this College, our hold on this planet has increased.

Speech given by President John F. Kennedy at Amherst College in Massachusetts in honor of the poet Robert Frost at the groundbreaking of the Robert Frost Memorial Library.

The speech is included in a collection of noteworthy eulogies titled *Farewell, Godspeed: The Greatest Eulogies of Our Time* (Copeland, 2003) and in William Safire's collection of great speeches, *Lend Me Your Ears* (Safire, 2004).

October 26, 1963 was a beautiful New England fall day. The ground-breaking ceremony was held outdoors, with a very modest platform that seated eight. The president spoke briefly at the groundbreaking.

The President's Remarks at the Library Groundbreaking

MR. MCCLOY, PRESIDENT PLIMPTON, members of the Trustees, Ladies and Gentlemen: I am privileged to join you as a classmate of Archibald MacLeish's and to participate here at Amherst, and to participate in this ceremony. I knew Mr. Frost quite late in his life, in really the last four or five years, and I was impressed, as I know all you were who knew him, by a good many qualities, but also by his toughness. He gives the lie, as a good many other poets have, to the fact that poets are rather sensitive creatures who live in the dark of the garret. He was very hard-boiled in his approach to life, and his desires for our country. He once said that America is the country you leave only when you want to go out and lick another country. He was not particularly belligerent in his relations, his human relations, but he felt very strongly that the United States should be a country of power and force and use that power and force wisely. But he once said to me not to let the Harvard in me get to be too important. So we have followed that advice. "Home," he once wrote, "is a place where when you have to go there they have to take you in." And Amherst took him in. This was his home on and off for 22 years. The fact that he chose this College, this campus, when he could have gone anywhere and would have been warmly welcomed, is a tribute to you as much as it is to Mr. Frost. When he was among you, he once said, "I put my students on the operating table and proceeded to take ideas they didn't know they had out of them." The great test of a college student's chances, he also wrote, is when he knows the sort of work for which he will neglect his studies. In 1937 he said of Amherst, "I have reason to think they like to have me here." And now you are going to have him here for many, many years. Professor Kittredge, at Harvard, once said that they could take down all the buildings of Harvard, and if they kept Widener Library, Harvard would still exist. Libraries are memories and, in this library, you will have the memory of an extraordinary American, but more than that, really, an extraordinary human being; and also, you will have the future, and all the young men who come into this library will touch something of distinction in our national life, and, I hope, give something to it. I am proud to be associated with this great enterprise. Thank you.

Archibald MacLeish, lawyer, poet, and public servant, a star in his own right, played only a supporting role to President Kennedy at the convocation. MacLeish, however had won three Pulitzer Prizes and had, until 1962, taught as the Boylston Professor of Rhetoric and Oratory at Harvard University. His sparkling, witty convocation speech deserves reproduction in this collection.

Frost and Stone
The Convocation Address

Archibald MacLeish
Reproduced from the *Amherst Alumni Quarterly*, Fall 1963

MY PRESENCE HERE today is proof—if any is needed in a college as civilized as Amherst—that you can't learn by experience. By which I mean that this is not the first time I have assisted a President of the United States to start a library. It was some twenty odd years ago at Hyde Park in the State of New York where a building had been constructed to house the papers of Franklin Delano Roosevelt—which was all very well except for two facts: that I was Librarian of Congress at the time, having just been appointed to that office by Mr. Roosevelt, and that the Library of Congress, down at least to the date of my appointment, had itself been the usual repository for Presidential papers. Mr. Roosevelt's invitation to me to speak at Hyde Park – if "invitation" is the word I want—was, I dare say, kindly meant: there was to be nothing personal about the affront. But it is one thing for an invitation to be kindly meant and another thing altogether to accept it in kind—particularly when it involves a speech by the director of the library to which invaluable papers ought to have gone, celebrating the opening of the library to which they are going. I made, I am told, a memorable impression. Indeed, my friend and classmate, Dean Acheson, on whose unfailing candor I have always been able to rely whether I wanted to or not, assured me on my return to Washington that no public servant in the history of the Republic had ever appeared to better advantage with his pants firmly caught in the crack of the door. There are differences, of course, between that day and this. I don't work for Mr. Kennedy—or if I do, it is from the private heart, not from public office. And as for the Library of Congress, it has long since grown accustomed to the alienation of hoped-for papers, some having been alienated as far west as Independence, Missouri. But whatever else is altered, the fact remains that a library, or the idea of a library, is here again in process of inauguration by a President of the United States and that I seem again to be part of the proceedings. If precedents still mean anything in this revolving world, the probability must be very great indeed that no good will come of it. No good, that is, to me. Amherst can be more hopeful and so too can this October valley and the old, soft, lovely hills off to the west of it where I have lived for half a biblical lifetime. The people of this countryside may forget in ordinary human course what anyone says on this occasion, but they will remember for many, many years that a young and gallant President of the United States, with the weight of history heavy upon his shoulders, somehow found time to come to our small corner of the world to talk of books and men and learning. I say "small corner" not in modesty but in Yankee modesty—which is a different thing. We may not be as conspicuous at this end of the Commonwealth, Mr. President, as some you must have heard of at the other, but we bear up. We remind ourselves that it was a citizen of this very town of Amherst who was described by a famous daughter as "too intrinsic for renown," and we like to think that even now, a century after Edward Dickinson's death, there are still men in these valley villages and up along the Deerfield, Bardwell's Ferry way and in the hills behind, who deserve the tribute of Emily's unfractured crystal of pure poetry, pure praise. But whether we are right or not—whether we and our neighbors are too intrinsic for renown or merely too remote for notoriety—we know an honor when we see one, and your presence here we take to be just that: an honor to this College and these counties and ourselves. Not to mention Robert Frost, for Frost, of course, is another matter—as he always was. There is an old Gaelic tale of the West Highlands called "The Brown Bear of The Green Glen" which has a whiskey bottle in it so definitively full that not a drop can be added, and so fabulously copious that nothing is lost, no matter how you drink it. Frost's fame is like that bottle: it can't be added to because it is full already, and it won't draw down however it is drunk. We may name a library for him. We may go farther than that: we may give his name to the first general library ever to be called for a poet in America—which is what this library will be. We may pass even that superlative of honor: we may designate as his the first general library but one in the entire world to bear a poet's name—the one being the A. S. Pushkin State Public Library in farther Kazakhstan in the U.S.S.R. We may do what we please. Nothing whatever will have happened to the bottle: it will merely continue to be full. This, I suggest, is a phenomenon which might well concern us on this particular occasion—the secret of that bottle. Is it the mere bulk and body of the fame which keeps it so miraculously brimming—the fact that no poet in English, with the single exception of Yeats himself, had as much fame in his lifetime as Frost had at the end of his? Is it the quantity of the reputation, the number of people who knew Frost's name or recognized him on the streets or crowded into those wonderful talkings which some called readings, and lined up afterward for autographs they rarely got? I doubt it and so do you. We know a little in our time and country about fame in bulk and its effect on lasting fame. At least we know what happens when a whole new industry is established, dedicated to nothing but the manufacture, in larger and larger quantities and in shorter and shorter periods of time, of crude, bulk reputation: we have seen its fruits. (Try not to see them!) If great actresses are in short supply, as they invariably are, two or three to a century being about all the natural processes can produce, the industry will assemble you a dozen assorted Greatest Actresses in a single season, inflate them with adjectives and launch them like blimps to float about for a year or three or maybe five or longer. But then what happens to them? Or to the greatest novels, the greatest plays, detergents, sedatives, cigarettes, laxatives, which circle with them? Or even to the greatest men? And even when they are great. For the industry processes everyone, true as well as false. Let the actual thing itself appear—Keats's seldom-appearing Socrates in fact and in the flesh – and the assembly line will multigraph him and pass him current by every mechanical means until nothing is left of the single, human fact of the man himself but his bubble reputation in as many million mouths as the new technology can activate. It takes an Einstein to survive it. And even Einstein had reason to be grateful for the isolation of his vast achievement out among the galaxies of space and mind where the copywriters couldn't follow. Yet Frost, too, survived, and with no such adventitious aid. Everything about him—the seeming simplicity of his poems, the silver beauty of his head, his age, his Yankee tongue, his love of talk, his ease upon a lecture platform—everything combined to put him within easy reach. No one in my time upon this planet was so pursued by fame as Frost—so "publicized" in the specific sense and meaning of that word. But even now, months after his death, the "public image," as the industry would call it, has already begun to change like the elms in autumn, leaving enormous branches black and clean against the sky. Frost too, it seems, but in a different way, an opposite way, is "too intrinsic for renown"—too intrinsic for renown to touch. Something in the fame resists the flame as burning maple logs—rock maple anyway—resist the blaze. And what it is, I think we know. At least there is an evening, not many years ago or many blocks from here—an evening others in this room remember—which might tell us. It was his eightieth birthday. Frost had been in New York where every possible honor, including some not possible, had been paid him, and, returning here to Amherst and his friends, he fell to talking of what honor really was, or would be: to leave behind him, as he put it, "a few poems it would be hard to get rid of." It sounds like a modest wish but Frost knew, as his friends knew, that it wasn't. Poems are not monuments – shapes of stone to stand and stand. Poems are speaking voices. And a poem that is hard to get rid of is a voice that is hard to get rid of. And a voice that is hard to get rid of is a man. What Frost wanted for himself in the midst of all that praise was what Keats had wanted for himself in the midst of no praise at all: to be among the English poets at his death—the poets of the English tongue. Which means something very different from being talked about or passed from mouth to mouth by reputation. Reputation—above all literary reputation—is a poor thing. It rises and falls. Consideration leads to reconsideration, fashions change and no one yet has heard the verdict of posterity because posterity has never come. Frost will be praised and then neglected and then praised again like all the others. It wasn't reputation he was thinking of that wintry evening: it was something else. To be among the English poets is to be—to go on being. Frost wanted to go on being. And he has. It is this fact—this actual and not at all imaginary or pretended fact—I wish to speak of for a moment: the persistence of this man. It has a certain relevance to what we do here. On the surface of these proceedings Frost's part in them is purely passive: nothing is asked of him but to receive the honor we now pay him and to relinquish a great name he does not own, having bequeathed it to the future—three syllables to be carved above a doorway…Frost and stone to age together. In fact, however, if one includes among his facts the fact I speak of, these roles are quite reversed: like the citizens of Colonus at the death of Oedipus in Sophocles' great play, the passive part is ours. He gives: we take. Not that Frost was Oedipus precisely—except, perhaps, in his constant readiness to talk back to sphinxes. But there is something in the ending of that myth that gives this myth of ours its meaning. You remember how it goes—the wretched, unhappy, humbled, hurt old king, badgered and abused by fate, gulled by every trick the gods can play him, tangled in patricide and incest and in every guilt, snarled in a web of faithful falsehoods and affectionate deceptions and kind lies, exiled by his own proscription, blinded by his own hands, who, dying, has so great a gift to give that Thebes and Athens quarrel over which shall have him. You remember what the gift is too. "I am here," says Oedipus to Theseus, King of Athens, "to give you something, my own beaten self, no feast for the eyes…" And why is such a gift worth having? Because Oedipus is about to die. But why should death give value to a gift like that? Because of the place where death will meet him:

> *I shall disclose to you, O son of Aegeus,*
> *What is appointed for your city and for you—*
> *Something that time will never wear away.*
> *Presently now without a hand to guide me*
> *I shall lead you to the place where I must die.*

And what is that place? The Furies' wood which no man dares to enter: the frightening grove sacred to those implacable pursuers, ministers of guilt, who have hounded him across the world.

> *These things are mysteries, not to be explained*
> *But you will understand when you have come there.*

The gift that Oedipus has to give is a great gift because that beaten suffering self, no feast for the eyes, faces the dark pursuers at the end. Frost, I said, was not Oedipus, and so he wasn't. But he too has that gift to give. And I can imagine some late student reading his poems in the library that bears his name and feeling, like Theseus, that the beaten and triumphant self has somehow, and mysteriously, been given him—a self not unlike the old Theban King's. Quarrelsome? Certainly—and not with men alone but gods. Tangled in misery? More than most men. But despairing? No. Defeated by the certainty of death? Never defeated. Frightened of the dreadful wood? Not frightened either. A rebellious, brave, magnificent, far-wandering, unbowed old man who made his finest music out of manhood and met the Furies on their own dark ground. We do not live, I know, in Athens. We live now in an insignificant, remote, small suburb of the universe. Reality, if one can speak still of reality, is out beyond us in the light-years somewhere, or farther inward than our eyes can see in the always redivisible divisibilities of matter that is only matter to eyes as dim and dull as ours. Homer's heroic world where men could face their destinies and die becomes to us, with our more comprehensive information, the absurd world of Sartre where men can only die. And yet, though all our facts are changed, nothing has been changed in fact: we still live lives. And lives still lead to death. And those who live a life that leads to death still need the gift that Oedipus gave Athens, the gift of self, of beaten self, of wandering, defeated, exiled self that can survive, endure, turn upon the dark pursuers, face its unintelligible destiny with blinded eyes and make a meaning of it…self, above all else, without self-pity.

President Plimpton's Address to the College

November 22, 1963

Amherst's president, Calvin Plimpton, spoke to the college community in the iconic setting of Johnson Chapel on Friday evening, November 22, 1963, after the news was received of President John F. Kennedy's assassination.

PRESIDENT'S MESSAGE[1]

FRIDAY, NOV. 22—The Reverend Lewis S. Mudge and President Calvin H. Plimpton, '39, conducted a short ceremony tonight in Johnson Chapel to commemorate the death of President John F. Kennedy, shot today in Dallas, Texas. The Student Council requested Dr. Plimpton to address the student body.

Members of the College community filled the Chapel to honor the late president and to hear Dr. Plimpton. Reverend Mudge offered the opening prayer. The proceedings follow.

The Rev. Lewis S. Mudge, Minister to the College: "Our Father and our God, look down in mercy upon us who scarcely yet can understand the tragic events of this day. Be compassionate to those whose family joy has been so swiftly turned into mourning. Grant unto our new President strength,

---

1   The Amherst Student, XCIII no. 19 (Nov. 23, 1963), 1-2.

wisdom, skill, and faith. Grant that we may be drawn closer together by our common sorrow. And, if it be thy will, guide us and our nation in this troubled time until the day breaks and the shadows flee away, through Jesus Christ our Lord. Amen."

President Calvin H. Plimpton '39:

"Four weeks ago he was here. We saw him; we heard him; and we knew him. He was one of us, for he was our most recent alumnus.

"Remember the words of Archie MacLeish: 'The people of this countryside may forget in the ordinary human course what anyone says on this occasion, but they will remember for many, many years that a young and gallant President of the United States, with the weight of history heavy upon him, somehow found time to come to our small corner of the world to talk of books and men and learning.' Now he is gone. But I think we bear with pride our sorrows so sharpened by this very intimacy.

"I suppose I saw more of him than most of you, and I would like to tell you my impressions, one man looking at another man. He came back to our house twice. The first time he took off his coat, and we talked in our shirtsleeves. Mr. MacLeish, being a bit older, just took off his vest.

"Mr. McCloy, being the oldest of all, kept his coat and vest on. We talked about Adenauer, McNamara, Eisenhower, the atom bomb and Gilpatrick. It was high level, and it was good to hear. Then we drove to the library and joked and talked and came back to the house.

"What was the impression he made upon me? He had said in his speech that Robert Frost had toughness. But this was also the impression that Mr. Kennedy gave me: not tough in the sense of ruthlessness or boorishness, rather tough in the sense of purpose, of mission and of meaning business. Tough like a machine that has been honed down with all the frills removed, ready for action—action in mind, in thought; action in body.

"He had a certain leanness which I admire. He was born rich, but he worked harder than the poor. There was no softness about him. Becoming President and then being President is not a sweet indulgence of one's ego. He was ambitious, but his concern was not himself. He was physically lean, no extra flab, no paunch around his middle. And he was lean with words. His speech was no windy diatribe. And he was lean in personality. He was not a charmer, not smooth. There was no soft soap, no affectations, no 'side', no effort to seem important—rather this very strong sense of purpose, with no time to ask himself if he was happy. He believed he could do the job better than anyone else, so he moved briskly. What's the question? What's the response? His thoughts were clear, going immediately to the heart of the problem. It was a tough, yet supple mind.

"Mr. Kennedy enjoyed his visit. He met Mr. McCloy the next week in Washington and said how much he had enjoyed Amherst; said he hadn't known it was such a fine college, and he was very glad to had been invited.

"But in the midst of life there is death. That is the problem; that is the question. What is the meaning? Where is the sense? He's gone now, but not necessarily all of him, and there lies the sense. As we shed our tears, let us remember his toughness. Let us trim our paunches, curtail our self-indulgence, our petty searches for little concerns, our laziness. As Robert Frost said of tennis courts, "We're not on them to see if the lines are straight, but to play tennis." We are here to sharpen our wits and to strengthen our bodies. Let us remember to advantage our late, great President's toughness in mind, body and soul. Let us stand a moment in silence, to honor him; then let us go and do the work he couldn't complete."

Stewart Udall, a former Arizona congressman and secretary of the interior, was close to both Frost and Kennedy. In this essay, he offered an insider's viewpoint on Frost's ill-fated journey to Russia and Kennedy's speech at Amherst.

Poetry, Stalinism and the Cuban Missile Crisis

Stewart L. Udall
October 30, 1988

MANY AMERICANS REMEMBER Robert Frost reciting his poem "The Gift Outright" at John F. Kennedy's presidential inauguration in 1960. Few know the story of their later estrangement or its remarkable epilogue.

The estrangement began two years later, when Frost was serving as a consultant to the Library of Congress. I was an Arizona congressman at the time and invited the poet to an after-dinner dialogue at our home with Soviet Ambassador Anatoly Dobrynin. After Frost engaged the ambassador in a piquant exchange about the need for more constructive forms of rivalry between our two countries, I impulsively proposed that Frost accompany me on an upcoming trip to the Soviet Union and explore his ideas with Soviet poets and writers. Dobrynin liked the idea, but the evening ended with Frost, then in his eighty-eigth year, wondering whether he was "up to it."

The poet advised me a few days later that he would make the trip if the President wanted him to go. Kennedy promptly sent a note endorsing the mission—and plans were soon under way. When we left Washington, however, I did not envision that either of us would be invited to confer with Nikita

Khrushchev. On the plane I said as much to Frost and was dismayed to learn that he had his mind set on a "big conversation" with the Soviet leader. Frost saw himself as an emissary of mankind, not as an ambassador on another cultural mission. His yearning for an exchange with Khrushchev grew out of a conviction that his tie with Kennedy put him in a position to make a contribution to peace.

Through a quirk of cold-war history, Frost's wish was fulfilled and both of us, on succeeding days, had long audiences with Premier Khrushchev. We didn't know it at the time, but our host had given us walk-on roles in a prologue to the impending Cuban missile crisis of October 1962.

Robert Frost had been escorted to the Crimea, where he was to visit with Khrushchev at the premier's summer retreat on the Black Sea, by Alexei Surkov, a poet who headed the Soviet Writers Union. Frost had a fever when he arrived in the Crimea and announced from his bed that he could not make the drive to keep his appointment with the premier. Advised by Surkov of Frost's illness, Khrushchev sent his personal physician to treat the poet and then came to his bedside for a talk that lasted for nearly an hour and a half.

After a few minutes of get-acquainted conversation, Khrushchev asked the poet if he "had something special in mind." Frost was ready—and a dramatic photograph of this bedside meeting shows the ailing poet making a vigorous presentation to his host.

Frost defined a code of conduct that would enable two nations "laid out for noble rivalry" to steer clear of mistakes and misjudgments that would inexorably produce catastrophes. He argued that the leaders had a duty to resolve conflicts before they became inflamed and to create a climate of understanding in which wide-ranging contact and competition could thrive. If there was mutual restraint, both sides would soon recognize "that petty squabbles and blackguarding propaganda" had to be avoided. "Great nations admire each other and don't take pleasure in belittling each other," the poet asserted.

Frost then told Premier Khrushchev that the "high-minded" rivalry he had in mind would encompass sports, science, art, democracy. The great test, he said, would be "Which democracy is going to win?" The premier agreed but added that the "fundamental conflict between the two countries was peaceful economic competition." The discussion then touched on the Berlin impasse, the perils of nuclear war, the implications of economic competition—and the common cultural traditions of the United States and the Soviet Union. And both men, before their final handshake, expressed confidence in the future and in the capacity of their two countries to meet the challenge of what Frost called "a hundred years of grand rivalry."

When Khrushchev left the room, the poet fell back on his bed exhausted. He said to Frank Reeve, "Well we did it, didn't we? He's a great man all right." Robert was elated by his performance, and by the situation. At the time I was puzzled by the long hours Nikita Khrushchev spent visiting with the two of us.

Six weeks later, when President Kennedy informed a trembling world that the Russians were building launching sites for missiles in Cuba, I realized that the poet and I, like Rosencrantz and Guildenstern, had innocently walked onto a stage where a great struggle would soon occur. It was clear then that Premier Khrushchev's high-risk missile decision had been made many weeks before our arrival—and that our appearance offered him an opportunity to reassure President Kennedy that he was rational by talking earnestly about peaceful competition with his friends.

Khrushchev was using a Russian version of poetry-and-power to push his program of political reform. There is ample evidence that the very week we saw him, Khrushchev approved a new round of de-Stalinization involving the publication of works by controversial Soviet writers to help him consolidate his base of political power. En route to the Black Sea, Surkov, the cultural commissar, had informed Frank Reeve that he was on a "business" trip, and he was seen later having an intense discussion with Khrushchev.

That business, history tells us, resulted in a fascinating coincidence. October 21, 1962, the day on which President Kennedy alerted the world to the Cuban gambit that produced this century's first nuclear confrontation, was also the day on which Yevgeny Yevtushenko's daring new poem, "The Heirs of Stalin"—an emotional appeal for vigilance to "stop Stalin from rising again"—appeared in Pravda. And the same week, "One Day in the Life of Ivan Denisovich," a searing expose of Stalin's prison camps by a then-obscure novelist, Alexander Solzhenitsyn, was published.

But as we flew homeward, we knew nothing about Cuban missiles or Alexander Solzhenitsyn. And Frost unfortunately was not aware that, while we were aboard, a senator had put President Kennedy on tenterhooks by charging that Khrushchev was sending troops to Cuba and was demanding an immediate invasion of that island.

When we arrived in New York on September 9, Frost had been awake for eighteen hours and was utterly exhausted. I should have prevented press interviews, but his visit with Khrushchev was a front-page story that day, and many reporters were at the airport for more information about Frost's impressions of the premier. Suddenly, near the end of the questioning, Frost wearily blurted out: "Khrushchev said…he thought that we're too liberal to fight—he thinks we will sit on one hand and then the other."

I was appalled. Reeve and I both knew that Khrushchev had never said this. The phrase "too liberal to fight" was a cliché Robert had used for many years to tease his dovish friends at Harvard. Frost had misrepresented Khrushchev's position, violated his own rules for "magnanimous conduct" and embarrassed his friend, the President. The damage was done—the headline in the *Washington Post* the next morning read, "Frost Says Khrushchev Sees U.S. as Too Liberal to Defend Itself."

Kennedy was stung by Frost's statement. The first question he fired at me was "Why did he have to say that?" The depth of the President's resentment was manifest during the weeks that followed. There was no follow-up on Frost's trip: The poet was not invited to Washington either for a debriefing or to convey the "personal message" from Premier Khrushchev to Kennedy.

Frost, hypersensitive himself to slights, knew he had "crossed" Kennedy. I got the impression, however, that he anticipated all along that Kennedy would mellow and put aside his grievance once the Cuban confrontation was resolved. But this was not to be. The day the crisis was officially ended, Frost sent me this wire: "Will you tell the President from me today quote Great

Going unquote. All the situation needed was his decision on our part. You and I saw that Khrushchev was tipping westward with all his heart. His be some of the praise." I passed it along, but it did not evoke a reply.

When headlines in early December informed the country that Robert Frost was seriously ill in a Boston hospital, his room was showered with wires and flowers from Ambassador Dobrynin and from Americans in all walks of life. Ethel and Robert Kennedy sent flowers, but no message came from the President.

A month later the poet was dead. Ten months later the President was dead as well. But during that time, Kennedy had experienced a change of heart where Frost was concerned. At Amherst College, on October 26, 1963, he delivered a eulogy of Frost that I consider the most majestic speech of his public career.

JFK'S HANDWRITTEN EDITS[1]
to the Speech Drafted by Arthur Schlesinger, Jr.

AMHERST   AS, jr.

draft

This day -- a day devoted to the memory of Robert Frost --

offers an opportunity for reflection -- an opportunity to be prized,

I might add, by politicians no less than by poets. For Robert Frost

was one of the ~~unchallengeable hero~~s *granite figures* of our time in America. ~~He~~

~~carved his poetry in materials as subtle as the colors~~ of this New

~~England Indian summer, and as enduring as the granite of his~~ New

~~Hampshire~~ hills. He was supremely two things: an artist and an

American. As we reflect on his life and his work, we must inevitably

reflect on the abiding values of our American civilization.

A nation reveals itself, not only by the men it produces, but by

the men it honors. ~~A society~~ betrays its innermost se~~crets by its~~

~~choice of heroes~~. In America, our heroes have customarily run to

men of large and dramatic accomplishment -- ~~statesmen, explore~~rs,

~~generals, magnates, inventors, men of notable courage in war, men~~

~~of notable enterprise in pea~~ce. But today this College and this

country honor a man whose contribution was not to our size but to our

spirit -- not to our ideology but to our insight -- not to our self-esteem

but to our self-comprehension. In honoring Robert Frost, we pay

homage to the deepest sources of our national strength.

1   Annotated draft of Kennedy's Convocation speech prepared by Arthur Schlesinger, Jr.
     Reproduced courtesy of the John F. Kennedy Library, President's Office Files, Speech
     Files, Box 47.

2.

Strength takes many forms -- and the most obvious forms
are not necessarily the most significant. ~~We take great comfort
in our nuclear stockpiles, our gross national product, our~~ scientific
and ~~technological achievement,~~ our industrial might -- and, up to
~~a point, we are right to do so.~~ But ~~physical power by itself solves~~
no problems and secures no victories. What counts is the way
power is used -- whether with ~~swagger~~ and contempt, or with
prudence, discipline and magnanimity. What counts is the purpose
for which power is used -- whether for aggrandizement or for
liberation. ~~"It is excellent," Shakespeare said, "to have a giant's
strength; but it is tyrannous to use it like a giant."~~

The men who create power make an indispensable contribution
to a nation's greatness. But the men who question power make a
contribution just as indispensable -- for they determine whether we
use power or power uses us. Our strength matters -- but the spirit
which informs and controls our strength matters just as much. This
was the ~~greatness~~ of Robert Frost. He brought an unsparing instinct
for reality to bear on the platitudes and pieties of society. His sense
of the human tragedy fortified him against self-deception and cheap
consolation. "I have been," he wrote, "one acquainted with the
night." And, because he knew the gloom of midnight as well as the

high

~~blaze of~~ noon, because he understood the ordeal as well as the
triumph of the human spirit, he gave his age new strength with
which to overcome despair.   At bottom, he held and affirmed a
deep faith in the unconquerable soul of man.

It is hardly an accident that Frost coupled poetry and power;
for he saw poetry as the means of saving power from itself.   When
power leads man toward arrogance, poetry reminds him of his
limitations.   When power narrows the area of man's concern,
poetry reminds him of the richness and diversity of his existence.
When power corrupts — poetry cleanses —
~~When power intoxicates, poetry restores sobri~~ty.   For art
establishes the basic human truths which serve as the touchstone
of judgment.   The artist, forever faithful to his personal vision of
reality, becomes the last champion of the individual mind and
sensibility against an intrusive society and an officious state.

The great artist is thus a solitary figure.   He has, as Frost
said, a lover's quarrel with the world.   In pursuing his perceptions
of reality, he must often sail against the currents of his time.
This is not a popular role.   If Robert Frost was much honored when
he was alive, it was sometimes by those who preferred to ignore
his darker truths.   ~~Too often we do not honor our artists until they~~

...

4.

are dead and can disturb us no longer. Yet, in retrospect, we
see how the artist's fidelity has strengthened the fiber of our
national life. If sometimes our great artists have appeared
most critical of our society, it is because *their feelings are so strong*
that they cannot bear for it to fall short of its highest potentialities.

I see little more important to the future of our civilization
than full recognition of the place of the artist. If art is to nourish
the roots of our culture, society must set the artist free to follow
his vision wherever it leads. We must never forget that art is not
a form of propaganda; it is a form of truth; and, as Mr. MacLeish
once remarked of poets, "There is nothing worse for our trade than
to be in style." In free society, art is _not_ a weapon. Art does _not_
belong to the sphere of ideology. Artists are _not_ engineers of the
soul.

It may be different elsewhere. In Soviet Russia, Chairman
Khrushchev has informed us, "It is the highest duty of the Soviet
writer, artist and composer, of every creative worker, to be in the
ranks of the builders of communism, to put his talents at the service
of the great cause of our Party, to fight for the triumph of the ideas
of Marxism-Leninism." In democratic society, the highest duty

of the writer, artist and composer is to remain true to himself

and to his vocation, letting the chips fall where they may.

In serving his vision of the truth, the artist best serves his

nation.   And the nation which disdains the mission of art invites

the fate of Robert Frost's hired man -- the fate of having

> Nothing to look backward to with pride
> And nothing to look forward to with hope.

I look forward to a great future for America -- a future in which

our country will match its military strength with its moral restraint,

its wealth with its wisdom, its power with its purpose.

I look forward to an America which will not be afraid of grace

and beauty -- which will protect the loveliness of our natural environ-

ment, which will preserve the fine old houses and squares and parks

of our national past, and which will build handsome and spacious

cities in the future.

I look forward to an America which will reward achievement in

the arts as it rewards achievement in business or in statecraft.

I look forward to an America which will steadily raise the

standards of artistic accomplishment and which will steadily enlarge

cultural opportunities for all.

I look forward to an America which commands respect through

the world not only for its strength but for its civilization.

I look forward to a world which will be safe not for democracy and for diversity but for distinction.

Robert Frost was often skeptical about projects for human improvement. Yet I do not think he would disdain this hope. As he wrote during the uncertain days of the Second World War,

> We may doubt the just proportion of good to ill.
> There is much in nature against us. But we forget:
> Take nature altogether since time began,
> Including human nature in peace and war,
> And it must be a little more in favor of man,
> Say a fraction of one per cent at the very least,
> Or our number living wouldn't be steadily more,
> Our hold on the planet wouldn't have so increased.

5

ANNOTATED TIMELINE
Kennedy, Frost, and the Amherst College Class of 1964

Rip Sparks, '64

"We live forward, but we understand backward."
—Danish philosopher Søren Kierkegaard (1813-1855)

HOW REMARKABLE IT WAS for a sitting president, in the midst of grave international and domestic issues and a personal tragedy, to spend a beautiful fall day in 1963 at our small liberal arts college talking to us about the civic and ethical responsibilities of the privileged and the critical role of the arts and artists in the exercise of political power. We now appreciate the respect and gratitude that JFK had for the extraordinary, long-term government service of the Chair of Amherst's Board of Trustees, John J. McCloy. When McCloy invited the president to speak at the college, in Kennedy's own words, "…there is only one response. So I am glad to be here."

The speech JFK gave that day has been characterized as "the most majestic speech of his career,"[1] but it can also be understood as making amends

---

1   Udall, Stewart L. 1988. "Of Poetry and Power." *Los Angeles Times* endpapers section, 6 November 1988. http://articles.latimes.com/1988-11-06/books/bk-49_1_robert-frost

for breaking off contact and friendship with Robert Frost prior to the poet's death in January 1963. Based on documents that were not released to historians for years, in some cases fifty years, we can now appreciate how harmful, in Kennedy's view, were Frost's remarks to the press upon his return from a visit in September that included several hours talking with Soviet Premier Nikita Khrushchev. Unknown to Frost, Khrushchev was also pursuing a deliberate policy of brinkmanship by putting nuclear missiles in Cuba and wanted a private channel to assure JFK that the premier was rational. Khrushchev was also applying his own version of poetry and power, by authorizing publication of Russian writers as part of his de-Stalinization campaign.

JFK soon learned about the approach of Soviet freighters carrying land-based missiles to Cuba but did not know there were Soviet submarines equipped with nuclear-armed torpedoes to protect the ships from interdiction. Those thirteen days in October 1962 were more dangerous than we knew, and we now understand how critical it was that Khrushchev not misjudge JFK's resolve.

JFK faced troubled relations with China and the Soviet Union and trouble spots in Southeast Asia, Africa, and South and Central America. The disastrous attempt to depose Fidel Castro in Cuba occurred early in his presidency. The Soviets constructed the Berlin Wall and attempted to force the Allies to abandon the city and any progress toward eventual reunification of Germany. On the domestic front, the economy was still recovering from recession when JFK took office. Although laws had been passed against segregation in public transportation, schools, and businesses serving the public, attempts to integrate often met with violence and rioting. African-American churches and homes were bombed including the Sixteenth Street Baptist Church in Birmingham, Alabama, where four girls in Sunday school were killed.

There were big initiatives in space exploration, mental health, and overseas development (Peace Corps, Alliance for Progress) and hopeful visions and actions for equal opportunity and justice at home and for international cooperation in the arts and sciences and conquest of disease.

The president attended to the mid-term congressional elections of 1962 and was preparing for the presidential election of 1964. In midst of all this, John and Jacqueline Kennedy lost their newborn son in August 1963.

It was an incredibly event-crowded, inspiring, tumultuous, and dangerous time, yet the president made time to think deeply and speak eloquently about poetry and power in our democracy. The speech he gave that afternoon was his last. It is one to come back to, whenever we need a touchstone for our own times.

Notes: (1) The focus is on the years 1960–1963. (2) Footnotes are not provided for information that is readily available from multiple authoritative sites on the web. Footnotes are provided for information that is only available in print; or is available, but on less prominent web sites; or seems to be the most authoritative where dates or other details differ among sites.

1874	26 Mar	Robert Frost was born to William Prescott Frost, Jr., and Isabelle Moodie in San Francisco, CA.
1917	29 May	John Fitzgerald Kennedy (JFK) was born to Joseph P. Kennedy, Sr., and Rose Elizabeth Fitzgerald in Brookline, MA.
1959	Jan	Fidel Castro's revolutionary forces seized power in Cuba, President Batista fled.
	26 Mar	Press conference prior to Frost's eighty-fifth birthday gala. In response to a question regarding the alleged decline of New England, Frost responded, "The next President of the United States will be from Boston. Does that sound as if New England is decaying? … He's a Puritan named Kennedy. The only Puritans left these days are the Roman Catholics. There. I guess I wear my politics on my sleeve."[2]
	April	JFK letter to Frost: "I just want to send you a note to let you know how gratifying it was to be remembered by you on the occasion of your 85th birthday." [3]

---

2   http://www.poets.org/poetsorg/text/poetry-and-power-robert-frosts-inaugural-reading

3   *Ibid.*

1960	Feb	Sit-ins by African-Americans at segregated lunch counters began and spread to sixty-five cities in twelve southern states.
	April	An economic recession began that lasted ten months, until February 1961.[4] The Gross Domestic Product of the U.S. fell 1.6 percent in May. By the time of the November presidential election, the economy was shrinking 4.2 percent and unemployment had grown to 6.6 percent.[5]
	1 May	Gary Powers' U-2 spy plane was shot down over U.S.S.R.
	7 May	U.S.S.R. established diplomatic relations with Cuba.
	13 Sept	An Act of Congress authorized the president to present Frost a Congressional Gold Medal, "In recognition of his poetry, which has enriched the culture of the United States and the philosophy of the world."[6] JFK made the presentation in March 1962.
	19 Oct	Martin Luther King (MLK) was arrested in Atlanta, GA. JFK phoned his concern to his wife, Coretta Scott King. Robert Kennedy phoned the jurisdictional judge to secure MLK's safe release.[7]
	8 Nov	PRESIDENTIAL ELECTION. Popular vote: JFK won by 112, 827 votes, 49.72 percent to Nixon's 49.55 percent. Nixon carried twenty-six states, JFK twenty-two. Electoral vote: JFK 303, Nixon 219. More than 70 percent of African-Americans voted for JFK and provided the winning edge in several key states.[8]
1961	20 Jan	INAUGURATION. At Stewart Udall's suggestion[9], JFK had invited Frost to be the nation's first inaugural poet. In the glaring sunlight and wind, Frost had difficulty reading the poem he composed for the occasion, "Dedication"; instead, he recited "The Gift Outright" from memory, "The land was ours before we were the land's…"
	Jan	Frost later presented JFK with a manuscript copy of "Dedication." Excerpts: "Summoning artists to participate, In the august occasions of the state, Seems something artists ought

---

4   https://en.wikipedia.org/wiki/Recession_of_1960%E2%80%9361

5   https://www.thebalance.com/president-john-f-kennedy-s-economic-policies-3305560

6   https://www.gpo.gov/fdsys/pkg/STATUTE-74/pdf/STATUTE-74-Pg883-3.pdf

7   https://www.jfklibrary.org/JFK/JFK-in-History/Civil-Rights-Movement.aspx

8   https://en.wikipedia.org/wiki/United_States_presidential_election,_1960

9   Udall was a Democratic congressman from Arizona who knew Frost and supported Kennedy for president in 1960. President Kennedy appointed Udall secretary of the interior.

to celebrate. ...The glory of a next Augustan age, Of a power leading from its strength and pride...A golden age of poetry and power, Of which this noonday's the beginning hour." JFK's thank-you included the note: "It's poetry and power all the way!"

30 Jan STATE OF THE UNION MESSAGE TO CONGRESS[10] JFK announced measures to promote economic recovery, including speeding up already authorized programs in housing, education, medical facilities, and clean water. In foreign affairs, he identified troubled relations with China and the Soviet Union and trouble spots in SE Asia, Africa, S. and Central America, and Cuba, and then he pledged acceleration of the military's air-lift capacity and the entire missile program, including Polaris submarines. He asked Congress for new programs to assist the economic, educational, and social development of developing countries, including Food-for-Peace, Alianza para el Progreso, and the Peace Corps. Finally, he turned to possible areas of cooperation with the Soviet Union and other nations: space exploration, communications satellites, weather prediction, farm technology, and curing of diseases.

1 Mar JFK signed the Executive Order that established the Peace Corps and asked his brother-in-law, Sargent Shriver, to be its first director.[11]

17 April US-backed Cuban rebels landed at the Bay of Pigs and were defeated in three days.

4 May First Freedom Ride. Seven blacks and six whites left Washington, DC on two public buses to test the Supreme Court ruling that declared segregation in interstate bus and rail stations unconstitutional. In Alabama the Freedom Riders were severely beaten and one of the buses was burned.

4 June Vienna Summit. Khrushchev met JFK for discussion of international relations. JFK himself thought the meeting went badly. Kennedy later told *New York Times* reporter James Reston it was the "roughest thing in my life. He just beat the hell out of me. I've got a terrible problem if he thinks I'm inexperienced and have no guts. Until we remove those ideas we won't get anywhere with him."[12]

June-Nov U.S. and Soviet tanks faced off as Soviets constructed the Berlin wall.

---

10   http://www.presidency.ucsb.edu/ws/index.php?pid=8045

11   https://www.peacecorps.gov/about/history/founding-moment/

12   http://www.nytimes.com/2008/05/22/opinion/22thrall.html

25 Jul	JFK signed bill doubling Federal effort to decrease water pollution.[13]
Oct	JFK established the National Institute of Child Health and Human Development. His sister, Rosemary, was born with intellectual disabilities. His sister-in-law, Eunice Shriver Kennedy, was director of the family's foundation for advocating and supporting the identification of the causes, prevention, and treatment of intellectual disabilities.
30 Nov	JFK authorized CIA to covertly kill Castro and remove the Communist government from power.[14]

1962	8 Jan	In a Kremlin speech Khrushchev described the U.S. policy he intended to pursue. It became known as the "meniscus speech" because he used the analogy of filling a glass to the rim, forming a meniscus, keeping the enemy on edge about whether it would spill over into nuclear war. He saw this brinkmanship as the only way for the Soviet Union, the weaker superpower, to keep the stronger superpower off balance. This critical speech and other documents were not known to U.S. intelligence agencies and did not become available to historians until finally declassified in 2003.[15]
	26 Mar	JFK presented the Congressional Gold Medal to Frost in a ceremony at the White House.
	13-20 May	Khrushchev decided to place nuclear missiles and bombers in Cuba, according to his memoirs.[16]
	29 May	After meeting a Soviet delegation, Castro decided to accept the missiles and bombers.
	1 June	U.S. installed intermediate-range nuclear ballistic missiles in Turkey targeted at the Soviet Union. The Kremlin feared U.S. intentions because intermediate range missiles at close, fixed sites appeared to be intended for a first strike capability, rather than deterrence. If the missiles were not used first, they would be destroyed within minutes of the beginning of a conventional or nuclear war. The same could be said of the missiles in Cuba.
	11 June	JFK addressed the nation on radio about civil rights. Excerpt: "We are confronted primarily with a moral issue. It is as old as

---

13   https://www.jfklibrary.org/Research/Research-Aids/Ready-Reference/Selected-Milestones-of-the-Kennedy-Presidency.aspx

14   https://en.wikipedia.org/wiki/Cuban_Project

15   https://www.nytimes.com/2003/09/14/weekinreview/word-for-word-khrushchev-unplugged-middle-east-cuba-fine-art-political-bluster.html

16   Talbot, Strobe, ed. 1970. Khrushchev Remembers. Little, Brown, Boston. Page 494.

the scriptures and as clear as the American Constitution. The heart of the question is whether all Americans are to be afforded equal rights and equal opportunities, whether we are going to treat our fellow Americans as we want to be treated."

23 July   Geneva. Declaration on the Neutrality of Laos attempted to end the civil war by creating a government coalition that included the pro-American, pro-Communist, and neutral factions. However, the civil war resumed.

Summer   JFK asked the Secret Service to install a hidden taping system in the White House Oval Office and Cabinet Room, most likely in preparation for a memoir. Complete transcription and analysis of the recordings by historians did not become available until 2016.[17] [18]

Summer   With JFK's blessing, Secretary of the Interior Stewart Udall organized a goodwill tour by Frost to the Soviet Union scheduled in September.[19] It was fortuitous that Khrushchev was using writers to advance his own program of de-Stalinization. Works by the poet Yevgeny Yevtushenko and novelist Aleksandr Solzhenitsyn were published in officially-sanctioned journals. Solzhenitsyn's novel, *One Day in the Life of Ivan Denisovich*, was based on the author's own experience in Stalin's slave-labor camps and became widely read throughout the world.[20] [21] It was also important to Khrushchev, who knew JFK would soon learn about the placement of nuclear missiles in Cuba, that Frost and Udall conveyed to JFK that the premier was rational and very much in command of Soviet policy.[22]

---

17   Naftali, Timothy (editor). 2001. The Presidential Recordings. John F. Kennedy: Volumes 1-3, The Great Crises July 30—August 1962. Transcribed, with preface, notes, and list of people recorded on the tapes. W.W. Norton & Company, New York.

18   Coleman, David, Timothy Naftali, and Philip D. Zelikow (editors). 2016. The Presidential Recordings. John F. Kennedy: Volumes 4-6, The Winds of Change October 29, 1962—February 7, 1963. W.W. Norton & Company, New York.

19   Udall, Stewart L. 1988. Poetry, Stalinism and the Cuban Missile Crisis. *Los Angeles Times* endpapers section, 30 October 1988. http://articles.latimes.com/1988-10-30/books/bk-696_1_cuban-missile-crisis

20   Udall, Stewart. Robert Frost's Last Adventure. The *New York Times Books*, 11 June 1972. http://www.nytimes.com/books/99/04/25/specials/frost-last.html

21   https://en.wikipedia.org/wiki/Aleksandr_Solzhenitsyn#Biography

22   Udall, Stewart. *Ibid.*

6 Sept	Udall and Frost were invited to meet Khrushchev at his dacha on the Black Sea. Frost was too ill to make the twenty-minute drive to the dacha. Neither Udall nor Frost knew that Soviet technicians were preparing missile launching sites in Cuba and the missiles were being crated for shipment by sea.
7 Sept	To Udall's surprise, Khrushchev arranged to come to Frost's bedside. The meetings with Udall and Frost lasted for a total of five and a half hours. The discussions were cordial, and Khrushchev listened intently to Frost elaborate on how the ideas and deeds of poets and political leaders shape the character of a country. Khrushchev gave explicit messages to each for JFK. Udall later reported that Kennedy's inevitable reaction to the missiles and bombers in Cuba was critical to Khrushchev. Khrushchev was gambling that the missiles would constitute a worldwide strategic breakthrough for the Kremlin, but they might precipitate a nuclear holocaust.[23] Udall reported that after returning to his Moscow apartment, Frost hosted a news conference, and the story in the *New York Times* the next day accurately reflected the highlights of the Frost-Khrushchev conversation: "Frost and Premier Khrushchev had agreed on the need for rivalry and magnanimity in relations between the two countries."[24]
9 Sept	Sick and exhausted from the eighteen-hour return flight to the U.S., Frost wearily blurted out to the reporters at the airport: "Khrushchev said…he thought that we're too liberal to fight—he thinks we will sit on one hand and then the other." Both Udall and the interpreter, Frank Reeves, reported that Khrushchev said no such thing, but the *Washington Post* headline was "Frost Says Khrushchev Sees U.S. as 'Too Liberal' to Defend Itself."[25] When Udall returned to Washington, JFK said curtly, "Why did he have to say that?"[26] There was no further communication from JFK to Frost.
15 Sept	Soviet freighter was photographed transporting missiles to Cuba.
20 Sept	JFK mobilized the National Guard to enable African-American Air Force veteran James Meredith to enroll and take classes at the University of Mississippi, after four unsuccessful attempts by Meredith and a riot that killed two people and injured dozens.

---

23   Udall, Stewart. *Ibid.*

24   Udall, Stewart. *Ibid.*

25   Udall, Stewart. *Ibid.*

26   Udall, Stewart. *Ibid.*

14 Oct	U-2 photographed missile sites and nuclear-capable bombers in Cuba.
16 Oct	Most of the members of JFK's executive committee of the National Security Council favored a military strike on the bombers and missile sites in Cuba. JFK decided to try a blockade of Cuba before a military attack.
22 Oct	5 p.m. Prior to the public broadcast of his plan, JFK briefed Senator Richard Russell (R, GA), Chairman of the Armed Services Committee. Russell urged "stronger steps." 7 p.m. Kennedy addressed the nation on TV and described the blockade. He also issued a warning: "It shall be the policy of this Nation to regard any nuclear missile launched from Cuba against any nation in the Western Hemisphere as an attack by the Soviet Union on the United States, requiring a full retaliatory response upon the Soviet Union."
24 Oct	With the U.S. Navy blockade of Cuba in place, Soviet ships reversed course. U.S. subsequently allowed a few ships not carrying nuclear weapons to pass on to Cuba.
26 Oct	Khrushchev sent a private letter to JFK stating that nuclear missiles would be removed from Cuba if U.S. pledged never to invade Cuba.
27 Oct	Khrushchev's second, public letter added that U.S. missiles in Turkey would have to be removed. Later that day, a Soviet commander in Cuba, without specific authorization, fired a SAM missile that brought down Col. Rudolf Anderson's U-2 that was on a photographic mission.[27] Khrushchev announced they accepted the U.S. offer to never invade Cuba in exchange for removing nuclear weapons from Cuba. The U.S. later removed the missiles in Turkey, but this was not publicly mentioned.
6 Nov	Midterm congressional elections. Republicans picked up four seats in the House, but Democrats retained strong majorities in both houses of Congress. In the Senate, Democrats had a net gain of four seats. Gains of liberal Democrats later allowed passage of the Clean Air Act and the Civil Rights Act of 1964.[28]

---

27   https://nsarchive2.gwu.edu/nsa/cuba_mis_cri/dobbs/anderson.htm

28   https://en.wikipedia.org/wiki/United_States_elections,_1962

1963	29 Jan	Frost died of complications from prostate surgery at age eighty-eight.
	5 Feb	JFK delivered "Special Message to the Congress on Mental Illness and Mental Retardation" that recommended programs for maternity and prenatal care, community mental health centers, research, and special education.
3 April–10 May		Southern Christian Leadership Conference (SCLC) and the Alabama Christian Movement for Human Rights (ACMHR) launched the Birmingham campaign, with lunch counter sit-ins, marches on City Hall, and a boycott of downtown merchants. Birmingham Commissioner of Public Safety, "Bull" Connor, directed the police and fire department to use dogs and high pressure fire hoses on a mass demonstration by school children, and the scenes were aired on national television. Robert Kennedy sent his chief civil rights assistant to facilitate negotiations between the white business community and prominent African-Americans that resulted in "The Birmingham Truce Agreement" on 10 May.
	11 May	Segregationists bombed the hotel where King and others had stayed, the home of the hotel's owner, and the parsonage of King's brother. Riots began because of eye witness accounts of the involvement of the Birmingham police in the bombings. JFK ordered 3,000 federal troops into position near Birmingham and prepared to nationalize the Alabama National Guard.[29] [30]
	11 Jun	JFK called for legislation on civil rights "…giving all Americans the right to be served in facilities which are open to the public—hotels, restaurants, theaters, retail stores, and similar establishments…"
	12 Jun	Medgar Evers, African-American Army veteran and civil rights leader was assassinated in Jackson, MS, by Byron De La Beckwith of the White Citizens' Council, triggering civil rights protests. La Beckwith was not convicted until 1994.
	7 Aug	Patrick Bouvier Kennedy was born to President Kennedy and his wife, Jaqueline, five and a half weeks early. The infant suffered from the No. 1 killer of premature babies at that time, hyaline

---

29 http://kingencyclopedia.stanford.edu/encyclopedia/encyclopedia/enc_birmingham_campaign/index.html

30 https://en.wikipedia.org/wiki/Birmingham_riot_of_1963

membrane disease, and died thirty-nine hours after birth.[31]

28 Aug	On the centennial of the Emancipation Proclamation, 250,000 people joined the March on Washington for Jobs and Freedom. Martin Luther King delivered his "I Have a Dream" speech on the steps of the Lincoln Memorial.
15 Sept	A bombing killed four young girls in Sunday school at the Sixteenth Street Baptist Church in Birmingham, Alabama. Riots resulted in deaths of two more African-American youths.
24 Oct	JFK signed the Maternal and Child Health and Mental Retardation Planning Amendment to the Social Security Act—the first major legislation to combat mental illness and intellectual disabilities.
26 Oct	JFK was awarded an honorary Doctor of Laws in a Convocation at Amherst College. He then gave what Stewart Udall considered "the most majestic speech of his public career."[32] He spoke of the relationship between poetry and power and a view shared with Frost that power must be exercised, but wisely—tempered by a moral restraint inspired by the arts and a liberal arts education. He also spoke of the obligation of those "given a running start in life" to serve the public interest. In a very brief second address at the groundbreaking for the Robert Frost Library, he said Frost "…felt very strongly that the United States should be a country of power and force but should use that power and force wisely." Of the library, JFK said, "…all the young men who come into this library will touch something of distinction in our national life, and, I hope, give something to it."
31 Oct	In a special ceremony, JFK signed legislation (separate from the 24 Oct Amendment to the Social Security Act) that provided funding for construction of facilities for research, prevention, care, and treatment of intellectual disabilities.
22 Nov	On the first swing of his reelection campaign, JFK visited Texas, where he had carried both the popular vote (by 2 percent) and all twenty-four electoral votes in 1960. He was assassinated in Dallas. That evening, Amherst President Calvin Plimpton

31 Levingston, Steven. For John and Jackie Kennedy, the death of a son may have brought them closer. *Washington Post Opinions*, 24 October 2013. Adapted from the e-book *The Kennedy Baby: The Loss That Transformed JFK.* https://www. washingtonpost.com/opinions/for-john-and-jackie-kennedy-the-death-of-a-son-may-have-brought-them-closer/2013/10/24/2506051e-369b-11e3-ae46-e4248e75c8ea_ story.html?utm_term=.7595392ba4da

32 Udall, Stewart L. 1988. "Of Poetry and Power." *Los Angeles Times* endpapers section 6 November 1988. http://articles.latimes.com/1988-11-06/books/bk-49_1_robert-frost

delivered a brief memoriam in Johnson Chapel, concluding, "Let us remember to advantage our late, great President's toughness in mind, body and soul. Let us stand a moment in silence, to honor him; then let us go and do the work he couldn't complete."

1964   June   Graduation of the class of 1964 and commencement of varied careers.

FIFTY YEARS LATER

2014   Jan   Amherst '64 alumni continued research and planning for their fiftieth reunion. Theme: The World We Inherited; the World We Will Bequeath—and What We Can Still Do About It. Planning teams addressed four areas: The State of Our Democracy, the Environment, Healthcare, and Education.

30 April—2 May   Ten Amherst '64 alumni undertook a study trip to Washington, DC, to investigate the reasons for political dysfunction and what might be done about it.

28 May—1 June   Fiftieth reunion of the class of 1964. Molly Fowler, documentary filmmaker and wife of deceased classmate, Jack Levine, filmed reunion activities and interviewed class members for a film with the working title *Reunion*. Over the next four years, Northern Light Productions was contracted to produce a film and the working title changed several times (*The President and the Poet*; *The Last Speech*; *JFK: The Last Speech*).

2017   29 May   Official year of celebration of the centenary of JFK's birth began.

2018   6 May   The documentary film, *JFK: The Last Speech*, premiered at the JFK Library in Boston, Massachusetts.

REFERENCES, WITH NOTES:

Coleman, David, Timothy Naftali, and Philip D. Zelikow (editors). 2016. *The Presidential Recordings. John F. Kennedy: Volumes 4-6, The Winds of Change October 29, 1962—February 7, 1963*. W.W. Norton & Company, New York.

Cuban Missile Crisis Timeline. Harvard Kennedy School of Government, Belfer Center for Science and International Affairs. Scroll to 4 June 1961, Vienna Meeting of Kennedy and Khrushchev: http://www.cubanmissilecrisis.org/background/timeline/

Fursenko, Alexsandr and Timothy Naftali. 2006. *Khrushchev's Cold War: The Inside Story of an American Adversary*. W.W. Norton & Co., New York. The following information is from the book jacket, the introduction, and Wikipedia. The authors were able to access documents from the top decision-making organ of the Communist Party of the Soviet Union (the Presidium of the Central Committee) that were finally declassified in 2003. These documents explained the plans and actions of Khrushchev and the U.S.S.R. during a time of brinkmanship and the imminent threat of nuclear war. Aleksandr Fursenko (1949—) is Chairman of the Academic Council of the Foundation "Centre for Strategic Research North-West." Timothy Naftali (1962—) is a Canadian-American historian at New York University. See also his co-edited, six-volume transcription and analysis of the Kennedy tapes referenced below and above in this list.

Levingston, Steven. "For John and Jackie Kennedy, the death of a son may have brought them closer." *Washington Post Opinions*, 24 October 2013. Adapted from the e-book *The Kennedy Baby: The Loss That Transformed JFK*. https://www.washingtonpost.com/opinions/for-john-and-jackie-kennedy-the-death-of-a-son-may-have-brought-them-closer/2013/10/24/2506051e-369b-11e3-ae46-e4248e75c8ea_story.html?utm_term=.7595392ba4da

Naftali, Timothy (editor). 2001. *The Presidential Recordings. John F. Kennedy:* Volumes 1-3, The Great Crises July 30—August 1962. Transcribed, with preface, notes, and list of people recorded on the tapes. W.W. Norton & Company, New York.

https://www.poets.org/poetsorg/text/poetry-and-power-robert-frosts-inaugural-reading *Poetry and Power: Robert Frost's Inaugural Reading.* Second paragraph, beginning "On March 26, 1959, prior to a gala to celebrate his 85th birthday, Frost gave a press conference at the Waldorf-Astoria hotel in New York City…"

Reeve, F.D. 1963. *Robert Frost in Russia.* Little, Brown & Company, Boston, in association with *The Atlantic Monthly Press.* Reeve (1928–2013) was the guide and interpreter for Frost on the visit to Russia and the meeting with Khrushchev. Reeve spent time in Russia with his family as a research scholar. He was a poet, professor of Russian at Wesleyan University, and author of a book of literary criticism and of a half-dozen translations (excerpted from the book jacket).

Schwarz, Benjamin. 2013. "The Real Cuban Missile Crisis: Everything you think you know about those 13 days is wrong." *The Atlantic.* January/February 2013. https://www.theatlantic.com/magazine/archive/2013/01/the-real-cuban-missile-crisis/309190/

Talbott, Strobe, ed. 1970. *Khrushchev Remembers.* Little, Brown & Company, Boston. Talbot (1946—) is an American foreign policy analyst associated with Yale University and Brookings Institution, a former journalist associated with *Time* magazine, and a diplomat who served as the Deputy Secretary of State from 1994 to 2001. He was president of Brookings from 2002 to 2017. He did the translation and the editing. Edward Crankshaw wrote the introduction, commentary, and notes. Until 1968 he was a correspondent for *The Observer* and frequently visited Russia and Eastern Europe. He wrote a biography of Khrushchev (1966*), Cracks in the Kremlin Wall, Russia Without Stalin* and *Khrushchev's Russia.*

Thrall, Nathan and Jesse James Wilkins. 2008. "Kennedy Talked, Khrushchev Triumphed." The *New York Times Opinion*, 22 May 2008. http://www.nytimes.com/2008/05/22/opinion/22thrall.html

Udall, Stewart L. 1972. "Robert Frost's Last Adventure." *New York Times Books*, 11 June 1972. http://www.nytimes.com/books/99/04/25/specials/frost-last.html

Udall, Stewart L. 1988. "Poetry, Stalinism and the Cuban Missile Crisis." *Los Angeles Times* endpapers, 30 October 1988. http://articles.latimes.com/1988-10-30/books/bk-696_1_cuban-missile-crisis

Udall, Stewart L. 1988. "Of Poetry and Power." *Los Angeles Times* endpapers, 6 November 1988. http://articles.latimes.com/1988-11-06/books/bk-49_1_robert-frost

ALSO OF INTEREST:

Another speech has a claim to being JFK's last speech, although he never gave it. However, you can hear an electronically synthesized version in Kennedy's voice. A company in Scotland spent eight weeks recreating an audio by synthesizing 116,777 voice samples from 831 JFK recordings. The audio was published online by *The Times*.

https://www.thetimes.co.uk/edition/news/jfk-video-hear-kennedys-lost-dallas-speech-in-his-own-voice-xtkvhm255

http://www.businessinsider.com/jfk-speech-from-day-he-died-recreated-with-voice-tech-2018-3

It was the speech JFK intended to give in Texas to the Dallas Citizens Council, the Dallas Assembly, and the Graduate Research Center of the Southwest on the day he was assassinated. It was essentially the opening of his presidential election campaign and an accounting of his first 1,000 days as president.

https://www.jfklibrary.org/Research/Research-Aids/JFK-Speeches/Dallas-TX-Trade-Mart-Undelivered_19631122.aspx

Topics included the buildup of both nuclear and conventional forces, special forces, and airlift capacity; international military and economic assistance; space exploration; and the growing economy.

The opening paragraphs included material relevant to our time:

This link between leadership and learning is not only essential at the community level. It is even more indispensable in world affairs. Ignorance and misinformation can handicap the progress of a city or a company, but they can, if allowed to prevail in foreign policy, handicap this country's security. In a world of complex and continuing problems, in a world full of frustrations and irritations, America's leadership must be guided by the lights of learning and reason or else those who confuse rhetoric with reality and the plausible with the possible will gain the popular ascendancy with their seemingly swift and simple solutions to every world problem.

The last paragraph returned to familiar themes about power exercised with wisdom and restraint:

We in this country, in this generation, are—by destiny rather than choice—the watchmen on the walls of world freedom. We ask, therefore, that we may be worthy of our power and responsibility, that we may exercise our strength with wisdom and restraint, and that we may achieve in our time and for all time the ancient vision of "peace on earth, good will toward men." That must always be our goal, and the righteousness of our cause must always underlie our strength. For as was written long ago: "Except the Lord keep the city, the watchman waketh but in vain."

PART 2
Doing the Work He Couldn't Complete

———————

[Carrying the Torch]

6

THE LIFE OF AN ACTIVIST
Peace Corps & Other Adventures

———————

Ted Nelson, '64

PRELUDE: THE CHICKEN MUST DIE

In November 1964, in a small village halfway up a mountain in northwest Turkey, for the first time in my life I seriously thought I might die. A few weeks earlier, my wife and I had arrived there as Peace Corps volunteers. We were just settling in when a monster storm struck, leaving the entire village isolated. Normally treacherous mountain roads became impassable: nothing in, nothing out. Many of the stock animals perished in the initial onslaught. After the first few weeks, the only remaining food supplies were grain for bread and beans. Lots of beans.

The villagers generously shared what little they had, but after two weeks I could not force another bean down my throat, even if my life depended on it. And after three months of bread and water, having gone from 205 pounds down to 147 pounds, my life did depend on it. Fourteen weeks after the storm's onset, some of the hardier villagers finally managed the thirty-two-kilometer hike down to the market town, slogging back with fresh supplies. Boisterous celebration marked their return. Before long, four village men, led by the *mukhtar* (village leader), tromped into our house trailed by a noisy contingent of children.

The *mukhtar* stood front and center, a huge smile lighting up his old, craggy face. From behind his back, he pulled a ragged burlap bag with something moving inside.

"We were worried about you, so we bought you a gift." he said.

With that, he reached into the bag. Alarmed, I stepped back, no idea of what would emerge. He pulled out a CHICKEN—a scrawny, squawking, flapping, unhappy chicken. To me, it was manna; my stomach growled.

"Kill it!" my wife said, as she immediately set to boiling some water. The villagers looked on with great anticipation, curious as to how an American would handle this everyday task. The options were grisly. In training, I had learned to insert an ice pick up through the chicken's beak and into the brain, killing it instantly and preventing the bird from clenching its muscles and thereby becoming too tough to eat. I had no ice pick, and my axe, another option, was nowhere to be found. What to do?

My wife continued her harangue, encouraging me to dispatch the bird before it became an embarrassment. During a brief moment of critical thinking, I determined exactly what I would do. I took the struggling chicken to my work bench, and grabbed a hand saw from a nail on the wall. Anticipating coming events, the *mukhtar* and his buddies shrunk back, aghast. I raked the saw over the chicken's neck. Hideous sounds poured from its beak. Children screamed and ran crying from the house. The dulled saw blade took a few moments before cutting deeply enough to silence the bird. The head came off after about thirty seconds of sawing. Chicken blood covered my hands. The men stood there in shock. They had never seen a chicken decapitated with a hand saw. (In my own defense, this was before PETA. Hunger can overcome compassion.)

I said—in my elementary Turkish—"This is how we kill chickens in America, but our saws are much sharper."

The confusion hinted that I might not have expressed my thoughts precisely. In fact, several weeks later, the witnesses told me what I had said, "This is how Americans train chickens, but we use a sharper saw on our wives."

In discussing it amongst themselves, they were uncertain as to what I meant, but all agreed that my time in the village would make me a better person.

In a Turkish village, when a chicken is given as a gift, the donors traditionally stick around to share the meal. This time, no one stuck around. (Was it something I said?) On the other hand, I was glad they left. I was starving, and I had no intention of sharing that bird with anyone but my wife.

Feathers flew as I frantically plucked it and plopped it into the kettle of boiling water. Finally, it was done. Draining the water and laying the bird on a plate, I tore off a leg, and ignoring the heat, bit hungrily into the bird's flesh.

I might as well have bitten into a piece of cement. The leg was as hard as a rock. The chicken had its own sweet revenge, clenching its muscles so mightily in its death struggle as to become inedible. My wife experienced a brief moment of anxiety as I looked at her hungrily. Then we both laughed and laughed—until I could no longer feel the hunger.

I was in the throes of an adventure that had started with an unexpected handshake and would last a lifetime.

AMHERST COLLEGE, OCTOBER 26, 1963

On a glorious fall day in Amherst, a year before my experience with the chicken in Turkey, President John F. Kennedy arrived to speak at the convocation for the Robert Frost Library groundbreaking. Sparkling sunshine danced between the shadows of lazy clouds, warming expectant faces.

I was there. It was the second month of my senior year, filled with the angst of imminent graduation. My plans were set: the week after graduation, I would marry my girlfriend of three years and then launch my career as a management trainee for a major insurance firm. Yet, I wanted something more for my life, but I couldn't quite put my finger on it.

Kennedy's speech captured me. It wasn't just the elegance of his words or the eloquence of his delivery. When he spoke, quoting Frost, I felt goosebumps rise on the back of my neck:

The problems which this country now faces are staggering, both at home and abroad. We need the service, in the great sense, of every educated man or woman, to find 10 million jobs in the next two and a half years, to govern our relations—a country which lived in isolation for 150 years, and is now suddenly the leader of the Free World—to govern our relations with over 100 countries, to govern those relations with success so that the balance of power remains strong on the side of freedom, to make it possible for Americans of all different races and creeds to live together in harmony, to make it possible for a world to exist in diversity and freedom. All this requires the best of all of us.

And therefore, I am proud to come to this College whose graduates have recognized this obligation and to say to those who are now here that the need is endless, and I'm confident that you will respond.

Robert Frost said it:

Two roads diverged in a wood, and I–
I took the one less traveled by,
And that has made all the difference.

His words passed through my mind, reached my flesh. I felt disquietude, a deep, visceral connection. His words lit a fuse. Though I did not recognize it at the time, the arc of my life's journey had just been set.

Following his speech, Kennedy paused to shake hands and talk with a small group of students, myself included. He asked what our plans were following graduation and, nodding, received the expected: various flavors of graduate schools.

"No," he said firmly. "You're all going to join the Peace Corps."

We responded with mildly embarrassed laughter; he moved on.

Twenty-seven days later, an assassin's bullet ended President Kennedy's life: stunning, unbelievable. I was still numb when, at last, I got to bed that night. I slept fitfully. I woke at dawn, feeling strangely calm—a calm based on cold anger and unshakable resolve. I would join the Peace Corps. I would answer Kennedy's call.

That same day, I called my fiancée to ask her if she would consider a two-year honeymoon in the Peace Corps. To my delight, after only a brief discussion, she agreed. Her father was a Clancy and her mother a Kelly; of course, she would respond to Kennedy's call! We submitted our applications to the Peace Corps, and in that life-defining moment, we took the road less traveled by.

My Amherst education exploded in my mind. A nineteen-year-old freshman, a poor kid on scholarship, I was full of myself, confident I knew what this world was all about. Then, Amherst took me apart, challenging, questioning, analyzing assumptions and beliefs about the universe, the world, and my very essence. And Amherst, like all the king's men, could not put Humpty-Dumpty together again. But it left a powerful tool in the rubble: critical thinking. Critical thinking backed up by broad knowledge. My metaphorical torch had been forged in the heat of my education. With Kennedy's handshake and his wrenching death just three weeks later, the torch was lit.

In the spring of 1964, my wife-to-be and I received acceptance letters from the Peace Corps. We were assigned to an experimental rural community development program in Turkey. Turkey? We knew little about Turkey, and even less about rural community development! What had I gotten us into?

The Peace Corps had a wild idea: an American liberal arts college graduate with bare-bones language proficiency could accomplish something important in a small Turkish village. Send someone who knows a little bit about everything, but not much about anything—a BA generalist. What could go wrong?

PEACE CORPS AND THE POOR PEOPLE'S CAMPAIGN

Our Turkish honeymoon began at The Experiment for International Living in Putney, Vermont, the first stage of our training. Seventy newly minted BA generalists showed up for training. Several weeks later, fifty-eight of us went on to Turkey, including sixteen couples.

Training at the Experiment was rigorous, intensive, and disorganized. Our Turkish trainers, all city-dwellers, knew little of life in a rural village. The training schedule consisted of a half-day of Turkish language classes, and a half-day of work on community development projects in Calais, Vermont, then topped off with evening classes on Turkish history, culture, and development.

In a few of the Turkish villages, problems had emerged when the locals enticed some of the volunteers who preceded us into drinking (often *raki*, a powerful alcoholic beverage similar to anisette) or gambling (poker and bridge). And, many volunteers had to deal with the villagers' persistent efforts at conversion to Islam. The trainers asked each of us to formulate a personal plan responding to these issues.

I grew up in Maine, and an old Maine friend of mine who had spent time in Northwestern Turkey told me that the residents reminded him of New Englanders: reticent, watchful, and wily, with a wry sense of humor. I identified with that, especially the wry humor part. This was good. I could work with this. Then, I remembered Robert Frost at Amherst, and I knew exactly how to deal with the problems.

Frost was one of my literary heroes, second only to Dylan Thomas. As a freshman at Amherst, I was a Frost stalker, wanting to see, hear, and absorb everything he had to offer. But over time, despite deep appreciation of his craft, I came to thoroughly dislike him as a person; an arrogant curmudgeon, he alienated me. One of Frost's most interesting accomplishments was the creation of his persona. He purposefully designed it and then promoted it for his artistic goals. But, this key unlocked my assignment. I, too, would create a persona, one that would preclude problems with drinking, gambling, or my religious conversion.

Drinking was easy. I don't drink. Never have. Telling the Turks I didn't drink would lead to suspicions and distrust. I announced I was allergic to alcohol, and it worked, perfectly.

Gambling was more formidable. How could I avoid gambling without being either fearful or aloof? I created a bombastic, outrageous persona in Frost's crusty New England image: a card player so skillful it would be dishonorable to gamble with the Turks. I proved it, with the help of my marked and stripped decks. I could read any card from the marked decks, and the stripped cards allowed me to instantly identify a card reversed from the others. I developed my card shuffling skills and magic tricks in high school and college; along with the marked decks, these skills led to some spectacular performances. The villagers soon realized I was not one to gamble with. In the local tea houses, they welcomed me as an honored kibitzer, a much safer and more effective role for a community development agent.

Surprisingly, religious conversion also turned out to be easy. When my wife and I first visited villagers' homes, we found hanging on the walls pictures of the founder of modern Turkey, Mustafa Kemal Ataturk (their George Washington), and next to him John F. Kennedy. The villagers loved Kennedy. When their efforts to win me over to Islam began, I reminded them that as JFK's torch bearer, I was duty-bound to remain faithful to his beliefs and mine. This worked well. Our discussions of religion continued, but proselytizing gave way to philosophizing.

So, I have Robert Frost to thank for my change-agent persona in the village. And, over the years, my feelings about Frost have changed. I no longer dislike him. An old man myself now, I have come to an enhanced appreciation of his humanity. He is just as loveable as I am. (To signal this change of heart to the world, my Michigan vanity plate stands as a continuing tribute to Frost: CURMUGN.)

Our first night in the village was dramatic. It was dark. I mean, really DARK—so dark I couldn't see my wife's face six inches from mine. No moon or stars. Just unseen clouds propelled by a cold wind. My wife and I were huddled in bed together, fully clothed, shivering beneath the blankets. We hadn't yet learned to stoke a night fire properly. That would be the first of many lessons learned the hard way.

Suddenly, above the sound of our chattering teeth and the rustle of the animals below us, a new and ominous sound emerged—frantic men's voices, chanting one sound over and over. Through the un-curtained window, we saw bouncing balls of fire coming towards us up the road. A few worried seconds later, the vision cleared revealing a mob of torch-carrying men, all shouting, "Dead!" "Dead!" "Dead!" and marching right up to our house. I turned to my wife, whose face I could now see reflected in the light from the torches and suggested that she go down and ask what they wanted. I can't repeat what she said to me.

By the time I reached the door, several men had already entered. I recognized the first man in, my landlord. "Mister Ded, Mister Ded," he said urgently, and conveyed a message that was clear even to my limited Turkish. A structure was on fire in the village and they wanted me to witness it. The villagers had trouble with the "T" in my name and Ted became Ded. Or Mister Ded as I was called for months. I attended the fire with the villagers, and my wife and I began our Peace Corps honeymoon.

We survived our intense, challenging, satisfying, horrifying, enlightening, and inspiring time in the village. The richness of this experience has blessed the rest of my life. What my wife and I accomplished in the village was, from beginning to end, a product of collaboration with the villagers. Our role was to help the villagers initiate their own development and their own advancement, to clearly define their problems and take action to solve them, using whatever resources were available. We were organizers and stimulators: gadflies. A great task for BA generalists. In context, we accomplished quite a bit. One of our biggest successes was in the solution to a horrific contaminated drinking water problem.

For years, the villagers had suffered under an appalling infant mortality rate. Well over half of their newborns died before reaching age two, most from diarrhea brought on by severely polluted drinking water. We helped in constructing a series of closed springs and fountains that protected the water from pollutants, particularly those resulting from the use of night soil (human excrement mixed with garbage) as a fertilizer. I like to think that if I returned to that village today, many of the residents would be descendants of those who were saved by our efforts.

At Amherst, I received one of the finest liberal arts educations available in the world; two gritty, challenging years in that small Turkish village in the mountains gave me a Ph.D. in the visceral arts: survival, self-knowledge, and personal confidence. Nothing I could have done in those six years that would have given me a better and more complete education than four years at Amherst and two years in the Peace Corps. I came out of Turkey a changed person. Physically, I was in the best shape of my life, forty pounds lighter than when I joined. Emotionally, I had begun to unravel the bonds of culture. I had discovered a level of common humanity that undergirds culture, a level deeper than social conventions. I had become a citizen of humanity, a gift I have come to cherish and one that served me well in my later involvement in the 1968 Poor People's Campaign.

In my two years of Peace Corps service, I made the transition from an intense and overwhelming experience of being "the other"—an unknown, untrusted and feared outsider among the tight-knit villagers—to the role of a unique, intriguing, and oddly likeable insider who tickled their funny bones and often made them shake their heads in wonder. My awareness expanded beyond the parameters of culture to the common humanity we shared. I went from being called Mister Ded to the much fonder and inclusive Turkish title of Older Brother. Over the two years, the villagers literally saved my life several times, and, in my own nuanced way, I returned the favor. And, in addition to all of this, I have some great tales to tell. It was a superb adventure.

I stayed in Turkey for another year as assistant director of the program, then moved to a Peace Corps staff job in Washington, DC. In early 1968, I took a leave of absence to work with the Southern Christian Leadership Conference (SCLC), organizing and conducting the Poor People's Campaign. I established and ran the Volunteer Speakers Bureau, a cadre of Washington, DC volunteers with knowledge of the issues and sympathy for the cause. I also gave them rigorous training in non-violence.

Two experiences from that time stand out. Early in the campaign, I accepted a speaking request from a church in Virginia. When I arrived, the church was half full, an all-white audience of around two hundred. I stood behind the altar rail and began my presentation. My introductory words induced nothing but silent glares. In the back of my mind, a big "Un-oh!" took shape. A beefy man in his thirties exited his pew, yelled "LIAR!" and ran at me. I stood transfixed. Leaping over the altar rail, he launched his right fist directly at my face. My jump backwards took some force from the blow, but he connected powerfully with my nose. I went down, his body on top of mine: blood gushed from my nostrils. The pastor and a group of parishioners rushed to my aid, pulled him off and helped me to my feet. The blood from my nose flowed copiously as I swung my head from side to side. The pastor and parishioners gathered around me expressing their shock, embarrassment, and apologies. I learned later that the church was the local headquarters for the John Birch Society. If you are a soldier in the army of non-violence, your bullets are your blood. It was glorious. I took full advantage of it.

On April 4, 1968, I filled another speaking assignment, this one from a black Baptist congregation in NE Washington. The meeting room in the church basement was packed. The pastor introduced me, and I was greeted with polite applause. Suddenly, in mid-presentation, the rear door to the meeting room banged open. A woman stood there, tears streaming down her face. "THEY KILLED MARTIN!" she wailed. "They killed Dr. King."

Dead silence gave way to a bedlam of moans and cries of disbelief. I experienced a shiver of fear, realizing that I was the only white man in the room. Then, from the shocked and grieving audience, an old woman emerged. She approached me with a slow, determined gait; her eyes never left mine. Directly in front of me, she stopped, raised her left arm, and placed her warm hand on my cheek. She held it there. "You are safe here," she said. "You are safe here."

In the last Sunday sermon of his life, Martin Luther King Jr. said:

"We are coming to Washington in a poor people's campaign...We are coming to demand that the government address itself to the problem of poverty. We read one day: We hold these truths to be self-evident, that all men are created equal, that they are endowed by their creator with certain inalienable rights. That among these are life, liberty, and the pursuit of happiness. But if a man doesn't have a job or an income, he has neither life nor liberty nor the possibility for the pursuit of happiness. He merely exists...We are coming to ask America to be true to the huge promissory note that it signed years ago. And we are coming to engage in dramatic non-violent action, to call attention to the gulf between promise and fulfillment; to make the invisible visible."

Before Dr. King's death, he and the SCLC had planned a march on Washington called the Poor People's Campaign. It was a multiracial protest to raise awareness of discrimination in the workplace and the need for living incomes and affordable housing. We built Resurrection City, with a population of three thousand, on the National Mall between the Washington Monument and the Lincoln Memorial. Poor people from all across the country came to tell their stories and make their demands, and we had fifty thousand supporters in reserve. The campaign peaked on June 19, 1968, with the Solidarity Day Rally for Jobs, Peace, and Freedom, when the residents of Resurrection City were joined by the fifty thousand in a huge rally.

After that, it went downhill. I have a jumble of memories, mostly of physical sensations, from that time: the burn of teargas, police on horses, batons, arrests, mud, and bruises. With the loss of Martin Luther King and Robert Kennedy, a strong proponent of the campaign, the planned end stages of the Poor People's Campaign never materialized.

THE COMMUNE

Following the Campaign, I started the Education for Involvement Corporation (EIC), a 501(c)(3) minority-controlled nonprofit, a commune, aimed at effective citizen involvement in racism and poverty.

EIC had a strong Board of Directors, chaired by the Hon. Edward W. Brooke of Massachusetts and made up of some of Washington, DC's top religious, political, and community activists. Almost all of EIC's staff and supporters were refugees from the Poor People's Campaign—experienced, tough, and dedicated. We organized ourselves into an urban commune and thus began another great adventure. I spent the next seven years as a resident of the commune and director of the nonprofit, a consuming seven years that included the end of Johnson's presidency, all of Nixon's tenure, and the end of the Vietnam War.

Protests, the culture wars, Watergate, Vietnam, the draft, hippies, pot, incredible music, riots, moon landings, free love…and so much more. The commune, a crucible, mixed all these ingredients. We lived, worked, loved, laughed, and cried together. We talked, argued, and processed everything. It was exhausting and uplifting. There were weddings and divorces; I was involved in both. Eventually, everyone had sex with everyone else. Of course, we had to talk things out, endlessly. Early on, we believed that sex would be the big problem. Over time we discovered a much deeper and more divisive issue: differing standards of personal hygiene.

We worked hard. The commune, which ranged from twelve to nineteen members over its term, was the hub for all of EIC's services. We presented workshops, conducted training programs, organized protests, lobbied politicians, and created multimedia support materials for our efforts. The commune was an experimental family, always exploring new and possibly better ways to communicate and better ways to get along. I had an amicable divorce and later remarried. There were births, but no deaths. There was learning and change, heartbreak and love, victory and defeat—everything you would expect from humans living and working together. More than anything else, it was FUN! (A deliciously exquisite benefit of this experience is that my memories are better than my fantasies.)

The commune disbanded shortly after the end of the Vietnam War and Richard Nixon's resignation from the presidency. My second wife and I moved to California. I became executive director of the Human Behavior Center (HBC), a branch of Psychiatry and Psychology Associates in Long Beach. This was California when the human potential movement was in full flower. Sunshine, the Pacific Ocean, and fresh-squeezed orange juice made it perfect. I loved it.

NEW LOVE, NEW PURPOSE

When I turned forty, my then-wife suggested it was time for me to make some money. Following an implausible series of events, I ended up with a store on Hollywood Boulevard, just two blocks from the Chinese Theatre. It became an awards business, and by 2000, the business had grown relatively stable and modestly profitable. In 1985, my second wife left me. Yes, the one who suggested I go into business. She fell irretrievably in love with a Scotsman, my oldest son's soccer coach. Unfortunately for her, she left before the business became profitable.

My life as a lover of women turned into a series of fender-benders. Women have little patience for a man who cannot look them in the eye and say, "I love you." As the millennium turned, I broke off a relationship that had stumbled on for over a decade. I remember the moment of my greatest despair, because I recorded it in one of my infrequent journal entries:

> I felt it building up inside me as I watched the last bright crescent of sun slide quickly into the Pacific—a soft fur-ball of a thing expanding in my gut, something that had finally caught up with me. The view was from the open window of my bedroom. I shivered as the first cool breezes of the evening goosed the skin on my bare arms. *It's over*, I thought. *I may not have lived my last, but I have loved my last.* My body told me it was time to mourn.

> I want to find love. I want to be embraced by the consuming intensity of it, to feel once again the visceral joy of completeness that comes with being madly in love with a kindred spirit, to burn one more time with this sacred and sacramental fever. But the fur ball is in me now, telling me it's over. *Give it up, old man. Let it go. You had a good run. Let it go.* I shivered again as my body took the full measure of this advice and as soft tears baptized my cheeks.

Approaching sixty, I had a galaxy of nagging diminishments: worn body parts, problematic but controllable diabetes, a tendency towards inertia, waning enthusiasm, and the reflection in the mirror only one step removed from road kill. I loved my work and my now-adult children, but my spirit was in crisis. It was one of my darkest moments.

I don't believe in miracles, but...

The day after my journal entry, I received a call from a New York journalist writing a book about a 1976 Peace Corps murder in the Kingdom of Tonga. I recalled it vividly; a male volunteer had repeatedly stabbed a female volunteer, killing her. After the murder, the Peace Corps sent me to Tonga to conduct an in-country training program for the newest group of volunteers, and to help the then-current volunteers deal with the emotional aftermath of the event. While there I met a woman, a volunteer. From the first moment I laid eyes on her, I was smitten. We had an intense romance that lasted for almost three months. But when I returned to the States, neither of us was in a position to carry the relationship forward. Nevertheless, her memory never left my mind or my heart.

I was stunned by the call. As the journalist listed the people he had already contacted, he spoke her name. I broke in, saying, "I will not say another word to you unless you give me her phone number."

He refused, pleading journalistic ethics. However, he agreed to contact her and give her my number. For a few moments, I reconsidered the possibility of a god.

THE FLINT ADVENTURE

After six months of impassioned emailing, phone calls, and a carousel ride of chaotic emotions, we reunited in Flint, Michigan. Despite our mutual fears, it exceeded all expectations. I became a regular commuter to Flint in pursuit of love.

Five years later, we were married. Ten years after that, I left my adult children managing the business, and retired to Flint. My wife, Jan Worth-Nelson, and I assumed leadership of the oldest neighborhood news magazine in the country: *East Village Magazine* (*EVM*). *EVM*, a nonprofit monthly publication, has served the city of Flint for more than forty-one years. With the collapse of *The Flint Journal*, Flint's only daily newspaper, *EVM* and its online version (eastvillagemagazine.org) have taken on an expanding role in the Flint community.

Coinciding with our take-over of *EVM*, the Flint water crisis exploded on our beat. Ironically, fifty-two years after my Peace Corps experience in Turkey, I found myself and my now battered torch in Flint, Michigan, involved in another drinking water fiasco. In Flint, all the roads in our country's road map of historical social conflicts cross. Poverty, racism, ignorance, disease, corruption, incompetence, they all have made dramatic appearances on Flint's stage. To be an activist in Flint is to be long-suffering. So, it doesn't surprise me that a half-century after shaking JFK's hand at Amherst College, I have become an unpaid volunteer working on another water crisis in another perfect job for a BA generalist.

The fight goes on. President Kennedy's challenge continues. The need for Amherst's army of BA generalists with critical thinking skills persists. The Kennedy-Frost messages are even more relevant now than when they were first spoken.

I suspect that the arc of my life nears completion. Still, I hold the torch as high as my arthritis allows. I have no intention of letting go of that torch or of passing it on. Though it is covered with dents, scratches, and the grit of long engagement, I carry it with pride. When finally I fall, YOU MAY NOT pry that darkened torch from my cold dead hands. It dies with me. It's personal. You have your own torch. The time will come, if it hasn't already, when you infuse it with your own precious flame. If you dare.

CIVIC ENGAGEMENT AND THE LIBERAL ARTS

There are always battles to fight. The common humanity we share, its diverse perspectives and experiences, ensures an ongoing context of combativeness. We are by nature contentious. In a way, Frost's claim of "a lover's quarrel with the world" holds for each and every one of us. Each of us is more or less unique, and every one of us is the artist of our own existence. Yet we all share the same palette, the same human nature. Shakespeare knew that "all the world's a stage." It's inevitable that, as we bump and grind through our brief appearance on life's stage, our performances strike sparks. We are all artists, quarrelling about life, seeking to make our contributions. It is, by nature, a truculent and dramatic process, and the outcome is never certain. We share the hope that the process will lead to progress, that we will survive, overcome, and advance. Winston Churchill, commenting about Americans, said that we always get things right in the end, but only after trying everything else first. Let us hope.

Power and poetry, art and civic engagement, politics and progress—the dialogue continues and the process plays out. I enjoy my small but satisfying role in the drama. President Kennedy's words changed my life in ways I never expected, and in ways I have never regretted.

The adventure goes on.

7

TRUTH TO POWER

Steve Downs, '64

ON OCTOBER 26, 1963, when President Kennedy spoke at a convocation to celebrate the groundbreaking for the Robert Frost Library at Amherst College, he described the arts as providing a control on our use of power.

He said, "*[Artists] determine whether we use power or power uses us... art establishes the basic human truth which must serve as the touchstone of our judgement.*"

At the time, I did not understand what he meant. Now, more than fifty years later, I think I am beginning to figure it out.

Perhaps it's odd that I was so slow to understand. My father died in World War II before I was three years old. I do not remember him. I used to ask my mother why my father died—why, if Hitler was such an evil man, was he able to come to power in Germany? And my mother responded that good Germans who could have stopped him instead did nothing. (Like many of my mother's generation seeking explanations for the war, she may have been echoing Edmund Burke's observation that "the only thing necessary for the triumph of evil is for good people to do nothing.") I grew up understanding that the most dangerous people—the people who in a sense killed my father— were the good ones who could have stopped tyranny but instead did nothing.

In 1961, I spent the summer in the highlands of the Cameroons, West Africa, building a clinic with a program called Crossroads Africa. My mother, a doctor working at Harlem Hospital, prodded me into going. She said I was very "white" and needed a little "blackness" in my perspective. She was right. I was white, privileged, and fundamentally clueless. She was inspired by the black minister, James Robinson, a friend of the family. He founded Crossroads to get white and black Americans engaged in Africa through work projects. Crossroads was so successful that it became a model for Kennedy's Peace Corps a few years later.

In the Cameroons, our group of eight Americans, split about equally between blacks and whites, talked about the experiences of being black in America and of facing the toxic power of racism. We talked about the experience of being white in America, blinded to the injustices in society by the whiteness of our skin. I began a long journey to understanding how little I really knew. I learned that if you wanted to know the truth about life, you had to listen to the authentic voices of people who are actually living it.

———

ON NOVEMBER 22, 1963, I was walking past the Octagon on the Amherst campus when I heard that President Kennedy had been assassinated. I remember the exact spot. Kennedy's inauguration speech resonated in my head: "*Ask not what your country can do for you. Ask what you can do for your country.*" My father had died in the service of his country, and I felt called to serve my country also and thereby acknowledge, or perhaps honor, his sacrifice.

In his convocation speech, Kennedy had called on Amherst students to recognize their responsibility for the public service adding, "*Privilege is here and with privilege goes responsibility.*" I certainly felt my responsibility to contribute something, but I struggled with what exactly it was to be.

My solution, in 1964, was to join the Peace Corps. I was assigned to serve in the Indian Himalayas, primarily as a youth worker and beekeeper. I knew nothing about beekeeping when I started, but after on-the-job training in this delicate art, I came eventually to love the little critters. I did not know much about the country I was serving, but my Indian counterparts were happy to teach me. I caught bee swarms in my hat; crossed a Himalayan mountain pass in a blizzard; rode third class on trains and learned lessons of life from beggars. Eventually, in small ways, I learned to see life through the eyes of another culture, and at the same time to escape from my own culture for a while. The experience was liberating.

In India, I became interested in how laws designed to help people often became barriers instead. When the time came to leave, I decided that I would become a lawyer and help people make the laws work for them, rather than becoming obstacles in their path. I graduated from Cornell Law School in 1969. In 1975, I found the perfect job, one that I loved every day. For the next twenty-eight years I was chief attorney for the New York State Commission on Judicial Conduct, disciplining and removing bad judges.

My commission was to be the voice for those who were abused by the New York State court system. For nearly three decades, I listened to stories of abuse daily and came to understand the limitations of our judicial system. Many of those stories featured judges enforcing the laws unjustly. I began to think of justice as the art of treating equally people who society had deemed to be unequal.

One case involving Troy City Court Judge Henry Bauer arose just as I was about to retire, and it haunted me. Like all cities, Troy had a significant population of marginalized folks—black, poor, immigrant, or mentally ill—whom the police tended to harass with minor charges like "open container" offenses and loitering. The police claimed these actions were required to "clear" the streets. Judge Bauer began setting high bails on these minor charges—ten, fifteen, or even twenty thousand dollars—and he sent the defendants to jail without representation. After a few weeks, Judge Bauer would bring the defendants back to court, still unrepresented, and gave them a choice: guilty now and get out of jail or remain in jail waiting for a trial that might be months away. Bauer was so polite and seemingly considerate of the defendants he was harming. He seemed to feel that his method was more efficient. The defendants were all going to end up with a jail sentence anyway, so why waste time going through the formalities? Just put them in jail at the beginning and after they had served their time, then let them out by pleading guilty. It was much more efficient. Naturally, most of the defendants pleaded guilty to get out of jail, even when they had done nothing wrong.

When called before the Commission, Judge Bauer insisted that everything he did was legal. The law, he argued, gave him discretion as to the amount he could set bail, to the appointment of counsel, and to the scheduling of trials. But, in fact, the net effect of Judge Bauer's conduct was a giant injustice machine that generated wrongful convictions and mocked the procedural safeguards of American justice. The Commission eventually removed him from office.

Other judges had engaged in similar misconduct and were removed as well. But in Bauer's case, a public defender had been assigned to his court to represent the indigent. This individual watched the poor and marginalized being abused daily, apparently without objecting. Oddly, the public defender in the court was highly regarded. He did a good job for his clients, but only for clients that were specifically assigned to him by the judge. As he saw it, the ones who were unrepresented were not his problem. At the Commission hearing, he even testified as to what a fair judge Bauer was. So the public defender believed there was no reason for him to protest the injustices he witnessed because Judge Bauer had not specifically appointed the defender's office to represent the abused defendants. Meanwhile, the prosecutor handed out guilty pleas as though the only important thing in the judicial system was to get a conviction rather than doing justice.

The Bauer case represented for me the elaborate walls that society erects to prevent the marginalized from being heard. It wasn't just Judge Bauer—it was the whole community. And it wasn't just Troy—it was virtually every community nationwide. Each of the marginalized defendants in Bauer's court had a story to tell about the circumstances that brought him or her into court; the court was determined not to hear these stories. Instead, the court convicted the defendants according to the biases placed on them by society. That society could coerce convictions so easily without ever actually listening to the defendants amazed me.

———————

IN MARCH 2003, when the second war in Iraq was starting, I wanted to protest this impending war, but the Commission's staff had to follow the same rules as the judges. We weren't allowed to engage in political activity. I had the urge to walk around a local mall wearing a Give Peace a Chance T-shirt as a "non-political" protest. That way, I would not be entirely complicit in supporting the coming war. I knew it was sort of lame, but I was about to retire so I did it anyway. Within fifteen minutes, mall security accosted me. They told me to take off the peace T-shirt. When I refused, I was arrested. The arrest became international news, broadcast on CNN. Hundreds of folks from Albany rushed to the mall wearing peace T-shirts, trying to get arrested. The mall dropped the charges against me. So, in a strange way, I received my credentials as an activist on the very eve of my retirement from the Commission. It was the first protest I had ever attended.

Newly empowered by my arrest, I decided that in retirement I would try to serve the wrongfully convicted population. I was privileged to have a law license and "with privilege comes responsibility." I felt responsible to use it in a way that would represent innocent people. To me, the wrongfully convicted were the poets who spoke the authentic truth about our dysfunctional legal system. Without their voices, I felt we could not make progress in reform.

Eventually, working with a group of formerly convicted individuals who had been exonerated, known as ICHTY (It Could Happen To You), I drafted a bill to create a Commission on Prosecutorial Conduct that was as similar as possible to the legislation that supported the Commission on Judicial Conduct. Why, I argued, should we have a Commission to give oversight and discipline to judges, but not one for prosecutors? The prosecutors were at least as important as judges, if not more so, in our system of justice. As of this writing, we are still trying to get the Prosecutorial Bill through the New York

State legislature. But the driving force behind the bill comes from the stories of the folks wrongfully prosecuted or convicted. By the time I became involved with ICHTY, I was familiar with wrongful convictions on the federal level.

In 2006, I volunteered to assist in the defense of a local imam, Yassin Aref, who was accused of terrorism. He was placed in solitary confinement. For months before his trial, I visited Yassin for ten to fifteen hours a week and came to know him well. He was a beautiful and brilliant person. Although he spoke little English, he had an intense desire to communicate, and in his broken English he told me fascinating stories about his life as a Kurd in Iraq before he came to the U.S. in 1999 with his wife and children as United Nations refugees. He told me he really wanted to be a poet. I asked him why. Yassin said that poets were the most dangerous people in society. They could tell truth to the dictator, and if they were very good (and popular) they could escape execution.

"Poets starve in this country," I told him. "They are mostly ignored."

"You do not live under a dictator," Yassin said.

The charges against Yassin were based on a months-long elaborate FBI entrapment scheme. Critical parts were secretly recorded and videotaped. Yassin was accused of being a witness (the Muslim equivalent of a notary) for a loan between a secret FBI informant and a member of Yassin's mosque. According to the sting protocol, while witnessing a series of repayments of the loan, Yassin would overhear background conversations between the FBI informant and the mosque member. He would learn that the funds for the loan had been obtained from the (fake) sale of a missile to terrorists. Yassin's having witnessed the repayments with knowledge of the source of the money would supposedly constitute a crime: material support for terrorism.

Yassin, however, was never clearly told about the sale of the missile during the sting. He never said anything to indicate that he had heard the garbled background conversations, and he never gave any support whatsoever to terrorism. It was a classic frame-up. The FBI agents acknowledged afterwards that they had slipped incriminating information into conversations in a way that Yassin would not notice, so as not to "spook" him.

Yassin was charged with twenty-eight counts of material support for terrorism, one count for each of the repayment meetings. After viewing all of the evidence, the jury found Yassin not guilty on all counts except the final one from the June 10, 2004 meeting. During this last meeting, the FBI informant told Yassin directly, "I buy chaudries; I sell chaudries; they make money for me, so I can make you a loan too."

The prosecution claimed that the word *chaudry* was a code word for "missile." There was no proof that Yassin was ever told the supposedly coded meaning of the word *chaudry*. Nonetheless, the jury convicted Yassin on the basis of that one conversation. We were confident the conviction would be reversed on appeal.

After the defense and prosecution filed appeal briefs with the Second Circuit, the prosecutor filed a secret brief that the defense was not allowed to see. Then the Justice Department from Washington filed a top-secret brief that even the local prosecutor was not allowed to see. After oral argument, we—the defense—were excused, and the prosecution presented a secret argument before the court. The Second Circuit's decision either ignored or misrepresented most of the points raised by the defense. Apparently realizing that there was no evidence that Yassin was told the meaning of the code word *chaudry*, the Court said nothing about the June 10 conversation—the one conversation for which Yassin was convicted. The Court simply said that there was enough evidence from all the other conversations that the jury *could have* found Yassin guilty, thereby ignoring the jury's not guilty finding on all the other counts.

In other words, the Second Circuit convicted Yassin based entirely on evidence for which the jury had already found him not guilty. The conviction seemed legally bizarre. I became convinced that the FBI and the Courts had deliberately framed and convicted an innocent man. It changed my life.

Yassin was sentenced to fifteen years in prison and sent to a special Muslim prison in Terre Haute, Indiana, called the Communication Management Unit. The Unit severely restricts the inmates' contacts with the outside world. Later, we found out that the government had mistakenly identified Yassin as another person, Mohammed Yassin, who was associated with Al-Qaeda. Mohammed Yassin was killed in Jordan *after* Yassin's conviction. This misidentification may have been unethically and secretly conveyed to the courts during the trial and appeal. However, the government did not see fit to reverse Yassin's conviction. Yassin, along with the presumption of innocence and the rule of law, were merely collateral damage in the War on Terror.

Yassin is one of the lucky ones. He will complete his sentence in October 2018. Then, he will probably be deported to Iraq. His wife wants to go with him, so we are getting them both Iraqi passports. Three of his children are now Americans, and plan to come back to the U.S. for graduate school. The fourth child still has no citizenship from any country; we continue to work on U.S. citizenship for him.

There are many others who are much worse off.

———

IN THE COURSE of our work, we became aware of hundreds of other cases similar to Yassin's, in which the Justice Department targeted and convicted innocent Muslims. We began to call these cases "preemptive prosecutions." Innocent Muslims were being convicted in show trials, without any crime having been committed.

These actions were based on the government's suspicion of what the target might do in the future. After 9/11, the Bush Administration charged the FBI with preventing the next terror attack before it occurred. Vice President Cheney reportedly said, "If there is even a one percent chance that someone may engage in terrorism, we have to respond as if it is a certainty." Cheney's so-called "one percent doctrine" meant that convicting 99 innocent Muslims was preferable to allowing one terrorist to go free. We found hundreds of victims of preemptive prosecution all over the country—over 700 by our latest count.

In 2008, four friends and I formed an organization called Project SALAM (Support And Legal Advocacy for Muslims) to study preemptive prosecution.

We began giving presentations around the country at mosques, churches, conferences, and schools to warn Muslims about FBI entrapment schemes, like the one involving Yassin, targeting impressionable young Muslims. Because names so powerfully evoke personalities, we made a point to speak the names out loud: Aafia Siddiqui, Dr. Rafil Dhafir, Fahad Hashmi, Shifa Sadeqee, Matin Siraj, Tarik Shah, Keifa Jayyousi, Ahmed Abu Ali, Ziyad Yaghi, Hatem Farez, the Newburg 4, the Ft. Dix 5, the Holy Land Foundation, the Virginian Paintball Network, and hundreds more.

My wife cut up a Tyvek roll into 3-inch by 6-inch strips: 155 panels, each with the name of a preemptively prosecuted prisoner. She lovingly sewed them into three large wall panels that were held upright by 4-foot by 6-foot plastic pipes. The whole wall could be disassembled into a ski bag that we called our missile launcher. The wall could be assembled in five minutes for a stunning backdrop to any presentation. It made a portable "wall of shame" to illustrate the magnitude of the problem, and the wall was soon too small. We dragged it all over the country for dozens of presentations. After presentations, people would come up from the audience to touch a loved one's name, take its picture, or just cry. Prisoners wrote to me, asking to be put on the wall because they "did not want to be forgotten." People asked me to bring it to presentations. There were only names on the wall, but the names so strongly evoked the actual people that folks later remembered it as a wall of faces. The wall became our poem of defiance, where "As long as these persons' names and stories are spoken, you cannot obliterate them with the label 'terrorist.'"

———

YASSIN'S INFLUENCE ON my life did not end after his conviction. On the day after his trial ended, I went to visit him in jail. He said to me, "I want to fire you as my attorney." I was stunned. Then he added, "I want to hire you as my brother. I have no other family in this country, and at this point I think family will do me more good than lawyers."[1]

We grinned at each other in agreement. I pushed a stack of yellow pads toward him and said that this would be a good time for him to start writing the story of his life. For the next six months, until he was sentenced, we exchanged drafts, sharpening his still evolving English, until he had written a 485-page story of his life, *Son of Mountains: My life as a Kurd and a Terror Suspect*. It is one of my favorite books, from a master storyteller. Project SALAM published the book; it is available electronically on Amazon.

We immediately sent copies of the book to journalists to generate publicity. One of the journalists was Laila Al-Arian, the daughter of the political prisoner Dr. Sami Al-Arian. Unbeknownst to us, he was under house arrest in Laila's apartment. Sami saw the book on her coffee table, realized our support for Yassin, and invited us (Project SALAM) to Virginia to meet with him in Laila's apartment.

Sami had been a distinguished professor at Southern Florida University, and an outspoken proponent of Palestinian rights. Militant Zionists pressured the Justice Department into bringing terrorism charges against him. The claim was that he was a member of Islamic Jihad, a group responsible for bombings in Israel. For six months the prosecution showed the jury lurid pictures of buses being blown up and Israelis driven from their homes, but no evidence that Sami had anything to do with this carnage. After six months of trial, the defense rested without calling a single witness. The jury acquitted Sami of most of the charges but were hung on a few minor charges. Rather than be retried on the remaining minor charges, Sami made a deal with the Florida prosecutor to be deported without having to cooperate in any further prosecutions.

---

1   As Yassin's "brother," I became responsible for his wife and four young children, who had no means of support. None of them (except the youngest, born in the U.S. while Yassin was in prison) had a green card. None of the children were a citizen of any country in the world. I learned from these four brilliant, charming kids what it meant to be a "dreamer" in America. Together, we had many adventures. The oldest two have now graduated from college. After a lawsuit against the U.S. government, they have finally become U.S. citizens. We hope the third child will soon follow the other two. Meanwhile, the community in Albany has raised roughly $10,000 annually, for over a decade, for their support.

But the Justice Department double-crossed Sami. A Virginia prosecutor, Gordon Kromberg, called Sami before a grand jury in Virginia to ask him, under oath, about all the matters on which a jury in Florida had just acquitted him. Kromberg had done this before with another acquitted Muslim, Sabri Benkala, and then convicted Benkala for perjury. Sami refused to testify before Kromberg's grand jury, citing his non-cooperation agreement with the Florida prosecutor. Kromberg then brought criminal charges for refusal to testify. However, the presiding judge, Leona Brinkema, saw the perjury trap that Sami faced from the Justice Department. She released Sami under house arrest to his daughter's apartment in Virginia, and quietly put Sami's file away in her bottom drawer. Sami remained under house arrest for the next five years, unable to work or lead a normal life, while his case quietly died[2].

IN 2010, SAMI, under house arrest, proposed that Project SALAM and some seventeen other organizations join together to form a new organization, the National Coalition to Protect Civil Freedoms (NCPCF). The mission of NCPCF would be to educate Americans about preemptive prosecution, profiling, and prison abuse including torture, solitary confinement, and the Communication Management Unit. A particular focus of the new group's activity would be to assist the impacted families of preemptively prosecuted men. These families were living under very difficult circumstances, often impoverished by the incarceration of their bread winner, shunned by society, and rejected even by their mosques, which were terrified of being associated with "terrorists."

In 2012, I became the executive director of NCPCF. I began to tour the country, telling the stories of the Muslims who were preemptively prosecuted. I asked to be named an interim director only. I felt strongly that these stories could best be told by authentic Muslim voices and the organization would be best run by the impacted families themselves. However, at that time, the

---

2   Finally, the Justice Department gave up, dropped the charges, and deported him to Turkey.

fear engendered by the FBI was so great that few Muslims were willing to speak out publicly or to become the unpaid director. Indeed, we non-Muslims did not know whether we might also become FBI targets. We hoped that our white skins might protect us. We were supporting Muslims who had been accused or convicted of being terrorists. Were we not then giving material support to terrorism? I used to say jokingly that I was running a support group for wrongfully convicted terrorists; I could tell from people's expressions whether they focused on the "wrongfully convicted" (sympathy), or the "terrorists" (fear).

Four events highlight my time as director illustrate the diverse nature of our work. The first was a press conference to help bring light to entrapment. One day, Lyric Cabral, a filmmaker, happened to meet a friend named Said Torres. Torres mentioned that the FBI was sending him to Pittsburg to entrap an individual, Khalifa Al-Killi, in a sting. When Lyric asked if she could film the sting, Torres agreed as long as the FBI was not informed. Lyric began filming. Khalifa quickly realized that the FBI was trying to entrap him. He reached out to Project SALAM and NCPCF for help. We held a press conference at the National Press Club in Washington to denounce the FBI's attempted entrapment of an innocent man. The day before the press conference, the FBI agents, who apparently knew of the press conference through wiretaps, arrested Khalifa on an unrelated gun possession charge.[3]

The NCPCF press conference eventually became part of the documentary film *(T)error* by Lyric Cabral and David Felix Sutcliffe. *(T)error* helped us tell the story of FBI entrapments and of NCPCF's efforts to stop them, and it won an Emmy in 2017.

The second highlight is the attempt to close the Communication Management Unit. In 2010, Yassin Aref became the lead plaintiff in a lawsuit brought by one of NCPCF's coalition partners, the Center for Constitutional Rights,

---

3   Months before the sting started, Khalifa had posted on his Facebook page a picture of himself holding a gun that a friend was using at a public shooting range. Long ago, Khalifa had been convicted of a felony. As a result, he was not allowed to "possess" a gun. Courts have ruled that simply holding a gun is sufficient "possession" to permit a defendant to be convicted. That simple act, holding a friend's gun for a photo, was enough to establish "possession." Khalifa was sentenced to eight years in jail.

to close the Communication Management Unit on the grounds that it had been illegally opened in the first place. I was proud of Yassin for being the lead plaintiff; he was being the true poet he always wanted to be—speaking truth to power—at a time when he was a vulnerable prisoner in the CMU.[4]

The third main work the NCPCF engaged involved Guantanamo. In 2014, Project SALAM and NCPCF wrote a report about preemptive prosecutions entitled "Inventing Terrorists: The Lawfare of Preemptive Prosecution." The report showed that 94 percent of the 399 terrorism convictions claimed by the government at that time were either completely preemptive prosecutions (72 percent) or had elements of preemptive prosecution (22 percent). Amazingly, this report made its way to Ammar Al-Baluchi, a prisoner at Guantanamo. He sent his lawyer to interview us as potential expert witnesses at his trial. This led to a series of public conferences in which the Guantanamo defense lawyers compared trials of terrorism cases domestically and at Guantanamo. The cases at Guantanamo are overshadowed by the routine torture of the prisoners. Since the U.S. government cannot admit to torture, the cases may never be tried, and the prisoners may live in that hell forever, until freed by death. Justice is a meaningless concept for them, and Guantanamo remains a symbol of our national disgrace.

The fourth milestone concerned our development as an organization. NCPCF held its first family conference for the families impacted by the preemptive prosecution of a loved one in 2012. At first, these shattered families had to learn to bond and begin their healing. In 2017, after the seventh conference, the families felt strong enough to go to Capitol Hill and lobby their representatives, some of whom were conservative Republicans, to demand fair and equal treatment for the Muslim community. And in 2017, NCPCF finally gained an executive director from the impacted families. Leena Al-Arian, daughter of the founder Sami Al-Arian, now serves as co-director together with her long-time friend, the activist, Dr. Mel Underbakke.

---

4   As of this writing the lawsuit has survived a motion to dismiss and is still pending—
     some seven years after it was brought.

I TELL STORIES of these marginalized people, particularly Muslims and exonerees, with great affection and respect. Despite all of their hardships, most of them still want America to succeed, albeit with a renewed commitment to justice and human rights. Individually, these folks are heroes. Collectively, their stories are authentic voices, the poetry of our time. As a lawyer, I am often required to speak for a client, but the power of a story is in its authentic voice. I must honor that authentic voice when it is strong enough to tell its own story. In any case, I am grateful for my client's trust.

In his speech at Amherst, President John F. Kennedy said that "*art is not a form of propaganda; it is a form of truth.*" Today, we are swamped by propaganda intended to drown out the voices of the poets. In an age when truth is "classified," and lies are called "alternative facts," we need to hear the stories of people actually living the truth in order to determine for ourselves what is authentic.

Kennedy noted that poets' concern for justice must make them aware of how our nation falls short of its highest potential. We need to hear the truth of how we failed; how we, like the good Germans who did nothing to stop Hitler, have turned aside in the face of torture, repression, and racism, and pretended not to see. We are at risk of becoming the very monster we tried to defeat in World War II, full of our own imagined superiority, arrogance, corruption, and blindness to justice.

Yassin used to tell me that only the ignorant could be happy, because "once you know the truth, you cannot evade responsibility." And, as Yassin predicted, once I finally began to see the truth, I could not un-see it.

———

NOW THAT THE legal precedent has been set, our government can eventually move from targeting Muslims for ideological crimes to prosecuting non-Muslims for the same thing.

A new version of German Pastor Martin Niemoller's famous poem on the lack of solidarity during World War II could become a lament for our freedoms lost:

First they shot unarmed black citizens, and I did not say anything because I was not black.

Then they reduced income for the poor, deported the immigrants, and stigmatized the marginalized, and I did not say anything because I was not poor or an immigrant or marginalized.

Then they labeled innocent Muslims "terrorists," tortured them, and locked them up in dog cages in solitary confinement, potentially for the rest of their lives, and I did not say anything because I was not Muslim.

Then they eavesdropped on my communications and targeted me for prosecution because privately I told my friends I disagreed with the government's lies. They sent ingratiating informants, pretending to be my best friends, who infiltrated my social groups and organizations. The informants tried for years to goad me into saying incriminating words which they could secretly record and use as evidence against me. They threatened to label me a "terrorist" unless I informed on my friends. And I did not say anything because I assumed my white privilege would protect me.

Then they arrested me on a pretext charge, convicted me in a show trial, and sent me away for life in solitary. And nobody said a word because they had all been terrified into silence.

Fortunately, many poets today are speaking about the experience of women, blacks, LGBTQs, Latinos, immigrants, Native Americans, and others. These experiences are being forged into a new political awareness—represented in works like *Hamilton*—the yearned-for promise of equality for all.

President Kennedy was right when he said that poets are "indispensable" to society. Yassin was right when he said poets are the most dangerous people in society because they tell truth to power. Who among us is willing to be a poet and a teller of truth? Or, at this time, perhaps we are all required to be poets.

8

GIVEN TO ME

———————

Gene Palumbo, '64

IN MY FIRST YEAR AFTER AMHERST, I taught and coached in a Peace Corps-type program at Baghdad College in Iraq. Near the end of the school year, a senior member of the faculty showed me a letter he had written. It was a series of paragraphs about episodes in his life, each beginning with the words, "It has been given to me…" Over the years I've found myself thinking along those lines, realizing how much has been given to me.

In Baghdad, it was hard to keep up with what was happening elsewhere, so I wasn't prepared for what confronted me when I returned to the U.S.: the controversy over Vietnam and the need to decide how I would respond. To give myself more time, I took my grad school courses on an audit basis, instead of for credit, and so was able to spend nearly a year—the most important year of my life, one that I now see as something "given to me"—doing little else but reading and thinking about whether I could ever kill someone. In the end I decided I couldn't, so I filed with the Selective Service System as a conscientious objector (CO). When I advised my local draft board of my decision, I was told—and this is a direct quote—"You can't be a Catholic *and* a pacifist. You're a communist."

Eventually I was granted CO status, which included a two-year alternative service requirement. How would I fulfill it? I kept returning to Albert Camus's "The Unbeliever and Christians," a talk he gave at the Dominican monastery of Latour-Maubourg in the wake of World War II. It was time, he told the monks:

> [To] get away from abstraction and confront the blood-stained face history has taken on today. The grouping we need is a grouping of [people] resolved to speak out clearly and to pay up personally.

I felt it was important that conscientious objectors show that we were willing to pay up personally; after all, as COs we were saying, "It's not that we're unwilling to die; it's that we're unwilling to kill." One way to make that point, I felt, was to volunteer with a service agency in Vietnam, since the work could well have involved some risk. But my draft board rejected my request. Why? Working in Vietnam was what I wanted to do, and the board wasn't about to grant any wish of mine.

We'd had an ugly, multi-year fight. It began with them rejecting my CO application out of hand, but ended, many appeals and confrontations later, with their decision to draft me—they actually sent me an induction notice—being annulled. While the Selective Service System's own regulations said that people should be given alternative service assignments that best utilized their experience, education and training, the chairman of the local draft board had angrily promised me, "You're going to wind up emptying bedpans, driving a truck or tending a garden." He kept his word—or tried to—with the assignment he gave me; but I refused to accept it, and he lost on that one, too. I ended up working at a community agency in Harlem.

It turned out to be a blessing that the CO application process dragged on for so long. In those years of riots and of cities burning, John Lindsay, the mayor of New York (where I was living), had established the Urban Action Task Force in an effort to keep New York from ending up as devastated as Newark and Watts were. During the long wait for a decision on my application, I was given a chance to participate in the task force's work.

That meant being out on the streets of some of the city's roughest neighborhoods until late at night, meeting with community people—sometimes amidst tension and danger—and trying to deal with volatile situations. It proved to be an extraordinary experience, something else that was "given to me." Lew Feldstein, a Lindsay aide, described it well in a documentary film about those years:

> [We] were locked to the central core of history and the issues in this country: race and Vietnam. All the issues were being fought out in this city…
>
> [Lindsay's] qualities…were ones that you could stand up behind: the adamancy, the belief in principles, the sense of justice, the sense of rightness, the sense of the possible, the sense that individuals could make a difference, that an entire city could make a difference…*It was like this big cable going through history, going through your life, with a surge of electricity going through it, and you grab it. And it doesn't happen often in your life. But in those years, we grabbed it.*

Later, in the seventies, I lived on New York's Lower East Side, freelancing as a print and radio journalist and working part time in the legal services branch of the federal anti-poverty program. Late one Friday night, as I was walking home from the subway, I passed a building near the Bowery where, judging from the noise inside, a riot was about to break out. The front door was open. I poked my head in and saw someone trying to break up a fight between two very angry people. I asked if I could help. Without knowing it, I had walked into a house of hospitality that was the headquarters of the Catholic Worker movement.

Soon I was spending a lot of time there. You never knew who you'd bump into—Dorothy Day, home from one of her many travels; César Chávez, visiting the east coast "office" of the United Farm Workers (i.e., the Catholic Worker's musty basement); Fr. Daniel Berrigan, back from a prison term for an anti-Vietnam protest; or new arrivals like Robert Ellsberg, who'd just taken a leave from Harvard following his sophomore year.

Robert told me about a time when, still a boy, he'd been asked by his dad to help out with a big photocopying project. Sure, he'd answered. Turned out his dad was Daniel Ellsberg, and Robert's job was to copy the Pentagon papers for the *New York Times* and the *Washington Post*. That and so much more, especially the lifelong friends I made, was life at the Catholic Worker —another gift "given to me."

One Saturday morning in 1978, I got a call from a friend at Fordham University: come to the Bronx immediately; there's someone here you'll want to interview. I grabbed my tape recorder and microphone and hurried to the subway. Waiting for me at Fordham was Álvaro Argüello, a Jesuit priest who'd flown in from Nicaragua to denounce the murder of his brother by the Somoza dictatorship, which had held power there for more than forty years. His brother, a businessman, was no lefty, but he'd made the mistake of criticizing the dictatorship. That was all it took. As I spoke with Fr. Argüello, the world of Latin America began to open to me.

A few months later I was in Puebla, Mexico, covering a three-week meeting of Latin America's Catholic bishops. There I met Óscar Romero, the outspoken archbishop of San Salvador. He had denounced human rights abuses by the Salvadoran military, and as a result was getting death threats. On one occasion a reporter, without alluding directly to the threats, asked him, "Are you really going back to El Salvador?"—as in (but not actually saying): "If you do, they're going to kill you."

"I know what you're getting at," said Romero, "but, you know, they say I'm the pastor, and the pastor is supposed to be there for the flock. And the flock is back in El Salvador. So, yes, I'm going to return." A year later, he was shot dead as he celebrated Mass in the chapel of the cancer hospital where he lived.

I arrived in El Salvador just after his assassination, thinking to cover the country's civil war. Who would have guessed that it would continue for another twelve years—or that I'd end up staying for the rest of my life?

———

I COULD CITE many examples of what was "given to me" in covering the war, but I'll mention only one: meeting Enrique Álvarez Córdova, a multi-millionaire coffee grower who, having made his fortune, decided to go into public service. As minister of agriculture in the early 70s, Álvarez had designed a program to deal with the country's most pressing problem: land reform. Tens of thousands of farmworkers, denied access to land, were unable to feed their families properly. But when the landholding powers-that-be saw his plan, they said, don't even think about it—we're not going there.

So Álvarez quit the government and undertook his own land reform: the workers on his prize-winning *hacienda* would now become its owners. He didn't stop there. When Archbishop Romero asked him to help in a last-ditch attempt to stave off the looming civil war, he accepted; and when the effort failed, he did something which, given his conservative and privileged background, boggled many minds: he accepted the presidency of the Democratic Revolutionary Front (FDR), a left-of-center opposition group. It was non-Marxist and non-violent, but it was strongly anti-government.

Álvarez didn't last long. Ten months later, as he and other FDR leaders were meeting one morning in downtown San Salvador, four blocks from the U.S. embassy, the Army moved in with troops and a tank and surrounded the meeting site. The leaders, Álvarez among them, were seized and dragged off; their tortured bodies were found the next day.

I am reminded of my last interview with him, not long before his death. It took place in the United States, where he had gone to tell people, in Washington and at the grass roots, about the war. I was in the U.S. at the time, and went to cover a three-day conference at which Álvarez spoke. On the final morning I awoke early and couldn't get back to sleep. I decided to take a walk on the conference grounds, and bumped into Álvarez, who was doing the same thing. It was just after 5 a.m. I said to him, "How about an interview—not about the FDR platform, but about your life?" He said yes.

His story was so compelling that I forgot I was holding a microphone and doing an interview—something that's only happened to me on one other occasion in all my years as a journalist. At the end of the interview, I asked him the same question we'd asked Archbishop Romero the previous year at the Puebla conference: "Are you really going back to El Salvador?"

There was no doubt that if he did, a major effort would be made to hunt him down. I will never forget his reply to my question. He prefaced it by describing, in English, what the previous months, as president of the FDR, had been like:

> When I took this decision [to accept the presidency], I realized all the risks that I would have, but—and this is very import-ant—these six or seven months that I've been really working full time for this, I have found out something that is very beau-tiful, I would say. You forget about everything else. You don't care about your own safety, you don't care about pleasures, you don't care about anything else. You're just completely absorbed by this kind of work…So I am not worried about [the danger]. I am conscious of it, but I am even thinking right now about going back to the country if my presence there is needed.

I learned later that he had re-entered El Salvador clandestinely and had lived in a series of safe houses until his death. I never saw him again.

———

IF I WERE ASKED, "What, more than anything else, has been given to you in El Salvador?" the answer would be, "Meeting my wife, Guadalupe Montalvo." As I got to know her, I finally understood something our class-mate, Tom Jacobs, had said to me thirty-five years earlier. At Amherst, and in our first post-Amherst years, he and I had talked at length about what we wanted to do with our lives. We thought it might be necessary to forego marriage and family; that would leave us freer to do the work which seemed most important (even if it didn't pay), and to take risks which, if we'd had spouses and children, we might have been reluctant to take. Then one day, after we'd been out of touch for a while, we got together and he told me something: he was going to marry. I didn't get it. How could he go and do that? What about all those dreams and plans, those conversations we'd had?

I asked him to explain. His reply was simple: "I met someone." Well, I, too, had had the experience of falling in love, but what always ended up prevailing was the conclusion I'd reached at Amherst: staying single made sense. It continued to make sense for another thirty-five years. Then came Guadalupe.

It would be hard to imagine two people with backgrounds more different than ours. The oldest of nine children, she had grown up in a rural area where subsistence farming was the norm and where the only accessible school ended at third grade. It wasn't an easy life, but the land was fertile and her parents were able to feed their children. Then came the war. Little by little, their once-peaceful region turned into a free-fire zone. Close friends and relatives from their village were killed, and her family came very close to death. Finally they were forced to flee with literally only the clothes on their backs. Left behind was the little they'd had: a few farming tools and a simple house they hadn't finished building.

When they fled, Guadalupe's mother was eight-and-a-half months pregnant, and had recently broken her knee in a fall. With her husband carrying her part of the way, it took the family an entire day to walk from their remote village to a road where they could flag a bus. Given their arrival after nightfall and a wartime dusk-to-dawn curfew, they settled down to spend the night huddled beneath a tree on the roadside.

In the village where they took refuge, Guadalupe and her brothers and sisters were mocked at school for being barefoot, for wearing ragged hand-me-downs instead of the school uniform, for not having knapsacks for their books, and for always being out on the streets trying to sell the baked goods their mother made to supplement what her dad earned as a sharecropper.

Guadalupe had a dream: she wanted her younger brothers and sisters to be able to get their high school degrees. But that seemed out of the question; the expenses it would have involved were something her family, so close to the edge, simply couldn't afford. So Guadalupe dropped out of school after ninth grade and went to work in a sweatshop, staying there for fourteen years and eking out just enough to pay for books and school supplies, and to see her dream realized. Perilous health conditions at the factory finally forced her to leave, but soon she was working in another one.

I had friends who'd met one of her younger sisters, and who often went out to the countryside to visit the family. They'd return to San Salvador with compelling stories about an extraordinary older sister—Guadalupe. I decided I had to meet her.

———

HOW TO CONVEY to you what she's like? Possibly others can do it better than I. After meeting Guadalupe during a visit to El Salvador, a friend spoke about her in a talk he gave at a college back in the U.S. After the talk, he was approached by a student who, the year before, had lived in El Salvador in a study-abroad program where Guadalupe was by then working as a cook. Weeping, the student said to him, "Guadalupe was my salvation during my time in El Salvador. She's the most incredible person I've ever met—and I can't believe you just talked about her!" She added that getting to know Guadalupe's family had been a life-changing experience for her.

A few years ago, Guadalupe and I were invited to give talks at Notre Dame University. A student who heard her wrote later:

> *Honestly, being in her presence that night was more than just a*
> *learning opportunity. Her experiences were striking in themselves,*
> *but the entire time she spoke, I just had this strange feeling of love*
> *emanating from her. It's hard to describe with words, but her story*

was so genuine and heartfelt. It took me through the joys and sorrows of human life, but to extremes that I had never experienced. Hearing her was a blessing and a challenge.

Another student added:

Hearing her story both in Spanish and English [I was translating for Guadalupe] made it that much more powerful. Her courage in speaking about the trauma she endured, and her grace and eloquence were amazing. I very much admire Guadalupe for what she has survived and for her effort to share her story with others.

As Guadalupe and I got to know each other, I finally began to understand—it had only taken me thirty-five years—what Tom Jacobs had meant when he explained his decision to marry by saying "I met someone." Now I, too, had "met someone."

Not that ours was an easy courtship, because Guadalupe resisted. She kept saying—you can't believe how insistent she was about this—"You're making a terrible mistake. You should find someone more *preparada*"—in other words, someone who'd had the chance to study and travel, to do the things she'd never been able to do. My reply was, "There's really only one difference between us: I've had some opportunities that you haven't had—and that doesn't matter."

It took a few years, but she finally allowed herself to be convinced by that argument, and on March 25, 2007, we went to the chapel at the hospital where Archbishop Romero had lived, and there, at the altar where he was murdered, we were married.

———

THERE HAD ALSO BEEN the question of further education—Guadalupe's. When I first raised the issue, while we were courting, she was adamant: no chance of that happening. Why? She hadn't been in school for nineteen years. "*Estoy oxidada,*" she said. "I've rusted over."

It didn't seem that way to me. I saw her as a natural "researcher." Without books or access to a library, she had made the best of whatever—or whomever—was at hand. There was, for example, the time when she heard a priest talking on the radio about a problem similar to one she was facing in her pastoral work at the local parish. One morning, after she'd finished her all-night shift at the factory, instead of returning home to the countryside, she got on a bus and went to San Salvador, tracking down the priest at his parish. He was about to leave, having gone in very early to say the 6 a.m. Mass. The poor guy was probably longing to go home and go back to bed. And here came this bright-eyed woman walking right at him: "*Hola, Padre.* I heard you on the radio. Could I ask you a few questions?" End of dreams (the priest's) of an early-morning *siesta*.

She kept returning after the night shift to ask more questions. The priest ended up admiring her so much that he arranged for a group of nuns to offer her a three-year high school scholarship at their motherhouse in Rome (myself, I think they were hoping to recruit her). She turned it down because taking it would have meant leaving her job, something that was unthinkable because her $145/month salary (and that was after fourteen years on the job) was keeping her family afloat.

And then, years later, I came along, trying to convince her to resume her studies. How to get her to give it a try? I had an idea. The students in the study-abroad program where she works had a late afternoon class in Salvadoran literature, given by an outstanding teacher. What better way to re-enter the classroom? The students were crazy about Guadalupe and delighted at the prospect of her being in their class. But she declined, and that, it appeared, was the end of it.

I'll come clean: with no other alternative, I stooped to conspiring—and against my future wife! I approached the teacher, María Ester Chamorro: would she personally invite Guadalupe to take the class, and be a co-conspirator in a maneuver I was planning? "Of course!"

Anticipating one of Guadalupe's responses—"I can't afford the books for the course"—I got the booklist from María Ester, bought them all, and took them to her home one night. Guadalupe and I arrived there the following morning. The overture was made, and pressed: "I'd love to have you in the class," said María Ester, "and so would the students." Guadalupe played her last card: "That's very nice of you, but I could never pay for the books." "You're in luck!" said Maria Ester. "I happen to have an extra set." Cornered, Guadalupe accepted; her "de-rusting" process was about to begin.

Later we found out about a good high school equivalency program. For eleven months, while working full time, she went to classes on Saturday, and studied every day till after midnight. Imagine her parents' pride when, one Saturday morning, we all climbed into my 1978 jeep and drove Guadalupe, in cap and gown, to her high school graduation.

What next? "What," I asked, "would you like to be?" During her twenty-three years as a catechist in her rural parish, she had done as much counseling as teaching. "What I'd really like is to be a psychologist, but I don't know if I could do it."

One day a psychologist friend turned up at a party at the study-abroad program. I told her about Guadalupe and her dream, but also about her doubts. "Would you speak with her about it, and then tell me what you think?" My friend wandered off toward the kitchen, where Guadalupe was washing dishes. An hour later my friend was back, blown away: "They should waive all the requirements, and let her start practicing now."

———

AND WHAT DOES Amherst have to do with all of this? A great deal.

If there'd been a prize freshman year for the member of our class who was the most lost and overwhelmed, I'd have won it easily. Academically, socially, emotionally, I was barely holding on, and wondered if I was going to survive. Our physics teacher, Arnie Arons, wasn't much help; one afternoon in his office, when I asked for help with that week's assignment, his reply was devastating: "You're in the wrong pew" (in other words, "You'll never make it here."). That almost pushed me over the edge. Eventually I began to get my bearings, but even with that, I was largely playing catch-up during my years at Amherst.

Even in the midst of so much pain, there was one thing I did "get," one thing that was "given to me." It has made possible so much of what's been good in the years that have followed. It was—and I hope this doesn't sound trite—the emphasis on truth, on intellectual honesty, on having the courage to follow the evidence wherever it leads.

That didn't come easily to me. I arrived at Amherst as a "cradle Catholic" and was forced to shed some beliefs that had been part of the bedrock of my life. In those days, it didn't take much to set me off. I remember the day in Humanities 1 when the professor, William Kennick, mused about the Catholic doctrine of Mary's assumption into heaven. What a shame, he said, that back then they didn't have the kind of scientific equipment we have today; if they'd been able to measure her velocity at "lift off," he said, we could easily calculate exactly where she is in the solar system today. You may smile, but I was so shaken that I transferred out of Kennick's section.

Having my beliefs challenged was hard, but by senior year I'd come out on the other side: having overcome the fear, I finally felt able to face what needed to be faced. I even signed up for a philosophy course with the same Kennick I'd fled freshman year, and sat through his famous demolition of Aquinas's proofs for the existence of God.

For me at that time, Camus' "The Unbeliever and Christians" said it all:

> Between the forces of terror and the forces of dialogue, a great unequal battle has begun. I have nothing but reasonable illusions as to the outcome of that battle. But I believe it must be fought, and I know that certain [people] at least have resolved to do so…Perhaps we cannot prevent this world from being a world in which children are tortured. But we can reduce the number of tortured children.

In trying to help fight that battle, stripped of the comfort of my earlier beliefs, I could at least strive, along with others, for "atheistic sanctity" (Camus' *The Plague*). I was having to settle for less, but in time, I would come to see that "less" as enough: "In the midst of winter," Camus wrote, "I discovered that there was in me an invincible summer."

In subsequent years, I kept encountering people who saw things that way and were living it out. In that first post-Amherst year in Baghdad, I came across some words of the French novelist George Bernanos that have served as a kind of credo. Bernanos wrote them while in exile during World War II. I love these words for the primacy they give to truth, and for the terrible modesty of the hope they express:

> There is something worse than dying. It is to die deceived. It seems to me that I can help you, that we can help each other, not to be deceived—or at least, to be deceived as little as possible.

Later, in the years of Vietnam and my embrace of nonviolence, there was Gandhi: "If truth is not the law of our being, the whole of my message falls to pieces." And then there was this passage from Dag Hammarskjöld's diary, *Markings*:

> I do not know Who—or what—put the question. I don't know when it was put. I don't even remember answering. But at some point I did answer "Yes" to Someone—or Something—and from that hour I was certain that existence is meaningful and that, therefore, my life, in self-surrender, had a goal.

For me, a new dimension has been added during these years in El Salvador. What I've come to see here—and this is the basic message of what is called liberation theology—is that to really seek the truth, you need to be close to those who have always gotten, and are still getting, the short end of the stick. That finally came home to me in the words of a priest who'd been a counselor to one of the four U.S. churchwomen—women I had known —who were raped and murdered in 1980 by members of El Salvador's National Guard. "If you stand with the poor," said Fr. Michael Crowley, "if you identify with them, feel their insecurity, their rejection, you begin to understand in a new way."

The churchwomen had stood with the poor, identified with them, worked with them in conflict zones and refugee camps. This "new way of understanding" that Father Crowley spoke of, this new grasp of the truth—what did it mean for the churchwomen?

Ana Carrigan, who made a documentary film about them, put it well:

> I came to see that the meaning of their lives was so rich that death was not ultimately important. Every single day, when they got up, they had to know that that day might be "it," the end, as it had been for so many of their friends and so many people all around them. But it was like the biblical saying, "Death, where is thy sting?" It wasn't a factor for them. If it had been, they could never have done what they did. They simply couldn't have functioned.

———

ALL OF THIS has been given to me. It's been a long road, and it started at Amherst. Had it not been for what I began to learn there, I'm not at all sure that I would ever have gotten here. And for that, I'm very grateful.

9

"WITH PRIVILEGE GOES RESPONSIBILITY"

George Wanlass, '64

"I think of myself as being in a line of work that goes back about twenty-five thousand years. My job has been finding the cave and holding the torch."
—Walter Hopps

LONG AGO, I ATTENDED AMHERST COLLEGE, then went on to graduate school at both the University of Kansas and Stanford University. Disenchanted with the prospect of a future as a history teacher, I decided to go into agriculture, took a blind leap, and bought a dairy farm near Logan, Utah, the home of Utah State University.

FAMILY CONNECTIONS

My family's historical involvement with the state of Utah is deep. It began with John T. Caine II, my great-grandfather, one of the seven founding fathers of Utah State University. For years, he taught English, and he also served as treasurer. My grandfather, George B. Caine, headed the university dairy department and traveled throughout the state doing dairy extension work. My paternal grandfather, Will Wanlass, served as dean and interim president of the university. My grandmother, Marie Eccles Caine, and my mother, Kathryn C. Wanlass, distinguished patrons and supporters of the arts, initiated and supported my involvement with the arts.

Shortly after I arrived in Utah to become a dairy farmer, life propelled me toward further involvement with the arts—combining and continuing yet another strong thread of my family history. My great aunt, Nora Eccles, funded a new art museum at Utah State, the Nora Eccles Harrison Museum of Art (NEHMA). Also, my wife, Karen Carson, is an artist. Every day, I enter her studio and watch the creative process unfold. Creating art turns out to be much more difficult than I ever imagined, and I have found myself increasingly fascinated by the evidence of that work.

So, with the financial support of a family foundation, I became an art collector. With no other significant acquisition funding, and no one else at the university to do what I did, over forty years I have built a unique collection of the art of the American West for the NEHMA.

BECOMING A COLLECTOR

I tapped into a treasure trove of twentieth-century art created by an extremely creative group in the West. Wonderful, affordable things appeared in my travels to dealers and auctions, with little competition in the market. The demands of cattle ranching (no more milking!) consumed most of my time and energy. But whenever I went to Los Angeles, San Francisco, New Mexico, Seattle, or New York, I ran from gallery to gallery. I didn't have much time, and I wanted to see more, learn more, and acquire additions to the collection. Affordable and desirable art was available.

I have always maintained a mental vision of the collection I was building, an image of the whole toward which I'm striving. This vision is based on what I've seen and learned but remains open to new material. Here are some examples of the building process.

Years ago, visiting the daughter of the sculptor Adeline Kent, I selected a piece called *Gambler* for the Museum; no sale. Later, patience paid off and I purchased it.

Before she died, June Wayne, a very strong-minded woman, decided that she would not sell me a painting I had selected at her studio. Many years later, I contacted her daughter and bought *The Elements*, my original choice.

Lots of interesting material continues to pop up. In a small California auction, I noticed a work by an artist named Dooley Dionysius—reason enough to become interested. A little research revealed that he had worked as a Disney illustrator in the 1930s. Though very small, the painting was magical, and I added it.

I continue to seek work from many other artists. Perhaps at the right time, when the right material surfaces, I'll complete the collection I see in my mind. Meanwhile, as the collection grows, my ability to look at art and judge its value grows.

LEARNING ABOUT ART

The artists whose work I bought have trained me. These exceptional individuals exhibit a special sort of intelligence and creativity. Their language may sound foreign to us, but patience and attention to the art itself yields great dividends. I visit many of the artists; this provides the most memorable part of the collecting process.

I visited the painter Gordon Onslow Ford twice, at his home in Inverness on the Point Reyes peninsula of California. He explained his theory of *Line, Circle, Dot* and his approach to automatic painting, and even gave me a demonstration by laying paper on the floor and proceeding to apply paint from above. Ford had many works of art from his relationship with Andre Breton's surrealist circle. One, Charles Howards' *Visitation*, ended up in the NEHMA collection. I also later purchased two of Ford's own paintings.

I have always admired the curator Walter Hopps' eye for art. One summer, after picking up his catalog, "Visionary Art," I launched a search for work by the five artists in the group that I most admired. This led me to the homes of

Nic Hyde and of Bill Martin's widow, where I purchased two iconic works by artists of the movement. Subsequently, attending obscure East Coast auctions enabled me to add work by the other three: Cliff McReynolds, Tom Akawie, and Gage Taylor. A very satisfying conclusion.

My inveterate auction shopping has swallowed years of my life and damaged my eyesight. Obviously, an art collector needs to know how to look closely, but my absorption with art led to a peril or two along the way. Nonetheless, careful looking helped me find some unexpected treasures. For example, years ago, skimming an online catalog for an auction of Lincoln memorabilia, I came across a small plaster head of Lincoln. On its back was a fragment from Mount Rushmore and a signature that had been pressed into the wet plaster: Gutzon Borglum. I bought it for $65, and later learned that Borglum used these small, rare, casts to encourage donors to contribute to his enormous project.

Once, my ongoing education provided the opportunity to rescue an older artist from obscurity. Following up on a reference in an art history survey of the artists of the San Francisco Bay area, I contacted Robert Comings, who lives in Mendocino County, in the small town of Willits. What a treat! As a result, the museum in Utah added one of his paintings to its collection, and the attention re-energized his career.

ART AND THE COMMUNITY

Art can bring change to communities. A museum collecting American artists has an obligation to represent the spectrum of ethnic and racial groups that comprises American society. To this end, I have added work to the NEHMA collection by artists, men and women, of diverse ethnic and racial origin.

The limited exposure to arts education of most Utah residents initially posed an obstacle to the local success of the NEHMA collection. Early on, I realized the value of in-depth exposure to art beginning at a young age. I spent two years seeking art that was "beautiful" in one way or another, along with representational art that would help the staff engage with elementary schoolchildren. Students at a local elementary school chose a work of art from the collection, spent time with it, and wrote a poem about it. We published their poems, along with illustrations of the paintings they had selected. The poems reflected an interest and appreciation of the art, and to my surprise, the students picked almost exclusively abstract paintings. I have witnessed a whole class of fifth graders transfixed by Irving Norman's *Blind Momentum*.[1]

Similarly, one night I encountered a group of teenagers from the local "alternative" high school in the museum. Seven or eight of them clustered around Seymour Locks' sculpture, *The Claw*, studying it intensely. It consists of a redwood tree root clad in copper with multiple nails driven into the surface. Knowing that one provided the bait to draw young people into a learning experience involving art is satisfying.

Working with a family foundation, I still strive to bring arts experiences to young people: to three arts outreach organizations in Los Angeles, to children's theaters in Los Angeles and Logan, Utah, and to a special program that connects the Yellowstone Art Museum in Billings, Montana, with fourth and fifth grade students on the Crow reservation. My visits to the Crow reservation with arts educators have deepened my belief that arts education is essential for young people to develop fully. Students there find that art is a way of realizing their innate ability, of understanding that they can be creative, and as a result, their self-esteem grows. Arts education incrementally enhances the lives of these students.

RESEARCH TO COMPLEMENT ACQUISITIONS

Exposure to the art itself, however, doesn't meet all the needs of a community. A lack of literature about art and artists that would guide intelligent acquisitions was the greatest problem I encountered in making buying decisions. Consequently, I made an effort to develop a research library at Utah State University capable of supporting the collection that I was building. In the process, foundation resources made possible the purchase of three different collections of Beat poetry material that I stumbled upon. Not only was Beat poetry the most important literary development in the American West, its

1   http://www.irvingnorman.com/OIL_PAINTINGS_MASTER_PAGES/1960_blind_momentum.htm

history was closely intertwined with the art and artists found in the Museum. Together, the collection of Beat poetry, magazines, books, and ephemera at the university is now one of the largest in America.

And, with my mother's financial support, I also added the artist James Prestini's collection of more than 13,000 volumes, all related to design, to the Utah State Library. In addition to works on art, artists, and architects, he had books on birds, botany, cars, ceramics, insects, quilts, railroads, silver, and textiles: a remarkable collection. When catalogued, the library had duplicates of roughly half the titles; the duplicates then went to Montana State University in Bozeman.

CONCLUSIONS

On my ranch in Montana and at home in California, my personal art collection surrounds me. Living intimately with art, I profit from it in ways that are hard to understand and challenging to articulate. I just know it's happening. I can feel it. And I know that I have provided others with resources to help them forge a relationship with the arts: the art and library collections at Utah State.

Art provides special ways of looking at ourselves and at our world and enables us to come to some understanding of ourselves as human beings. Art brought something wonderful and valuable into my life. I believe that I have helped to bring others that same gift.

10

CARRYING THE TORCH— VIGNETTES

Just as our perceptions of the events of October 26, 1963, as recounted in Chapter 3 varied, Kennedy's call to action, to public service, resonated differently among the members of his audience.

In contrast to those who took immediate direct action, many internalized his message that "with privilege goes responsibility." For them, that message became a lifelong guiding principle; they found a unique, personal ways to fulfill their responsibilities. Nine of them tell their stories here.

My Year in Vietnam with MILPHAP Team 20

Thomas P. Jacobs, '64

I RECEIVED MY NOTICE from the Army toward the middle of my second year of residency in internal medicine at Columbia University, early in 1970. According to the Army, I would be going to Vietnam that summer. Neither Janice, my wife, nor I supported the war our country was waging in that poor country. I felt stupid; I had only applied to two research labs at the National Institutes of Health and had not applied to the Indian Health Service. Those were the preferred venues for most of my fellow residents to spend their two years of mandatory physician service during the war.

Newspapers had reported the massacres at My Lai late in 1969. The Kent State shootings that left four students dead and nine injured, simply for protesting the war, had occurred in 1970. Some friends, like Harry Pincus, had escaped the country, and others, like Gene Palumbo, fought their draft boards to establish themselves as conscientious objectors. I wrote to the surgeon general, General Thomas Whalen, telling him that he would likely have to prosecute me for refusing orders to go to Vietnam. Although I certainly did not expect it, he invited me to Washington to discuss the issues. Janice and I packed our new baby into the car early one morning and drove to the Forrestal Building in Washington for an 11 a.m. meeting. General Whalen listened to me with surprising interest and sympathy and offered me a chance to volunteer for the Military Provincial Health Assistance Program (MILPHAP)—a vehicle for assigning medical servicemen to the civilian health system run by the government of South Vietnam.

Later that week, I had a long discussion with a more senior Columbia physician who had spent a year in the Mekong Delta under MILPHAP. He described it as extremely worthwhile. With a new baby and another on the way, we decided it would be a reasonable alternative to three years in Ft. Leavenworth federal prison.

In July, Janice, the two babies, and I flew to San Antonio and rented a motel room to serve as our home during my six weeks of "induction training" at Ft. Sam Houston. Once there I learned how to salute; wear my uniform; finalize my "payroll signature"; make a will; disassemble, clean, and use an M-16; treat tropical diseases; assess war wounds; and crawl across a simulated battlefield with live machine gun bullets flying overhead. Janice was so anxious and distraught about our future separation that she needed a medical evaluation at the Army Clinic.

We got through it and flew back to New Jersey. On the afternoon of August 15, 1970, we had a long walk. I boarded a plane at Newark Airport headed for Travis Air Force Base in California. Within an hour after landing I was on another airliner with two hundred other servicemen for the twenty-two-hour flight to Vietnam.

The extremely steep descent we made into Ton Son Nhut Air Base outside Saigon gave me my first hint that we were entering a war zone. The pilot was making the plane less of a target for small arms and rockets. After twenty-two hours in an airplane, we all felt like zombies but were shuffled off to barracks.

Over the next four to five days we were fitted for tropical camouflage gear, helmets, flak jacket, and jungle boots, and we got our anti-malarial Dapsone and mosquito netting. We received our "in country" assignments and were offered a choice of weapons. (I chose an M-16.) I recall eating a decent meal at an officer's club in Saigon, but the plaza downstairs was full of prostitutes and beggars. I had no desire to have a local girlfriend and was not much for adventuring in Saigon. The next morning a Caribou cargo plane, designed for short takeoff and landing capabilities, brought me north, first to Nha Trang, then to my new home of Kontum, deep in the Central Highlands of South Vietnam. Formerly populated only by the aboriginal Montagnard peoples and located close to the tri-border area of Vietnam, Cambodia, and Laos, the French missionaries had brought Catholicism, a school and orphanage, and a small cathedral to Kontum. The years of war had brought an influx of ethnic Vietnamese soldiers and their families. Decades before, the Montagnards might have executed any Vietnamese found in the mountains, but the French colonization and then the war had forced them to accept the Vietnamese presence, but not with trust. As the French, and to some extent the Americans, protected the Montagnards from the Vietnamese, the Montagnards trusted us almost unconditionally.

I was delivered to my "hootch," or military hut, in an old but comfortable compound built by the French. I was assigned to MILPHAP Team 20, a part of MACV Team 41, an advisory team of U.S. Army and civilian state department employees. Working with the local civilians and provincial officials, the team's goal was to make the provincial civilian government "work." Team 41 included experts in road building, water delivery, farming, and of course intelligence, communications, weapons, and self-defense. It assisted both provincial and local hamlet governments. Most of the officers were on their second or third tour to Vietnam, and most were glad that I was there with them.

I was so wet behind the ears that on my second week the commanding officer upbraided me for failing to consistently address him as "Sir," which had never been part of my vocabulary. We were surrounded by fences made of concertina (coiled barbed) wire. Guards were on watch all the time, and at night the compound was lit by lights and parachute flares. Although nights were full of the sounds of bombs going off, I rarely felt in danger. Our air force was carpet bombing the nearby Ho Chi Minh trail and 105mm howitzers were behind us, "pinpoint" shelling local targets called in by spotters and detectors. Occasionally sappers, Viet Cong (VC) commandos, were caught in the wire, but none made it through during my tour. Every two or three weeks, usually on a Sunday, our compound took rocket fire delivered by local VC, who were not very accurate with these weapons. After a few minutes in our shelters, we would emerge and have a beer.

By far the best part of my experience was the work itself. My command consisted of two senior medics, a nurse, a radiology technician, and a lab technician. All of us knew why we were there, so there was little need for giving orders. My Vietnamese counterpart, a French-trained physician named Dr. Truong Cao Thach, was the only civilian physician for this, the largest but least populated province in South Vietnam. Bac Si (Doctor) Thach did most of the surgery and obstetrics, and I cared for the medical and pediatric patients at the province hospital. At midday I would travel with some of my team by jeep or helicopter to the surrounding village dispensaries, often bringing back especially ill patients to the province hospital. The NCOs (non-commissioned officers) in my team demanded that I bring my weapon on these excursions, but I never had to fire it. Native patients, reluctant to die away from their village and family, often refused transportation.

My greatest gift that year was the chance to work at Minh Quy almost every evening. Minh Quy, a large mission hospital, sat across the town of Kontum and was staffed by a mix of Western nurses and locally trained Montagnard nurses and aides. Dr. Patricia Smith had founded the institution several years before my arrival. Pat Smith was a member of The Grail, a Catholic women's service organization. They had sponsored her first trip to Vietnam to work in a leprosarium. She had volunteered to work there after completing her internship at the University of Cincinnati and then stayed on to offer her excellent medical care to the Montagnard peoples, who were usually the victims of discrimination at the "Vietnamese" (only) province hospital.

Pat and I would sit in the clinic for three hours in the evening drinking Kool-Aid and caring for 150 patients a day. Each scantily dressed patient came with a 3 x 4-inch card identifying his/her name and village. We recorded a brief history and a stand-up exam on two to three lines and then ordered the necessary lab tests or medicines. One of the Montagnard nursing nuns then took over, and all was accomplished by the next day.

One of the best helpers we had was Sister Gabrielle, a tiny force of nature who would not allow me to make a mistake. When Pat and I emerged from the clinic, Sr. Gabrielle would wait for me, smiling, together with three or four patients I had seen, to suggest alternate diagnoses: tetanus for the girl who would not open her mouth, meningitis for the child with a fever, tuberculosis for the old man losing weight. Almost invariably, she was correct.

Every day I saw a new case of plague, unique forms of tuberculosis seen only in such poor rural areas, and several different presentations of *vivax* and *falciparum* malaria. Everyone was poorly nourished, and all had Ascaris and hookworm gut infestations. By the end of the year, I knew I had begun to measure up to the local burden of illness when I made a diagnosis of acute appendicitis *and* intestinal tuberculosis in a young man.

When we made a diagnosis of chronic conditions that required special surgery or encountered war wounds we could not manage, we had wonderful help from a career Army surgeon. He often made Sunday visits to the hospital and took these complicated patients south to the evacuation hospital in Pleiku by helicopter for correction of their cleft lips, closure of their patent ductuses, or stabilization of their mangled feet.

I had studied Bahnar, the local language, since shortly after arriving in Kontum, and after six months felt sufficiently competent to ask some questions and understand the answers without an interpreter. I could ask medical questions, with the help of a dictionary and my two interpreters, Wun and Huim, and greet locals in their own language. While Vietnamese is a tonal language, most of the more than thirty different Montagnard languages, are based in an Indo-European structure and sound. Amazingly, at the Army base at Pleiku there was a lending library, and it was there that I obtained and read Bernard Fall's incisive books about the French war against the Vietnamese. When I compared my own experience in Vietnam to that of the French, it was clear that we were doing no better for the people we had come to "save from Communism."

The beauty of the county was boundless. The jungle swallowed up most of the scars of warfare in a year or two. The young Vietnamese women wearing their traditional long white *au dai's* appeared almost like angels. A helicopter trip to the dispensary in the mountain village of Mang Buk was like flying into Shangri-La. At the former site of one of Teddy Roosevelt's tiger hunting lodges, one saw green terraced rice fields set in a secluded valley, drenched by both northern and southern monsoons each year. More ominously, a fortified compound for the local American Mobile Advisory Team (MAT) team dominated the middle of this small village. Riding above the jungle in an open Huey as the sun was setting in the mountains was as enchanting a vision as I have ever had. The very warm welcome Americans received from almost any Montagnard man or woman almost relieved me of my ambivalence about my mission: furthering the aims of the U.S. State Department in supporting a generally corrupt government, which was sure to lose in the long run.

I learned that I was not entirely a coward when it came to accepting some physical risk. One slow and hot Sunday afternoon, my team drove down to the Dak Blah River to swim where several of the local women were washing clothes. The river was swift, but deep only near the shore. My 220-pound NCO, Wilkerson, stood on the shore, complaining that he could not swim. After we teased him into the water, he lost his footing, panicked in the deep water, and was swept downstream. Calling on my Junior Red Cross lifesaving technique, I jumped off my rock, swam to him, and talked him into holding onto my arm, and not my head, as I swam to shore. We kept him out of the water after that.

Months later, a firefight erupted just outside our compound at 11 p.m. Our master sergeant had been hit and lay dead or dying outside the wire. Despite continued sporadic fire, I ran to him, confirmed his death, and stabilized Gloria, the missionary nurse from Wisconsin. They had been ambushed riding home from Minh Quy on her scooter. She had been hit in the back of the neck. We called in a Medivac Huey, and I rode with her through the night to the evacuation hospital on the coast in Quin Nhon, where she died.

A few months after Gloria died, I learned I had no taste for real combat. One night during a drinking contest, I won a ride in the open back seat of a Piper Cub "spotter plane" piloted by Captain Tigh, the chief of a small contingent of Forward Air Controllers who located the enemy in the jungle, usually by drawing small arms fire. We flew north of Dak To to the Tumerong Valley, a secure VC base. To avoid enemy fire, we dipped and curved constantly at treetop level, and I nearly threw up. Tigh called out coordinates to the Air Force over the radio and dropped colored smoke grenades through the trees. I could see nothing but jungle. We approached a ridge. Suddenly the engine went off, and we went into a steep dive. I heard a loud explosion next to my right ear, then another on the left. "This is it" was the only thing that went through my mind. To my surprise, the engine came on and we pulled out of the dive. I learned later, to my great relief, that the explosions were from the small wing rockets carried on these little planes. A minute later, two F-16s shot across our field of vision to drop bombs on the areas marked with smoke. On the trip back to Kontum, I didn't say much but was sweating the entire time. We found several new bullet holes in the underside of the plane after landing. I never accepted another ride. By the end of my tour, all four of the Forward Air Controllers assigned to our compound were dead or missing. They were real heroes and proved it every day. When I confessed the experience to Janice, she was understandably angry; she even recruited my good friend and fellow medical resident Kenny Prager to write to admonish me for being so foolish.

When the Montagnards wanted to celebrate, they had a "rice wine party." We were often invited. A week before the party, twenty to thirty tall pots were filled half way with mountain rice, then palm leaves were stuffed on top, and the pots were then filled with water. By the end of the week, a not very tasty alcoholic beverage was ready, along with dozens of flies and other vermin either dead or swimming on the surface. Bamboo straws were inserted to the bottom, and a small bamboo stick with a 1-inch perpendicular "measure" was laid across the top of the pot. The pots were all lined up, and every male at the party had to drink off one measure from each of the two dozen or so pots! We all tried to be good guests, but I don't believe I ever got past six or seven measures. Along with the rice wine, the mountain rice was cooked by stuffing wet rice into a bamboo husk and putting it into the fire for an hour. Meat was rare, mostly consisting of anything you could gnaw off the roasted carcasses of small birds, which had been brought down with a crossbow.

Singing and dancing were always part of these celebrations. We were often "gifted" with necklaces and bronze bracelets, some of which I still wear on holidays to remember these fine people. I always felt grateful and honored to have been asked, but almost always had diarrhea for a few days afterward.

The lack of available protein led to small stature and a great deal of chronic illness in the local Montagnards and Vietnamese. Universal worm infestation contributed to the visible malnutrition. I was not surprised when I watched a small group of girls out in the fields catching grasshoppers and eating them whole right on the spot. My interpreters were always grateful for any meat that I could carry away from our dining hall; they would always save it for their children. When a Special Forces party killed a mountain buffalo, supposedly belonging to the VC, out in the mountains and brought it in for the New Year's party, they celebrated loudly and long into the night. I was amazed whenever I passed through Saigon to find Vietnamese boys measuring as tall as six feet, clearly the result of better nutrition and much less hookworm and malaria.

I enjoyed the younger career Army officers on our team. They came from all over; most were ROTC graduates, and they worked hard at their jobs. They taught me a great deal about how the Army ran, and I exchanged books with some of them. Our conversations often ran to counting our many blessings for being in a war zone: a never-ending supply of ammunition, $65 a month hostile-fire pay, access to cheap goods, which could be ordered from the Post Exchange in Japan, and a chance to win medals. There was a small photographic studio on the compound, and I learned how to develop, frame, and crop black-and-white photos, which comprise the best of the small collection I brought home. Through the post exchange I ordered a Pentax camera (only $120) and left my Instamatic behind forever. Janice chaffed at the unnecessary expense until she saw the first photos of our boys after I returned home.

There was no TV, and we had only the U.S. Army radio station for news, along with the ubiquitous daily distribution of the military newspaper *Stars and Stripes*. Most music was from tape cassettes, and a small number of recordings were played over and over (think "I Want to Get out of this Place" and "I'm Leaving on a Jet Plane" as premier examples). The only time I listened to the radio was for the Fight of the Century between Ali and Joe Frazier, which, of course, was broadcast in the morning. Every week or two a movie was shown in the building used as a chapel. Most were war flicks like *The Bridge at Remagen*, though I was captivated by the movie version of Hardy's story *Far from the Madding Crowd*. I kept up with my medical and endocrine journals in the evenings. Once every month or two a "show" would be flown in, mostly bands of Filipino ladies in scanty costumes. They caused much raucous cheering, but they left as soon as the show was over. Janice sent cassette tapes with the boys' voices on them. I loved playing them over and over, until I got a recording of Christmas morning, during which the Christmas tree fell over to sounds of crying and weeping. I found it too sad to ever listen to twice. We exchanged letters on an almost daily basis, though they would arrive in Kontum in batches of five to ten at a time every week or two. My mom and dad wrote from time to time, and a friend sent me a copy of a beautiful letter from Fr. Dan Berrigan, a much-publicized Jesuit war resister who was in hiding at the time, and who much later became part of our worship community.

Most of us counted each day in country and knew exactly how many days were left till DEROS (Date of Estimated Return from Overseas). A few days before an officer's departure, there would be a Short Timer Party, celebrating not only the person leaving but publicizing the next in line. Drinking games helped pass the time, and I learned to down a flaming shot glass of Scotch quickly during one of these exercises. Late in the year, my three-man team won a timed drinking contest. I remember being held up in the shower with my clothes on. I awoke in my bunk the next morning, probably less hungover than I would have been had I not vomited up most of the liquor—or at least so I am told. We all make mistakes, and I am not immune.

As advisers, we were not in Vietnam to engage the enemy, but the mortality rate among my little advisory group—in the range of 5 percent—seemed high. Though flipping over a jeep by going too fast around a curve was one way to die, most who died were the young men on the MAT teams out in the villages. They led the men of the village out on patrols and ambushes, and likely faced even higher danger because of the ambiguous relationships of some villagers with the VC. Even though travel in the province became visibly more dangerous with each passing month, our HES (Hamlet Evaluation Score) submitted to MACV headquarters in Saigon suggested each month that travel was becoming gradually safer. If the scores worsened, the commanding officers assumed that they would be replaced. It was no surprise that Johnson and Nixon told the American people that we were winning, whatever that meant, while over a million Vietnamese people were dying. On a later trip to Washington, DC, I visited the striking Vietnam Memorial to those killed during the war. I found the names and recalled with some sadness almost all of our lost soldiers.

The futility of the war was obvious from my first week in the country. The number of old tractors and trucks rusting in the fields, all donated by the U.S. government, was astounding. The ARVN (Army of the Republic of Vietnam) troops worked carefully to not engage the enemy in the field, except when under the indirect command of U.S. Army officers eager to get their medals. The presence of the U.S. officers would assure that mortality was high on both sides. Because the wages were good, many Vietnamese worked for the Americans in office jobs, as interpreters and translators, or as laborers or drivers. Some of these employees, it appeared, were dependable sources of information for the local VC, but given our woeful lack of knowledge of their language and culture, how would we know?

"Protecting" a village from enemy influence or preventing the villagers from providing a source of food for the enemy, often meant rounding up the villagers and forcing them to live in Relocation Camps. In the camps, cut off from their usual food sources and dependent on a supply of bulgur wheat and other unfamiliar foodstuffs, often in inadequate quantities, nutrition was worse. Crowding led to more infectious disease. Plague was a much higher risk in these villages because the new quarters were at ground level (and close to the rats) rather than in typical Montagnard dwellings, which were typically raised five to ten feet off the ground.

When August of 1971 rolled around, and I was the next Short Timer, I felt tremendous ambivalence about leaving. I could hardly wait to see Janice and my boys, but I knew that I would also miss so many of my new friends, and that I could do little to protect them when we Americans finally left. I understood that back in America, the chance to treat and usually cure so many sick people on a daily basis would never again be part of my professional life. At the time, I felt conflicted as well, as I still do, about my own role in prosecuting and perhaps prolonging the war. I recall Robert Frost's answer to a question about why he was not more politically active: "I do good by doing well." I have never wholly agreed with Frost, though by doing well as a physician in Vietnam, I could tell myself that I helped many people live.

Did I answer John F. Kennedy's call to ask "what could I do for my country" by serving in the armed services in a war—as my father and grandfather did? I had willingly become an agent of the State Department. Could I have done more to end the war by refusing orders and forcing the Army to prosecute me with the attendant expense and publicity and the inevitable time in a federal prison? I have no answers to these questions, and I still admire classmates like Gene Palumbo and Chuck Phillips who fought the government to become conscientious objectors.

Even though I was coerced into serving with the Army in Vietnam, I am much richer for the experience. I lived and worked in an entirely different culture. I saw firsthand medical problems and effects of the kind of poverty that we do not have in the United States. I met many good people working to make life in Kontum better for all and learned that many of them carried on in other places after they had to leave Vietnam. In 1975, Pat Smith was forced to leave. When she came to live in Seattle where I was finishing a fellowship, we resumed our friendship, including both our families. I still correspond with Sister Gabrielle, now in her eighties, and send her some support to help her continue to train village midwives in Kontum. Best of all, I recall on an almost daily basis the warmth and welcome of the Montagnards, who may have been the last people on earth to love all Americans.

From Art History to Biomedical Research

Doug Lowy, '64

THE IMPORTANCE OF PRESIDENT KENNEDY'S visit to Amherst became magnified because his death in Dallas followed so soon afterwards. Although I did not attend his convocation speech—I was away that weekend visiting my girlfriend in the Catskills in New York—two parts of the written version resonated with me: the importance of service and the celebration of Robert Frost's art and his freedom of expression.

I became an art history major at Amherst because I was attracted to the visual arts and in awe of artists, whose talents far exceeded my own in this domain. This major enabled me to have an even greater appreciation for artists and for the changing tastes in art and the reputations of artists over time, and, in addition, to spend my junior year in France, with Steve Mitchell '64. Paradoxically, that year away from Amherst gave me a far greater appreciation of its educational principles, as I found, to my great disappointment, that the teachers of "higher education" in the country of Camus and Sartre did not seem interested in students developing and honing their own thoughts. Instead, the teaching there emphasized rote learning and the objective reality of history ("the French renaissance began in January 1515 when Francis I came to the throne"). By contrast, Amherst taught me the utility of curiosity and how to learn for myself.

Both of my parents were physicians—general practitioners—and despite majoring in art history, I assumed I would also become a practicing physician, so I took enough science courses at Amherst to be able to apply to medical school our senior year. I decided to go to New York University School of Medicine when I was accepted there, largely because I liked the idea of going to the same medical school that my mother had attended. It turned out that the teaching at NYU was oriented towards research. Instead of being didactic, the courses that appealed to me the most were taught first from the perspective of "how do we know what we know?" and second with the goal of trying to understand the mechanisms underlying the phenomena being described.

I tried my hand at research while still in medical school; that led to my going to the National Institutes of Health (NIH) for research training as well as clinical training in internal medicine and dermatology. I started my own laboratory in 1975 at the National Cancer Institute (NCI) at the NIH, and I still work there. Being at the NIH has given me tremendous freedom for conducting the research. Most of my work has been fundamental—studying viruses and genes that are involved in cancer. I thrive on discovering new phenomena and understanding their mechanisms. And some of my research had clinical relevance, like developing the technology that underlies the three FDA-approved preventive HPV vaccines.

HPV infection causes several different kinds of cancer but cervical cancer is the most important globally, accounting for almost 10 percent of women's cancers worldwide. Cervical cancer is especially common in low and middle-income countries, areas that lack the resources needed for high quality cervical cancer screening. My role in the development of HPV vaccine involved me directly in global health issues because the vaccine has the potential to drastically reduce the worldwide incidence and mortality from this cancer.

Another Amherst alumnus, Harold Varmus '61, asked me to become the Deputy Director of the National Cancer Institute in 2010 when he became the NCI Director. When Harold left in 2015, I served as the Acting Director for the next two and one-half years then resumed my role as Deputy Director when Ned Sharpless became NCI Director in October 2017. These positions gave me the opportunity to help shape many aspects of cancer research.

In retrospect, Amherst prepared me for many of my activities. As a scientist, a liberal arts education prepared me to identify problems, to describe them, and how to solve them. As an administrator, American Studies and Professor Ben Ziegler taught me the importance of understanding opposing perspectives. I learned consensus-building: a critical foundation for working effectively and efficiently with others and a necessity (at least for me) for leading a large organization and working with others outside that organization.

I am as excited to go to work today as I have been for more than forty years, and I still think, "I have miles to go before I sleep."

A Continuing Journey

Pat DeLeon, '64

LIFE IN THE RUSSIAN ORTHODOX CHURCH home where my maternal grandfather was the priest forms my earliest memories. Russians who had lost all material possessions when the Communists came into power made up our neighborhood. For a while, I was an altar boy. When my grandfather died, his colleagues came from all around the world to honor him in their processional around the church.

I will never forget the time that my Russian-born grandmother, with at best a grammar school education, showed me a photograph of her countrymen who had been hung; she simply said, "Those are your relatives."

I grew up in a very political family. My mother was the second female attorney in the State of Connecticut. In her final years, she told me that she had failed the bar the first time. Forty years after the written exam, the letter arrived informing her when her oral exam was scheduled. "If I were a man, they would have simply asked me where I was the next day and rescheduled the orals. Instead, they failed me."

She passed the second time.

My father, born in Italy, proudly received his Certificate of Citizenship on May 16, 1934. A star athlete and academic, he graduated from Amherst and became a lawyer. I did well in school and ended up following my father's footsteps to Amherst.

Amherst was, without question, a time for soul searching. I met some fascinating and truly wonderful people, while silently trying to figure out the larger picture of how to make a difference. While at Amherst I found out I had significant hearing loss and had always excelled at lip-reading. Several courses at college were especially difficult to handle, especially oral Spanish. Prior to coming to Amherst, I had always worked diligently in school. I was starting to feel burned out, but when Professor Robert Birney exposed me to the fascinating world of psychology, I was back on track.

Prior to Professor Birney's mentorship, I had taken up photography. For four years, I spent many days and nights covering the activities of the College on the Hill. On the beautiful autumn Saturday, October 26, 1963, when President John F. Kennedy came to our convocation and groundbreaking for the Frost Library, I was the student photographer. I probably had one of the best seats in the house. Over the years, my photographs have been highlighted in different venues, almost never, however, with the correct attribution. (I have learned to value the accomplishment rather than the attribution, which has proved to be very useful in "getting things accomplished.") Senator Ted Kennedy publicly displayed one of my photos of his brother in his office waiting room.

Amherst exposed us to fascinating visionaries, such as President Kennedy, Robert Frost, and Archibald MacLeish, and I had the opportunity to photograph them and, at times, to talk with them. In retrospect, the call to take "the road less traveled" and "ask what you can do for your country" significantly influenced my personal journey. I still recall walking to the campus darkroom on November 22, 1963, when I learned the devastating news of the president's assassination.

After Amherst I debated about going into law and politics or psychology. I wrestled with the options over the summer after Amherst before deciding to take the road less traveled—in my family at least. I enrolled in the clinical psychology program at Purdue University. At Purdue, I never felt as if I were taking a formal course. Instead, it was one fascinating learning experience after another.

At the very end of my clinical psychology internship at Ft. Logan, Colorado, I received a call from the Peace Corps inviting me to interview because I had earlier filled out an application to become a volunteer. That invitation led to my wife and me becoming Field Assessment Officers (FAOs) for Fiji and the Philippines, with projects based out of the Big Island of Hawaii. I had a fascinating exposure to different cultures and an opportunity to make a real difference, much as President Kennedy had envisioned that October day.

Next came working for the State of Hawaii Division of Mental Health during the de-institutionalization movement, another Kennedy initiative. We even had a write-up in *Time* magazine about our successful efforts to integrate chronically hospitalized individuals into the community. At that time, one had to be a physician with a master's in public health in order to be appointed director of mental health. So, changing my career direction, I enrolled in the University of Hawaii School of Public Health while continuing to work for the state.

My public health internship on Capitol Hill began the first day of the infamous Watergate hearings, and thirty-eight-plus years later, I retired as U.S. Senator Daniel K. Inouye's chief of staff.

Capitol Hill is a fascinating environment, as a number of our colleagues, including some who have served as elected officials, have discovered. Staff are extraordinarily bright, dedicated, and professional; one quickly forges life-long friendships. Public service is not a job; it is a way of life. I finally did get that law degree, too. One also quickly learns that senators and congress-persons hire individuals who have value systems that are very similar to their own. Although I would not claim the same distinction, some of my senior colleagues frequently would recall that their bosses had never second guessed their judgment.

Not surprisingly, Senator Inouye was especially close to Senator Ted Stevens of Alaska. Both were World War II veterans and they represented small, geographically isolated states, Hawaii and Alaska, populated with indigenous constituents—Native Hawaiians and Alaskan Natives—who historically have been significantly underserved (e.g., health disparities). Senator Inouye was also extremely close to both President Lyndon Johnson and Senator Ted Kennedy as they all had a passionate interest in serving the historically underserved, immigrants, rural Americans, the elderly, children, and native peoples, and in encouraging women in science. Education and never forgetting where one came from were viewed as the keys to providing a decent quality of life for *all* Americans.

As I look back, a number of programmatic initiatives that we established have had, without question, a profound impact upon many lives. For example, today Hawaii is experiencing a Native Hawaiian resonance—a direct outgrowth of the native Hawaiian education programs and the vision of the *Hokuleʻa* sailing around the world, guided solely by the stars and ocean currents. Other work has addressed the facts that Native Hawaiians had the highest incidence of cancer of any population in the world, and that more than 80 percent of Native Hawaii children failed their first hearing test—it's hard to do well in school if you cannot hear the teacher. I am also particularly proud of our Pediatric Emergency Medical Services initiative, which recently celebrated its thirtieth anniversary. Over the years, it has significantly enhanced the quality of care for children in distress worldwide. It grew out of an experience with my young daughter in a major city emergency room —once again, I guess "the doctors were wrong." As the senator frequently said, "Not seeking credit allows one to accomplish that which many would never consider."

Today, at the Uniformed Services University, I hope to emulate that special mentoring I received from Robert Birney and Purdue's Clifford Swensen. "Privilege is here, and with privilege goes responsibility." Aloha.[1]

---

1   Pat DeLeon is the former president of the American Psychological Association.

Kennedy, the Liberal Arts, and My Path

Paul Stern, '64

IF I HAD BEEN IN THE GYM to hear what JFK was saying to encourage our generation to, as he said in his inaugural address, "ask not what your country can do for you, ask what you can do for your country," I might not have been very impressed. I might even have found it a bit hypocritical. I was already involved in trying to do for my country, particularly on what were then called civil rights issues, and I didn't see the president doing much to address them. Instead, I was outside the gym with about thirty other Amherst students holding picket signs saying how we wanted *him* to do more for the country.

Civil rights issues were rampant and destructive. One way to demonstrate my concern was to help build racially integrated campsites in Tennessee in a remote part of the Great Smoky Mountains. It was the summer of 1963, and I jumped at the opportunity because it could be done before I started my summer job and because it would let me contribute to the cause without joining the freedom rides that were common that summer. I didn't feel quite right about Northerners going South to protest when there were so many unaddressed racial inequality issues in the North. But outside the spotlight, I thought I could help build something that could last. Although we tried, we couldn't stay out of the spotlight. One night, the county sheriff raided our integrated group, and we all spent a night in jail. A couple of days later, the campsite was destroyed by fire. The fire was probably set by Klan members who, a few days later, openly rode around the county courthouse in their hoods while our group leaders faced trumped-up charges.

So instead of attending the president's speech, I was out with the picketers expressing our dissatisfaction with what we saw as Kennedy's lack of effort on key national issues. If I had heard him talk about the importance of the liberal arts, I probably would have had a much more positive reaction to his message. The Amherst approach to liberal arts education has had a profound effect on my life and on the lives of many of my classmates up through today.

In the early 1960s, required courses in writing, history, physics, math, and physical education dominated the Amherst freshman curriculum. The sophomore curriculum continued that emphasis, though with slightly more room for electives. The courses were designed to shock students. For example, instead of focusing on Greece and Rome, and medieval times in the Sahara region, the history courses focused on unfamiliar periods and regions like the ancient Middle East and Asia. And our first writing assignment was so strange that we had whole dorm meetings in an attempt to decipher it. All of this was a stretch intellectually for most of us, and perhaps more importantly, it forced most of us to have substantive interactions with classmates with different backgrounds and interests. Because of the small size of our class (about 270) by spring of freshman year, we had met just about all our classmates.

The liberal arts approach forced us to seek connections among ideas from different domains, and the social context forced us to do this with people from very different backgrounds. It was not always pleasant. For example, I was a kid from a Jewish background and a low-income housing project on New York's Lower East Side. I had been assigned to room with a guy from Philadelphia's Main Line who had personal experience with debutante parties. It didn't last a week. He engineered a roommate switch that made daily life more pleasant for both of us. But the hothouse approach certainly did expand our horizons and provide lifelong contacts with people of all sorts.

My liberal arts education did not lead me easily into a professional niche. I followed my interests in psychology into graduate school and then into teaching at a liberal arts college. But during my first post-Amherst decade, I continued to search for a career that would better connect me to the major issues facing the country and the world. By the mid-1970s, I had focused on global environmental issues, which at first did not seem connected in any way to my doctoral training in psychology. Eventually, after reading Garrett Hardin's famous essay, *The Tragedy of the Commons*, which highlighted some of the reasons underlying environmentally destructive behavior, it hit me that the root problems of the environment were behavioral and could be investigated from that perspective. Following that, I focused on developing what I have called the science of human-environment interactions and bringing that science to bear to find ways that humanity can live within our planet's limits.

I organized an ongoing activity at the National Academy of Sciences to advance that mission. I also applied my training in research to find ways to reduce household energy consumption and to encourage public participation in environmental decision-making. My Amherst experience prepared me well for thinking about such problems, which require transdisciplinary perspectives.

In some ways, the effects of the liberal arts education on my cohort can best be seen in the program for our fiftieth class reunion. The theme was "the world we inherited and the world we'll leave behind," and one of the subprograms led eventually to the documentary *JFK: The Last Speech* and this accompanying book. I was asked to lead the subprogram on the environment. Working with classmates with backgrounds in ecology, oceanography, law, environmental history, and other fields, we put together a one-hour program focused on climate change—unfortunately our generation's prime environmental legacy. The room fell silent when we put up the following graph, showing that 74 percent of all carbon dioxide emissions from human activity since the start of the industrial revolution around 1750 have occurred *after* we graduated in 1964. We need to see a huge and rapid reversal of the historical trend to achieve global atmospheric conditions that can support the kind of clean world we grew up in.

ANNUAL EMISSIONS REDUCTIONS TO STAY WITHIN 1 TRILLION TON CARBON "BUDGET" THROUGH 2100

Annual carbon dioxide emissions, in billions of tons of carbon

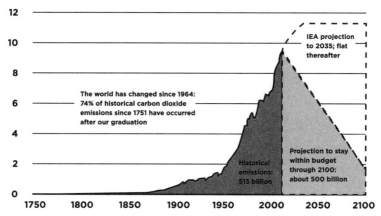

Sources: Daniel Raimi and Michael Vandenbergh. For historical emissions, the Carbon Dioxide Information Analysis Center national time-series data. Available at http://cdiac.ornl.gov/trends/emis/tre_coun.html. For projections, IEA *World Energy Outlook* 2013 Historical emissions were tallied from 1751-2012, and IEA projections were used to estimate annual growth in emissions each year from 2010-2035, when IEA projections end. Emissions after 2035 were assumed to remain constant.

Working on the program prompted a few of us, who were not scientific collaborators before the reunion, to continue working and publishing on ways to move the policy conversation on climate change in more productive directions. One of the results was a coauthored article in the leading journal, *Science.* We deconstructed the arguments of skeptics of scientific conclusions about climate change. We argued that people should think about climate change as a problem of decision-making in an environment of uncertain but increasing risks, rather than a venue for arguing over whether certain "facts" have been established.

Did those of us outside the gym come in and join the larger group, or have those inside come out? It really doesn't matter. As Calvin Plimpton, then the president of Amherst College, said only three weeks after Kennedy spoke: "*let us go and do the work he couldn't complete.*"

Our work continues.

You Go to Amherst College. Period.

Stephen Eaton Smith, '64

I DID NOT WANT TO go to Amherst College. I attended a public high school that stood in the shadow of the college. A little further away was the University of Massachusetts (UMass), where the parents of most of my close group of high school friends worked. The first girl I ever kissed was the daughter of the UMass head football coach. The daughter of the president of UMass was an early eighth grade date. My dad left his veterinary practice and absorbed a pay cut to become a professor at UMass so that his kids could go to UMass tuition-free. Of my high school friends, only four had Amherst College connections: one was the daughter of the dean of admissions Eugene S. "Bill" Wilson; one was the son of Rick Wilson, head basketball coach and coach of the freshman football team; one was the son of Fred Turgeon of the College's theater department; and one was the daughter of Steve Brown, the college physician.

I did not want to go to Amherst College. My UMass connection was strong. Amherst's reputation and its culture were anathema to all that I knew and felt. Amherst students were sophisticated preppies from elite schools far away. Nationally, they represented the intellectual cream of the crop; they all were wealthy. I was none of the above. I was an uncertain, naive, and un-traveled kid from a small town, the product of the Pioneer Valley in western Massachusetts that stretched along the Connecticut River from Greenfield in the north to Springfield in the south. That valley was my world. I had never been west of New York City. I played tuba in the high school orchestra and was an All-Western Mass guard on the football team. I was smart enough to get good grades but not intellectually curious. I led a simple, comfortable, sheltered, jock life. I was wary of Catholics and knew that if John Kennedy was elected, we'd all be governed from the Vatican. Already, thanks to the Irish-Catholics running the state government in Boston, my parents complained about having to go to New Hampshire to purchase birth control.

I did not want to go to Amherst College. Then a few things converged. First, in the fall of 1959, the Amherst tuba player, for whatever reason, failed to appear for the academic year. J. Clement "Pop" Schuler, the college's orchestra director, who also directed my high school orchestra, asked me to fill the tuba seat for a concert. I did. The guys in the orchestra were strange, but they didn't seem to have two heads. Next, Amherst freshman football coach Rick Wilson's son and I were football teammates, so Coach Wilson attended our games that fall. Perhaps he noticed me. Finally, my dad and Dean Wilson met each other when they took their back-to-back turns as president of our high school's PTA. I applied to the college to see what would happen. Shockingly, I was accepted. My instincts were still shouting UMass, though. At least, they were until the day our high school dietician sat me down in the school cafeteria and said (and I remember each word), "Stephen, you've been accepted at Amherst College. When you're accepted at Amherst College, you go to Amherst College. Period."

I still did not want to go to Amherst College. I contacted Dean Wilson and said that I'd come if I could room with an athlete, so I would have someone to relate to. That request accommodated, I matriculated in the fall of 1960. My athlete roommate measured up to every concern that I had. He came from an elite prep school far away. His father's chauffeur drove him to school, then unloaded all of his trunks and suitcases, filling his dresser and most of mine. His mother's maid had sewn matching curtains and bed spreads for our room, and my roommate instructed me to not put my shoes on the bedspread. He had been educated to date by the Jesuits and had considered going to a Jesuit college; his priest recommended that he go to a place like Amherst, where he would have a chance to practice his conversion skills. He told me that I was not allowed to use the word "God" in my cussing. By the time I went to bed that first night, he had hung a crucifix over my bed. We arranged a separation of church and state by second semester, and having absolutely nothing in common, the relationship ended with the school year.

I am very glad I went to Amherst College. As a local kid, I was already steeped in the poetry of Robert Frost. He sometimes came to our high school to read to us. In my view, by deciding to go to Amherst I was forsaking my destined road and "taking the road less traveled." We were all acquainted with, and could relate to, "After Apple-Picking" and the sentiments expressed therein, thanks to Atkins Apple Orchard in town. And as graduates leaving friendships developed over a dozen years, and heading off in different directions, the uncertainty of it all had us all feeling a bit queer—kind of like the little horse in "Stopping by Woods on a Snowy Evening"—living in that space of neither here nor there.

I struggled with the core curriculum but was comforted to discover that many of us did. We read letters written by the crusaders of the eleventh and twelfth centuries, read Dante's writings, struggled with three papers a week in English, and fought off language and physics lab. After freshman year, Bucky Salmon, an aide to General Dwight Eisenhower during WWII, enlightened us about that war and his experiences, and Henry Steele Commager amazed us with his note-free and wandering lectures about American history. We felt the intrigue of Machiavelli in political science and the manipulation of Pavlov's dog in psychology. I learned about guns and boats in history, and about guns and butter in economics. Thanks to a philosophy course taught by a visiting professor from Harvard Divinity School, I learned that Christianity was just one philosophy among many, and I questioned my own Protestant upbringing and childhood suspicions of Catholics.

I entered the college feeling uncomfortable about what I was taking on and feeling alone in that discomfort. I left four years later feeling quite the opposite, accompanied by 250 others who, by that time, also felt a lot better about themselves. I left with a body of learning referred to as "the liberal arts." I am immensely grateful for that beginning. Now, having practiced law for some fifty years, I can categorically say that among the requisite skills of my profession, substantive knowledge of the law is of the least importance. More important are the abilities to communicate and to listen well, to comprehend and appreciate different values and points of view, to be a critical thinker and creative problem solver, and to make connections across complex ideas. I have Amherst College to thank for ferreting out these skills within me, and for encouraging me to become as proficient in them as possible. I am very glad I went to Amherst College.

Late Bloomer

Don Lombardi, '64

IN THE EARLY SIXTIES, JFK's fresh image made me and many middle-class people my age proud to be Americans: his intellectualism and quest for leadership, his championing of the arts, sciences, and space exploration. Truthfully though, neither he nor my Amherst experience inspired me with a call to service. Like many other classmates, I was prepping for a next level of education and a post-graduate degree.

While much of my work has, indeed, involved social engagement and service, my political and social consciousness originated in the *late* sixties. The assassinations of John and Robert Kennedy, Malcolm X, and Martin Luther King, Jr.; the racial upheavals of the late sixties; and especially the Vietnam War—Mr. Kennedy's war—broke the spell of the Eisenhower-Kennedy years and provoked a shift away from the contentment, simple patriotism, and conventional middle-American attitudes we grew up with. In graduate school at MIT, I participated in demonstrations, agitated against the Vietnam War, broke from a traditional lifestyle, and adopted an anti-institutional frame of mind.

After several years in graduate school, life in the lab proved too confining. I quit and got a job at MIT's Education Research Center developing an alternative undergraduate curriculum where formal learning was organized around socially impactful projects. Ray Pariser, my boss, mentor, and friend until he passed away in early 2017, inspired me with his lifelong commitment to learning, teaching, and service. He worked on projects to address world hunger and environmental resources until his late nineties.

I was asked to develop an environmental science curriculum for a boarding school on Thompson Island in Boston Harbor. The island had a rural landscape, surrounded by ocean, with the city skyline a couple of miles away. I went to a conference on urban outdoor education to see what we might do with it. Only one person spoke convincingly about how outdoor education needed to be adapted for inner-city children: Arthur Wellington Conquest III. He had grown up in East Harlem, had become Outward Bound's first African American instructor, and then started his own wilderness school. I brought Arthur to Thompson Island to see how we could implement his principles.

Arthur was appalled by the school. Through his eyes I saw that it was a racist and sexist environment, and generally destructive to the kids, functioning more like prison than school. We put together a list of particulars and presented these to the school's board of directors with a demand that they close the school lest we send our memo to the *Boston Globe*. They obliged. Arthur and I had a plan to turn the island into an outdoor education center for Boston's inner-city kids.

Judge Arthur Garrity's 1974 federal court order to desegregate the Boston schools gave us an opening. We proposed that an outdoor education experience would help children learn to learn together, and we secured numerous grants to do so. This thrust me into civil rights and community organizing a decade later than my more forward-thinking Amherst classmates who had participated in the freedom rides of the early sixties. We brought children together from more than 100 schools across diverse Boston neighborhoods for a program that linked outdoor experiences with team building, problem-solving and academic skill development. There was intense resistance in certain neighborhoods like South Boston; rock throwing street demonstrations periodically interrupted our work as we transported children to our boat. It was a good way to spend my thirties.

After the Thompson Island experience, social impact has been an element of all my subsequent careers. In the early eighties, I advocated for bicycling rights with the Boston Area Bicycle Coalition. In the mid-eighties, I started the Chitin Company, which recycled crustacean shell by-product from the food processing industry into cosmetics, water purification technology, and agricultural supplements. We made only a few bucks when we sold the company to DuPont. However, I profited greatly from learning about patents, transactions, academic-industry collaborations, product development, regulatory affairs, manufacturing, and marketing.

In 1991, I took my newfound expertise to Boston Children's Hospital, became their chief intellectual property officer and established the first technology transfer office in a U.S. pediatric hospital. Our aim, as mandated in federal legislation, was to translate publicly funded research discoveries into actual products that can benefit the public. My next fifteen years at BCH were like a non-stop continuation of my graduate education, and we brought a number of new pharmaceutical products into the commercial pipeline. Interestingly, almost all of these became products for *adult* healthcare, because of the small and challenging market for pediatric medical products.

To better understand the needs and challenges of developing products that benefited kids, I began working more with clinicians than with researchers. Dr. Michael Shannon, chief of emergency medicine, had been treating children with lead poisoning using a drug that could reduce their lead burden tenfold lower than the medicine that was then standard treatment. However, the drug came only as a huge pill that needed to be ground up and suspended in liquid. It had a strong rotten egg odor and was difficult to get children to swallow. Michael's efforts to find a company to develop a child-friendly formulation failed. The reason? The patient population, in Michael's words, was "too young, too poor, and too black" to create a viable market. I decided to help. I found a company that would develop a formulation, convinced an angel investor to create an LLC to manage development, and helped find receptive ears at the FDA. Sadly, Michael passed away in the prime of life, and the project foundered.

Michael's passion, and that of other clinicians I had worked with, inspired me to found the Institute for Pediatric Innovation to remedy the gap in drugs and medical devices for treating children. This nonprofit organization works with clinicians at pediatric centers nationally to identify unmet needs, generate commercially feasible product concepts, and then partner with companies that can bring the products back to the pediatric community. A drug that we reformulated has reached the market, and we are now forming a spin-off company to commercialize a portfolio of new pediatric medical devices.

In the last two years, I've been inspired by working with a young man from Afghanistan. Mohammad Sayed lost his family and the use of his legs through acts of war at age six. He came to the U.S., survived a series of operations, and then started inventing devices to normalize life in a wheelchair. He also created Wheelchair Man, an action hero comic book series, to teach children in wheelchairs worldwide that they can participate fully in society. I helped him found the nonprofit Rim Power as a vehicle for realizing his vision.

Over time, I came to value my rigorous Amherst education in math, science, English, and humanities. It has provided a high level of adaptability through careers in science, education, business, intellectual property, and nonprofit management. When we reconnected in the early 2000s, my senior thesis advisor, Professor Allen Kropf, said my career exemplified what the college hoped the Core Curriculum would do—enable people to think on their feet. To which I replied wryly that its real value has been when I had fallen flat on my back.

Although my Amherst experience was overly cloistered and I feel an integration of the traditional liberal arts with practical engagement would have been valuable to me, I am pleased that Amherst now has a robust internship program. I have supported the program by sponsoring and mentoring a number of Amherst interns, and appreciate this opportunity to work with such smart, motivated young people.

Meeting Kennedy's Challenge in the Private Sector

Steve Drotter, '64

I SAW SENATOR JOHN F. KENNEDY marching in the Fall Foliage Parade on Main Street in North Adams, Massachusetts, in the first week of October 1954. He was the first important person I had ever seen up close. We had just moved to Massachusetts from the northernmost tip of Maine. Back in Maine, our town newspaper came from two hundred miles away; we couldn't get television reception, and the only radio station broadcast just during the day, in French. So, with almost no exposure to important people and events, I was thrilled to see JFK, not just because he was important, but because of how he carried himself. He projected a confidence and focus that said, "you can count on me." He had the appearance of a charismatic leader. That image has remained with me. I listened to his speeches, press conferences, and policy discussions with deep admiration.

Professor Dwight Salmon, the faculty advisor for our fraternity, invited his friend Robert Frost to the house. Frost came to talk with us shortly before he died. We all sat on the rug to listen to him. He wanted to answer our questions, not just talk about what was important to him. He was clear and concise in his responses; he projected strength and wisdom. It was an elevating experience. His deep, firm leadership was different from Kennedy's.

The conjunction of President Kennedy and the spirit of Robert Frost at the convocation for the Frost Library was a high point for me. I took Kennedy's challenge to us as an obligation. I had no interest in working in government or pursuing a political career, so it wasn't immediately obvious how I would meet the Kennedy challenge. I had grown up in a family of teachers, and I understood that teaching was an individualized way of delivering service. To make a wider impact, a business career seemed to offer the best opportunity, and I zeroed in on the human side of business: teaching.

As models, Kennedy and Frost didn't guide me on *what* to teach; their message, and their underlying influence, was on *how* to teach. In a business setting, whether one on one, with a small group or in a large classroom, there isn't any room for failure. Every student has to earn an A. Learning and developing the requisite skills and applying them are required for business and personal success.

Some students, for a wide range of business or personal reasons, don't want to engage in learning. They may have their minds focused elsewhere, or they simply don't want to change how they do things. In my business career, being tough enough to penetrate these barriers in a constructive way was a big part of the job. I had seen Amherst professors penetrate defenses, but often in a destructive way. That style would have gotten me fired. After experimenting with several styles, I decided to approach teaching my students as if I were their leader. To establish a climate of motivation, I set a clear purpose and direction, established a positive tone, and engaged everyone, not just the ones with their hands up. I encouraged intellectual risk-taking and acknowledged contribution. I wanted the students to feel that they could count on me to guide them through the learning. They needed to believe what I was teaching would help them. Kennedy did that very well, and I had watched Frost do the same, although in his more low-key manner.

During the course of my career, I consulted with over 150 companies in thirty-seven countries. I worked on the human side of business: developing leaders and planning succession, mainly at the highest levels. To help determine what and how to teach at each company, I regularly had considerable dialogue with those who were being led. What came through was the importance of their jobs, not just for feeding their families and driving a reliable car, but to their self-esteem and peace of mind. Achieving results, satisfying customers and earning recognition through achievement really matters. Income, health care, and pension plans are all part of the package. If businesses fail to provide these, government bears the burden.

Research on the causes of happiness has taught us that happiness comes from the pursuit of goals. For many of us, most goals are established at work. Teaching leaders to be more effective in setting goals, defining jobs, developing their personnel and creating a safe work environment is a worthwhile service. This is how leaders make their companies successful. Over time, the benefits of having a good leader at work become tangible. You feel it, hear it in the hallways, and see it on faces. Those faces are happy to be there. The effectiveness ripples through the community as well. If companies don't provide these things, then the government must. The negative effect on government and society from business failure—layoffs, plant closings, wage reductions, lost tax revenue—is immeasurable.

While I didn't consciously set out to use leadership training and development as my response to Kennedy's challenge at Amherst, it eventually occurred to me that many people in many countries had benefitted from this service that I provided. Thousands of leaders, responsible for millions of people and jobs, were my students. I had a great deal of leverage and used it.

I was a consultant, not an employee, and I can't take credit for the success or failure of businesses I served. I didn't set strategy, design products and services, make decisions, or sell. I measured my contribution in the only ways available: feedback from students, the business that hired me. Their feedback included reports of their progress, the number of times I was rehired, and they amount that companies were willing to pay me. Based on those criteria, my efforts made a difference.

I think President Kennedy would agree that this effort in private enterprise served society in the larger sense. He didn't really specify where we should perform our service. He did say that our relationship with the rest of the world mattered and must be strengthened.

In "Death of the Hired Man," Frost brought his poet's insight to the issues of work and self-worth:

"Surely you wouldn't grudge the poor old man
Some humble way to save his self-respect."

By teaching better management practices, particularly in the under-developed areas of the world, I hope I've done my part to meet the challenge.

Privilege and Responsibility

———————

Jesse Brill, '64

WHEN PRESIDENT KENNEDY spoke at Amherst in October of 1963, he underscored that each of us who had the privilege of attending a school like Amherst had a responsibility to give back.

I have been fortunate, some might say privileged, having gone to the best of schools on scholarships: Amherst and Yale Law School. I was a product of my times: self-reliant, hardworking, a perfectionist with the belief that I could accomplish anything, including making a lot of money. But I have always felt the need to give back. JFK articulated what many of us felt. We knew that our success in getting into the schools that we attended was good fortune, not because we were superior or "deserved it." We were the lucky few.

Instead of ruminating on Kennedy's speech, I would like to share a few life examples where I felt compelled to do some simple things. These were actions that others might not have thought of, and they show that we all can do things to give back, to make a difference.

CATCH A PURSE SNATCHER

In Manhattan in the late 1960s, my wife and I were walking down a street when we heard an old lady who was crossing the street cry out. Someone had grabbed her purse. My gut reaction was to catch the person and get her purse back. Since I was pretty fast, I knew I could catch him. I did and brought the woman her purse.

No big deal. It was something anyone could have—and should have—done. When you see a wrong, right it. It is important.

USE YOUR PLATFORM, WHATEVER IT MIGHT BE

Starting out with no money, sorting envelopes into zip code order on our living room floor, I created a respected legal publishing company. I was fortunate, and I felt an obligation to use the platform of our publications not just to tell lawyers and executives how to comply with SEC rules and developments—but to tell them to do the right thing. Here are a few examples:

Excessive CEO Compensation

In recent years, CEO compensation has risen to levels that are far out of line from past norms, causing serious socio-economic disconnects. A decade or so ago, my company's efforts made the *Wall Street Journal* in an article about the movement to limit CEO pay: "He (Brill) suggested directors include current and future compensation and dubbed the result a 'tally sheet.' Then he aggressively promoted the notion to the thirty thousand readers of his newsletters and Web sites, who include corporate lawyers, pay consultants and directors."[2]

As the *Journal* article shows, working from within can make a difference, and we continue to remind our readers of their responsibility to speak up when advising their clients.

"The Hot Dog and The Hungry"

(This was the lead piece from my newsletter's September-October 1992 issue. It has relevance today.)

As the various economic and social problems of society come closer to home and begin to have a more direct impact on corporate profits and all of

2   Joann S. Lublin and Phred Dvorak, "How Five New Players Aid Movement to Limit CEO Pay," *Wall Street Journal*, March 13, 2007, https://www.wsj.com/articles/SB117372189493934353.

our (and our children's) personal wellbeing, we should not ignore innovative, inexpensive yet potentially far-reaching solutions over which we may have some control. Many of our readers make annual gifts of stock or cash to our alma maters and various non-profit and civic organizations and institutions. Whether you are a large contributor or small, the following gift approach can have considerable impact.

A board member of a major sports arena recently was asked by a friend, the founder of a food program for the needy, what the arena did with all the cooked hot dogs, hamburgers, and other perishables left over after each game. The board member did not know but said he would find out. What he learned was that the food was simply thrown out.

Now, after every game, a truck from the local organization which distributes food to the needy pulls up to the arena, loads up, and delivers leftover hot dogs, etc. to many appreciative children and others who do not have any control over the situation they are in.

Many of us live in communities where there are now local organizations which are geared to picking up and distributing leftover food from restaurants on a daily basis. (Your local church or synagogue, which may even have its own food program, or your local welfare agency should be able to direct you to those food delivery organizations.) But, generally, the programs are limited to a few participating restaurants (and deliveries are often limited to the local soup kitchen, not reaching the young and the elderly—which could be reached through school food programs and volunteer "meals on wheels" deliveries).

Enter the Yale Alums

This writer woke up to this situation recently, at the very time that Yale Law School was soliciting contributions for his twenty-fifth reunion year. So, we asked Dean Calabresi what happened to the uneaten and leftover food after each meal in the law school dining hall—and, for that matter, all the other university-wide dining halls. As with the arena board member, the dean did not know but he immediately undertook to find out—and once again, learned that much of the time the food was simply dumped.

We then asked the dean what his reaction would be if we conditioned our twenty-fifth reunion gift on the law school:

(1) Developing a program for delivering uneaten and leftover food from all the university's dining halls to the needy in the community, including an effective delivery system to ensure that the food could reach those young and needy who do not go to soup kitchens;

(2) Developing and pursuing any necessary local health code enabling legislation or interpretations, especially provisions which would enable the distribution of served but uneaten leftovers (perhaps the greatest source of food, which the hungry would die for and raid garbage cans for but which purists might try to label as "unfit"); [Note that now the "Good Samaritan Food Donation Act" protects donors and recipients.]

(3) Expanding the program throughout the community with the goal that every restaurant, business, institution, etc. which serves food would be actively participating in the program; and

(4) Developing a model which other colleges and universities across the country could then adopt and implement in their own communities (and then export to other institutions in the area); and actively promote the program not only to the colleges and universities in the Ivy League, but across the country through the various national educational organizations (and their newsletters and other organs of communication).

Happily, Dean Calabresi and the Yale Law School immediately and eagerly embraced the project. (In fairness, Yale Law School already had in place a laudable program where students could donate the unused portions of their meal tickets.)

Enter All of Us

Our purpose in recounting this isolated incident, and naming Yale, is not to take any personal credit or to plug Yale Law School. Rather, it is to point out to our readers that if each of us were to ask the same questions of our own alma maters and other donees and institutions we are affiliated with, we could have a far-reaching impact in a very short time.

Don't overlook, also, our own companies and law firms, many of which not only provide food to employees but which are in a position to rapidly deal with any local or legal impediments (and inevitable bureaucratic inertia) that can easily be overcome with a little influence and standing. Those of our readers at airlines and food service companies in particular may want to explore ways to recapture all that untouched served food left on food trays.

Leftover Food at our Conferences

My organization hosts a three-day annual conference with over two thousand attendees. Each year we require the hotel to deliver all the leftover food from all the meals and events to local shelters. And at each conference we encourage our attendees to do the same whenever they have events. This is a simple thing that each person reading this can do by asking companies and organizations he or she is connected with to do the same.

STEP UP AND TAKE THE LEAD

For our Amherst Class of '64 fiftieth reunion, people were debating what to do for a responsible class gift. I have always felt that to make something happen you need to just take the lead and not wait for committees. So, a classmate, Vince Simmon, stepped up to provide at cost the LEDs to replace all the old campus lighting. And I offered to pay the expense of making the changeover, provided it was done in time for our reunion. It got done. We are now attempting to leverage this at Yale and other colleges and universities. Since there is a very short payback period from the electricity savings, this is a no-brainer. What it takes is an alumnus/alumna to urge his or her alma mater to do the same. (Vince will be able to show them how to do it for a lot less than those looking to make a profit may have estimated.) Again, here is something everyone reading this can do to make a difference.

BE AWARE OF PRIVILEGE—AND RESPONSIBILITY...

Based on what is happening today on football fields and around the country, I thought I would share the following.

I play softball three or four times a week. Frequently, I'm the only one on the field who is not of color. I drive an old beaten-up 1987 Mercedes that runs on biodiesel. My friends cringe when I make a U-turn to park in front of the ball field where we play. They cannot fathom doing anything like that: making a U-turn, not coming to a full stop at every stop sign, etc. They are always wary, expecting the police to stop them.

I want to share an incident that a black friend who is in his fifties recounted to me. This guy is bright, articulate, soft-spoken, and not in any way threatening. He drives a late model car which he keeps spotless.

One weekend afternoon, my friend was driving through a nice neighborhood in Oakland, California. Suddenly, an Oakland police officer stopped him and ordered him out of the car. The officer asked him in a challenging way how much he had had to drink. My friend responded politely that he does not drink.

The officer then ordered him to close his eyes and lean his head all the way back so that his eyes would be facing the sky when they were opened. The officer then ordered him to open his eyes. My friend, who has a great sense of balance, told me that even he felt a bit dizzy and disoriented, but he remained standing straight. The officer, now obviously frustrated and angry, demanded my friend's license. After calling it in, only to find that my friend had no record of any infractions, the office told him to get back in his car and go. No apology, never.

My friends of color all tell me that this is part of their experience. I sincerely doubt that any one of my white friends feels this constant nagging concern.

Something to think about.

OUR LEGACY

Our children and grandchildren now do their own caring things each in his and her own way. Let's be proud.

"The World We Inherited; The World We Will Bequeath" and What We Can Do About It

Charles Stover, '64

I FIRST USED THE PHRASE in the title above in the Spring of 2013 in an *Alumni Quarterly* note to the Amherst Class of '64 as a possible theme for our fiftieth reunion the following May. The phrase arose from the pit of my stomach—an undefined fear that our generation had perverted the legacy of post-war prosperity and bipartisan democracy we inherited from our parents who had struggled through the Great Depression and World War II.

The phrase became the theme for our fiftieth reunion, eventually building a network of classmates who re-engaged with our common past.

Old connections and new friendships evolved. We met with independent experts on our democracy and society. We learned from each other about the major challenges we were bequeathing to our children and grandchildren: climate change, weakened democracy, an unaffordable health care system, and an inadequate education system, along with enormously concentrated wealth and widespread poverty. The documentary film, *JFK: The Last Speech,* and this companion volume grew from that effort, and verify Kierkegaard's prophecy, "We live forward, but we understand backward."

"The World We Inherited; The World We Will Bequeath." What does this really mean?

To try to answer, I sat down for an intergenerational talk with my three adult daughters and a son-in-law. To summarize, I said:

Please remember, we inherited the past state of affairs from our parents. They didn't apologize for the devastation of WWII, the subsequent nuclear arms race—only modulated by mutually assured destruction—the Vietnam War and the social prejudices against women and minority groups. They also left us a booming manufacturing economy, rising wages and living standards, and a bipartisan political system able and willing to govern fairly. The bad came with the good. Our parents had done their best in difficult times.

Our generation is bequeathing to you a certain state of affairs—local, national and global. Our generation has produced great wealth, moving huge numbers of people out of poverty around the world. We live in a global information and technology age that has many benefits and has major opportunities and risks. We also inherited values. A penny saved is a penny earned; invest for the long term; hope for the best and prepare for the worst; a family inheritance is for the benefit of you and future generations; education is the most important investment; always do your best; your bond is only as good as your word; money is necessary but doesn't make you happy. But there are huge problems of which you are well aware. We transfer the responsibility for these affairs to you. You have inherited them; they are your responsibility.

Then I asked my children: *"What do you think that we have bequeathed to you?"*

They told me clearly:

1. *"Climate change is real—but people don't believe it is because they are not directly impacted. We're facing the largest challenge that humanity has ever faced."*

2. *"Society is facing scarcities in water and electric power. Population keeps growing and makes greater demand on resources. The old iconography of the American Dream is a cultural myth. It doesn't work in a world of finite resources."*

3. *"We need to adjust our customs and how we live. How much do we need? People don't have to own things—just to have access to them. They need access to education, shelter, health care, social relationships and social networks, and they need to be able to plan for the future."*

4. *"We were raised with a sense of responsibility for others. People bear responsibility for their fellow citizens. The role of government is trustee of public good; it must protect us for our survival."*

5. *"Race relations remain a huge issue; minorities and women are marginalized."*

6. *"We face many financial challenges. Colleges are no longer affordable. Most students must incur huge debts to advance themselves."*

7. *"We have an overabundance of ways to get and share information; social media pits you against others and is misused; we get overwhelmed and it's hard to concentrate—to read—to think."*

As I reflected on this interchange, I realized that Kennedy described our situation today in the speech he couldn't give—the one he planned to deliver at the Trade Mart in Dallas—on the day he was killed.

> This link between leadership and learning is not only essential at the community level. It is even more indispensable in world affairs. Ignorance and misinformation can handicap the progress of a city or a company, but they can, if allowed to prevail in foreign policy, handicap this country's security. In a world of complex and continuing problems, in a world full of frustrations and irritations, America's leadership must be guided by the lights

of learning and reason or else those who confuse rhetoric with reality and the plausible with the possible will gain the popular ascendancy with their seemingly swift and simple solutions to every world problem.

There will always be dissident voices heard in the land, expressing opposition without alternatives, finding fault but never favor, perceiving gloom on every side and seeking influence without responsibility. Those voices are inevitable.

But today other voices are heard in the land—voices preaching doctrines wholly unrelated to reality, wholly unsuited to the sixties, doctrines which apparently assume that words will suffice without weapons, that vituperation is as good as victory and that peace is a sign of weakness...

We cannot expect that everyone, to use the phrase of a decade ago, will "talk sense to the American people." But we can hope that fewer people will listen to nonsense..."

Today is not so different; the same lessons that helped us will help them. I was captivated by JFK's inaugural address, his approach to governing, and his speech at Amherst. After his assassination, however, it was President Calvin Plimpton's eulogy[3] that motivated me to action:

But in the midst of life there is death. That is the problem; that is the question. What is the meaning? Where is the sense? He's gone now, but not necessarily all of him, and there lies the sense. As we shed our tears, let us remember his toughness.

---

3   Speech by President Calvin H. Plimpton. Amherst College. Amherst, MA. November 22, 1963.

We are here to sharpen our wits and to strengthen our bodies. Let us remember to advantage our late, great President's toughness in mind, body and soul. Let us stand a moment in silence, to honor him; then let us go and do the work he couldn't complete."

I volunteered for the Peace Corps, lived in a small African village and assisted with the export of the local cash crop, peanuts. I continued with a lifelong career in public service, international development and related private business. My career grew out of going out to "*do the work he couldn't complete.*"

Today, young people are once again engaged; having seized the moral high ground of the human cost of gun violence, they are now learning to act. They are unwilling to trade away their morality for unrelated promises. They are speaking truth to power.

Just listen to them:

"I'm sick and tired of 'thoughts and prayers.' Thoughts and prayers don't protect us from bullets and shrapnel."

"I am here today, and you are all here today, because we do not want to die. I want every one of you to be [at your graduation]. And I won't tolerate anything less."

"I will not attend their early funerals. I will not watch them die in front of me. I will not live my life in terror of a murderer among us. I will not cower in the back of my classroom and watch my life be ripped from me. I will not ever let it happen to another school, to another city, to another state."

"Your children might become victims, too. You have the power to change this, and if you don't we will change you! We will vote you out."

"We are the ones most involved in this. We are the ones who lived through this whole tragic experience, and we are going to be the future leaders of America."

How familiar are their engaged, energized voices. How clear. How compelling.

I want the young people of today to hear Kennedy's message. Our children and grandchildren can count on support from those of us who embrace the principles of government and civic responsibility that President Kennedy articulated on October 26, 1963. President Obama, born in the year of JFK's inauguration, summarized those principles:

> To those of us of a certain age, the Kennedys symbolized a set of values and attitudes about civic life that made it such an attractive calling. The idea that politics in fact could be a noble and worthwhile pursuit. The notion that our problems, while significant, are never insurmountable.

> The belief that America's promise might embrace those who had once been locked out or left behind and that opportunity and dignity would no longer be restricted to the few but extended to the many.

> *The responsibility that each of us have to play a part in our nation's destiny, and by virtue of being Americans, play a part in the destiny of the world. [italics added]*[4]

Everyone needs constant practice to be a good citizen. First, it's an acquired skill, then it becomes a civic habit. Vote, vote, vote: in local elections, in state elections, in national elections. Vote in presidential years, and vote in

---

4   Barack Obama in his speech accepting the John F. Kennedy Profiles in Courage award at the John F. Kennedy Library, May 7, 2017.

off year elections. Making positive social changes, righting wrongs, shaping a positive future for ourselves and others—no matter how small the cause—all this brings its own rewards.

None of us are helpless in the face of power. Let us tune in, step up and speak our voices along with our children and grandchildren. Let us throw our hearts and minds again into preserving the vitality of our democracy, "*…let us go and do the work he couldn't complete.*"

PART 3

Looking Backward with Pride...
Forward with Hope

———————

[Passing the Torch]

11

THE PRESIDENT AND
THE POET

Robert Frost embodied F. Scott Fitzgerald's definition of genius: "The
test of a first-rate intelligence is the ability to hold two opposed ideas in
mind at the same time and still retain the ability to function." Frost
balanced his hope for "the glory of a next Augustan age" with a deep-
rooted Yankee skepticism. He realized the all-too-human temptations
to abuse political power and saw "art" in its broadest definition as
a countervailing force. The three writers in this chapter offer their
perspectives on Frost's concepts and Kennedy's articulation of them.

On Arts and Politics

———————

Joseph Kennedy III

RECENTLY, I VISITED AMHERST COLLEGE to commemorate a defining moment in a defining place for two extraordinary Americans: one, a proud Yankee poet, and the other a proud Irish-American president. Both were restless thinkers, rooted deeply and stubbornly in this New England soil. Both were lifelong students of the experience of ordinary men; they were explorers of the space between lofty vision and humble experience, between big dreams and hard realities. Neither aimed to proselytize or preach. Both strove simply to connect with our most basic humanity, our wants, our needs, pains and promises. In this shared effort, the poet and politician found common cause and mutual admiration for the other's art.

That common cause brought President John F. Kennedy to Amherst a half-century ago, to dedicate the site of the Robert Frost Library. On that occasion, he said:

> When power leads man toward arrogance, poetry reminds him of his limitations, when power narrows the areas of man's concerns, poetry reminds him of the richness and diversity of his existence, when power corrupts, poetry cleanses, for art establishes the basic human truths, which must serve as a touchstone for our judgment.

Over fifty years later, those words hit home for those gathered there, undoubtedly worried that our deeply fractured country had lost that touchstone for judgment.

It is no secret that we are in turbulent times, where a dark worldview has left many disoriented, searching for what binds us together in times that threaten to tear us apart. We are desperately hunting for common cause, for our better angels, for the decency that makes us proud to be part of these United States. In moments like this, the role for our liberal arts is critical, as precisely and as deeply needed as when President Kennedy spoke on the campus.

We trust our artists to expose the burdens that many of us carry along with them. We ask our artists to bravely share their vulnerabilities in order to help us recognize our own. We depend on them to remind us of our individual frailties; frailties that are not unique, but rather, if built upon, can fortify our common cause.

Nearly a century ago, Langston Hughes reminded America that "I too sing America," in a rebuke to a viciously segregated nation and a plea to his country to see his humanity and his dignity, not the color of his skin.

In 1969, Joni Mitchell faced a war-weary nation in the depths of Vietnam and asked, "Oh my friend, what time is this, to trade the handshake for the fist?"

And today, Chance the Rapper (yes, Chance the Rapper), looks at us and says,

"I know you scared

You should ask us if we scared too...

If you was there

Then we'd just knew you cared too."

forcing all of us to confront an enduring blind spot to the challenges facing minority communities.

POETS AND PAINTERS can see the world that surrounds them with a clear eye. Their empathy can translate despair into beauty. Their humanity finds color in our shadows. Their optimism orients us toward what is big and real and tough and worth fighting for, those values of justice and freedom and love. Art and academia don't just allow introspection, they require it. In so doing, they inspire us to create the tangible societal change that otherwise resides solely in our imagination. It's an ambitious assignment.

I don't believe that President Kennedy could have envisioned the change that would begin within the building he dedicated to Robert Frost in 1963. Students from nearly every state in this Union, and from fifty-four countries, challenge themselves from 8 a.m. until well past midnight.

They are students like Peter Tang, 2010 class president, who graduated and immediately entered teach for America in Memphis. Seven years later, Peter is still in Tennessee, working to strengthen the education system for low-income families. Or Carolyn Sufrin, a pre-med graduate who has dedicated much of her career to addressing the health care needs of incarcerated women. Or Josh Block, the ACLU attorney who has stood by Gavin Grimm's side through every level of our criminal justice system in the pursuit of lived-in legal equality for transgender students in America. Or Alexander Morton, who was a student when this library was dedicated and became a Peace Corps volunteer in Addis Ababa. His work in various government transportation agencies significantly contributed to the deregulation of the airline and trucking industries. He went on to visit nearly 80 percent of the world's countries throughout the course of his life.

For Peter, Caroline, Josh, Alexander, and so many other proud Amherst alumni, a lifetime of reflection began within those walls under Robert Frost's name. In dedicating that library to the revered poet, President Kennedy said:

> If sometimes our great artists have been the most critical of our society, it is because their sensitivity and their concern for justice, which must motivate any true artist makes them aware that our nation falls short of its highest potential.

That awareness is our ultimate American and human truth. We are, in fact, a work in progress, flawed and fragile, sometimes selfish and cruel. But like any great masterpiece, we defy our own limitations. In the moments that matter most, we expand and extend. We rescue; we protect, and we survive. We give; we open; we heal, and we help. That, more than any law or leader, more than even the most powerful movements or moments in our history, that is what drives us to progress. That is, in fact, the touchstone of our judgement.

No single person, no bully, no stubborn monster like prejudice or injustice, in the end none of it, none of it, can match the small personal courageous ways that Americans, with time, and persistence, and resistance and patience, choose goodness every single day.

In his poem that was left undelivered on a cold snowy day on the Capitol steps in 1961, when a young Massachusetts senator was set to become our nation's president, Robert Frost perfectly illustrated that optimistic calling. He wrote:

> There is a call to life a little sterner,
> And braver for the earner, learner, yearner.
> Less criticism of the field and court
> And more preoccupation with the sport.
> It makes the prophet in us all presage
> The glory of a next Augustan age
> Of a power leading from its strength and pride,
> Of young ambition eager to be tried,
> Firm in our free beliefs without dismay,
> In any game the nations want to play.

Poetry and politics may appear to live in dissonance, but excellence in either demands many of the same qualities: an embrace of human imperfection, a deep faith in the bonds of shared experience, an eye for opportunity that others might pass by, and a belief that this life, this earth, this fleeting time that we share together, is worth fighting for as hard as we can to get it right.

Frost and Kennedy on Poetry and Power in a Democracy

Robert Benedetti, '64

ON A VERY COLD clear morning, I attended President Kennedy's inauguration and witnessed Robert Frost reciting "The Gift Outright" on the steps of the Capitol. I also listened to Frost presenting his poems at Amherst, and attended the October 26, 1963, convocation where Kennedy spoke. My academic expertise does not include Frost's work or Kennedy's, but my personal experience does.

The relationship between politics and poetry is an ancient quarrel, to which both Plato and Aristotle contributed foundational arguments. Plato famously suggested that the poets should be excluded from the ideal city, though he recognized that poets provided a truthful description of the struggles that even heroes face, given the uncertainties of life and the reality of death. Plato was particularly interested in a rigorous civic education for a static state, establishing the norms of society rather than monitoring their implementation. On the other hand, the Greeks recognized that democracies would listen to poets, who described life as it was lived rather than as it ought to be.

In a unique contribution to this long-standing argument, Kennedy's remarks at Amherst linked power, poetry, *and a liberal education* for the benefit of democracy. Kennedy argued that those who were lucky enough to have a broad education had an obligation to serve our democracy by accepting power. But, he also argued that the insights of great artists, like Robert Frost, could counter the potential for power to breed arrogance.

He noted that "unless the graduates of this College and other colleges like it who are given a running start in life—unless they are willing to put back into our society those talents, the broad sympathy, the understanding, the compassion—unless they are willing to put those qualities back into the service of the Great Republic, then obviously the presuppositions upon which our democracy are based are bound to be fallible."

Kennedy then quoted Frost's famous lines about two roads diverging in a wood and urged that public service not be the less traveled by. In fact, Frost clearly suggested that the description of the road taken as less traveled was an afterthought of the traveler looking back.

Kennedy's pivotal argument was that artists, Frost and others, had a role in "saving power from itself." Kennedy specifically reminded his listeners that Frost sensitized society to platitudes, instilled a sense of tragedy, reminded us of the richness and diversity of experience, and established basic human truths. Only through the individuality of its artists can a democracy break through the public myth to learn the truth about the life that is lived within its borders.

Frost eagerly accepted the role of tutor to leadership, and his particular concern was the breadth of America's vision of itself. In "America is Hard to See" he focused on Columbus, implying the missed opportunity "to behold/ the race's future trial place, /a fresh start for the human race."

Frost feared that the initial opportunity of untouched America had become simply a locus to:

...spread the room
Of our enacting out the doom
Of being in each other's way,
And so put off the weary day
When we would have to put our mind
On how to crowd but still be kind.

For America to get beyond this pedestrian future, he believed that the nation needed bold leadership. In his view, civic engagement was not for everyone, but those who do have the gift to lead must grasp leadership just as poets pursue their calling.

In "How Hard It Is to Keep from Being King When It's in You and in the Situation,"[1] Frost tells the story of a king who voluntarily relinquishes his throne, escaping his kingdom with his son who wants to be a poet. The escaped king, enslaved as a cook for a second king, soon becomes that king's chief advisor. In the passages where the first king/cook advises the second king, one gets the sense of Frost's political outlook to the extent that he ever betrayed it. The second king asks the cook to tell him the rules for a wise reign and the ways to insure his people develop good character. His cook tells him to make the people "as happy as is good for them." He adds that the people should be consulted, allowing for "progress."

However, the cook suggests that while the ideal state may be one of "pliant permanence," a nation must run its natural course. Here Frost—who sounds more like his classical forbearers Plato and Aristotle than James Madison and the Founding Fathers—expects a state to progress:

Round and round in circles
From King to Mob to King
Until the eddy of it eddies out…

The cook then turns to a discussion of freedom. He warns against following a "right leader," no matter if he is Marx or Christ. Freedom is only found in "departure." While this term is not fully unpacked, Frost implies that appropriate rule would restrict discipline "in school and state" to that sufficient for individuals to become self-sufficient. In Frost's view, living unconstrained by authoritative social and political cues defines real freedom.

Frost made the case for leaders who strike balances between extremes, recognizing the nature of the context in which the challenge occurs. He

---

1   Robert Frost, *In the Clearing* (New York: Holt, Rinehart and Winston, 1962). 74-84.

championed the natural leader, even if at times that leader wants to refuse his responsibilities:

The only certain freedom's in departure.
My son and I have tasted it and know.

Civic engagement may not be for everyone, but those who have the talent cannot avoid taking the reins:

How hard it is to keep from being King
When it's in you and in the situation.

It's no accident that Frost's king is a leader and his son a poet. Both roles call for the same strength of character and willingness to engage the general in the specific.

For Frost, the purpose of education, then, is to find and refine the individual's innate abilities. In his collection of correspondence with Frost, Louis Untermeyer has many revealing passages about the poet's attitudes toward education. He quotes Frost:

> I still say the only education worth anything is self-education. All the rest consist of schoolwork, textbooks, training, aids to help distinguish one fact from another without helping us to tell true values from false. But that doesn't mean I don't believe in people learning as well as learned people. I'm for educated humanity all the time—except in an undiscriminating way. All men are born free and equal—free at least in their right to be different. Some people want to mix up the weak and strong of mankind; they want to homogenize society everywhere. That's why I'm against the homogenizers in art, in politics, in every walk of life. I want the cream to rise.[2]

---

2   Louis Untermeyer, *The Letters of Robert Frost to Louis Untermeyer* (New York: Holt, 1963), 376.

Frost was drawn to Amherst in part because the students were able and many were blessed with the courage to pursue a unique path. Like Kennedy, he wanted those with talent to succeed, in the arts and in statecraft. The hardheaded visionaries carried his hopes for the future. A broad education and "real life" experience would test their mettle and competition would bring the best to the top. This was his own life's experience and Frost would have others follow his lead.

Mark Van Doren, who read Frost's poems at his Amherst memorial, was a close student of his work. In his 1951 article for the *Atlantic*, he summed up Frost's philosophy of education this way:

> Frost's country is the country of human sense: of experience, of imagination, and of thought. His poems start at home, as all good poems do; as Homer's did, as Shakespeare's, as Goethe's, and as Baudelaire's; but they end up everywhere, as only the best poems do. This is partly because his wisdom is native to him, and could not have been suppressed by any circumstance; it is partly, too, because his education has been right. He is our least provincial poet because he is the best grounded in those ideas—Greek, Hebrew, modern Europeans and even Oriental—which make for well-built art at any time. He does not parade his learning, and may in fact not know that he has it: but there in his poems it is, and it is what makes them so solid, so humorous, and so satisfying.[3]

In a vignette quoted in Frost's obituary in the *New York Times*, Kennedy defined the common ground that politicians and poets share:

> There is a story that some years ago an interested mother wrote to a principal of a school, "Don't teach my boy poetry, he's going to run for Congress." I've never taken the view that the world of politics and the world of poetry are so far apart. I think politicians and

---

3   Mark Van Doren, "Robert Frost's America," *Atlantic*, June 1951 http://www. theatlantic.com/past/docs/unbound/poetry/frost/vand.htm.

poets share at least one thing, and that is their greatness depends upon the courage with which they face the challenges of life.[4]

Frost would have agreed!

———

AT KENNEDY'S INAUGURAL, both Frost and Kennedy called for the brightest and the best to rededicate themselves to America's historical destiny. The president's call for public service restated in concrete terms Frost's belief that the able must respond boldly to the special gifts of this nation. In a poem prepared for Kennedy's inauguration, Frost imagined a call for ambitious leaders who were sterner and braver, more willing to engage than criticize the state of political reality. Anticipating Kennedy to be such a leader, he predicted an "Augustan age" where power led from strength and American beliefs would be championed without "dismay."[5]

At Amherst, Kennedy went beyond a simple eulogy for Frost; using the moment to address the relationship of poetry and power, he testified to their shared hopes and concerns. Frost and Kennedy saw the political arena as requiring an artist's touch, including the artist's strength of character. Those most fit for statecraft had a breadth of education that encompassed all the liberal arts and sciences. They could be trusted to see clearly, to balance extremes, and to bring the country, in Frost's words, to "*A golden age of poetry and power.*"[6]

———

4   "Robert Frost Dies at 88; Kennedy Leads in Tribute," *New York Times*, January 30, 1963, http://www.nytimes.com/learning/general/onthisday/bday/0326.html.

5   Robert Frost, "For John F. Kennedy His Inauguration," *In the Clearing* (New York: Holt, Rinehart and Winston, 1962), 30.

6   *Ibid.*

A Witness to History
Robert Frost and Jack Kennedy, Then and Now

Paul R. Dimond, '66

THE WITNESS

The son of two schoolteachers, I grew up in Ann Arbor with one foot in town and the other in gown. On January 20, 1961, I watched President Kennedy's inauguration on a black-and-white TV. A frail old man tried to read a long poem he'd written for the occasion, the first ever for a president-elect. But he was blinded by the noonday sun. Then suddenly, eighty-six-year-old Robert Frost stood tall and recited from memory his 1935 poem "The Gift Outright." It fit the occasion—and the brief but compelling call of the new president to join in exploring a New Frontier—perfectly.

In the spring of 1962, I read in the *Ann Arbor News* that Amherst's Robert Frost would be speaking at Hill Auditorium, the magnificent 4,100-seat concert hall Albert Kahn built in 1913. A few weeks later, the *News* reported the great poet received an honorary degree at Michigan Stadium, the "Big House" built in 1927 by the legendary football coach Fielding Yost. I looked forward to attending Amherst College in the fall.

Unfortunately, I never met Frost. He was absent due to illness my first semester, and he died in January 1963.

Amherst's core curriculum composition course soured me on English, while the world history requirement led me to the archives in Converse Library and on to a history major. On October 26, 1963, John F. Kennedy spoke at our small college at a convocation on the occasion of the groundbreaking for the new Frost Memorial Library. I met the president and shook his hand. And then, less than a month later, he was gone, forever. For the following week, I watched the aftermath of his tragic assassination, the national mourning, on another black-and-white TV, with breaks only after midnight when the local stations signed off, appropriately, with the poem and song "High Flight."

At Michigan Law School, I continued my study of history in another library archive, this time in the original sources on the framing of the Civil War Amendments. This shaped several facets of my career. In the 1970s, I helped try five landmark race cases that challenged a closely divided Supreme Court[7] and served for two years as director of the Lawyers' Committee for Civil Rights under Law, first convened by President Kennedy in the summer of 1963. In the 1980s, I researched and wrote about enumerated federal powers as limited by our Constitution, including the individual liberties and equal rights guaranteed to each person against infringement by any legislature or public official, from county clerk to president. [8] In the 1990s, I served as special assistant to President Clinton for economic policy on the staff of the National Economic Council.[9]

In sum, after more than five decades witnessing history from such diverse perches, I have a unique perspective on this story of a poet and a president, then and now.

———

7   See Paul R. Dimond, *Beyond Busing: Reflections on Urban Segregation, the Courts, and Equal Opportunity* (Ann Arbor: University of Michigan Press, 1985), winner of the Ralph J. Bunche Book-of-the-Year Award.

8   See Paul R. Dimond, *The Supreme Court and Judicial Choice: The Role of Provisional Review in a Democracy* (Ann Arbor: University of Michigan Press, 1989).

9   See the preface, retrospect, and prospect added to the twentieth anniversary paperback reprinting of *Beyond Busing* (Ann Arbor: University of Michigan Press, 2005).

THEN: FROST AT MICHIGAN, 1921-26

In the fall of 1921, University of Michigan President Marion Leroy Burton launched a "grand experiment" in higher education, wooing Robert Frost from Amherst as a "creative fellow." As Burton wrote to former Michigan regent and governor Chase Osborn the donor who provided Frost's funding, "A real university should be a patron of art, literature and creative activity. We ought to have upon the campus persons of the rarest type of personality...who see visions and dream dreams, who are actually producing the results which influence the thought of nations."

Frost, in his acceptance letter, embraced the president's revolutionary vision "for keeping the creative and the erudite together in education where they belong; and [the creative can] make its demand on the young student." Frost also welcomed Burton's patronage, "the freedom to work at his own art without any classroom obligations." As Frost put it, the poet, the artist and the inventor in residence could "always be about" creating "definite deeds to be growing." Although originally envisioned as a one-year appointment with different creative fellows following every year thereafter, with Burton's help over the next five years Frost developed the fellowship into a more unique role. An acclaimed poet with no teaching responsibilities, present on whatever campus he chose, he wrote poems and inspired students to create while campaigning for his poetry and ideas at readings and events all across the nation.

In his first year, Frost regularly joined the meetings of the writers of Michigan's student literary magazine, *Whimsies.* He welcomed students to his rented home near campus to "say" a poem, and usually offered his encouragement "to keep it around for a while and deepen, deepen it." Town and gown welcomed his informal talks. On five occasions, the community filled the Hill Auditorium to hear Frost introduce and share the stage with his national poet peers.

Burton also hosted Frost at large dinner parties at the president's house, where the poet won over the guests by calling Harvard the Michigan of the East and saying a few of his poems. Burton concluded, "Robert Frost may be even more popular than Football Coach Fielding Yost." Frost replied, "Let's put that to the test: schedule a reading for me at the same time as a home football game. The stadium will be packed, but Hill will be empty, since even I will be at the game." Frost only proved the president's point; and the two men, each forty-seven years old, forged a bond that only death could sever.

The Whimsies honored Frost by dedicating the April issue of their magazine to him. The cover included the first verse from one of his earliest poems, "Revelation":

We make ourselves a place apart
Behind light words that tease and flout,
—But, oh, the agitated heart
Till some find us really out.

The poem hints at the larger challenge Frost and Burton faced. The English faculty was divided into two separate departments: literature, the academic department, and the non-academic rhetoric, composition, and journalism department. Many of the "academics" in literature, housed on the main quadrangle, objected to having any creative writer on the faculty, particularly Frost, a college drop-out who taught no classes but got paid as much as they did and stole the show with the students and the town. Such snobbery from pedants who created no new works of literature irked the poet. Frost also disliked his "shabby" office "firetrap" quarters on the "other" side of State Street with the non-academic rhetoric, composition, and journalism department.

Burton prized his poet friend so much that he changed his mind about rotating the creative fellowship annually. When Burton found another donor, he asked Frost to return for the next school year with more time reserved for writing poems. Frost was laid low by flu for much of the 1922-23 school year; he met infrequently with the Whimsies and hosted fewer guest lectures. Burton defended Frost's diminished public role by citing the Creative Fellow's primary duty, writing poetry. The president assured his restive regents and faculty that Frost's next collection of poems would bring great honor to Michigan.

When Burton couldn't raise donations to bring Frost back on a permanent basis, he asked the poet to recommend candidates for a one-year fellowship. Frost suggested the great American novelist Willa Cather, who had just won the Pulitzer Prize in fiction. The two feuding English departments joined to reject adding any woman, no matter how acclaimed, to their all-male faculty. This was not surprising, since at the time Michigan's student union didn't allow women in the front door either.

Frost dedicated his next book, *New Hampshire*, published in November 1923, to Michigan. With it, he won his first of four Pulitzer Prizes in poetry. Its most quoted poem, "Stopping by Woods on a Snowy Evening" ends with one of the most famous—and debated—last stanzas, "*The woods are lovely, dark and deep, / But I have promises to keep/ And miles to go before I sleep, /And miles to go before I sleep.*" Although most reviewers tried to make this poem a metaphor for confronting death, Frost favored the simpler calling of his solitary rider: get on with the chores and duties that lie ahead.

Rather than wait for donations to endow a special chair, Burton re-engineered the Lit School's budget to lure Frost back from Amherst. In the fall of 1924, the Regents approved the offer of a *permanent* position as a Fellow in Letters to Frost at a starting salary of $6,000 per year "out of University Funds." With Angell Hall now open, Burton also assured his now partner for life a new office in the heart of the campus. Frost would have responsibility for leading only one twelve-student seminar every other semester. Frost accepted, to begin in the fall semester of the 1925-26 school year.

In October 1924, Burton took to his bed, stricken by the chronic heart disease with which he'd long privately struggled; he died on February 18, 1925, at age fifty. The late president's public memorial service was delayed until May 28 so Frost could attend and deliver the eulogy to the forty-one hundred mourners who filled Hill Auditorium. The poet paid his kindred spirit the highest honor possible: Frost shared his maturing views on the academic role of the creative artist and students learning by doing that Burton and the fellowships at Michigan had done so much to shape.

Frost did return to Michigan for the 1925-26 school year. He joined the gatherings of both student literary magazines, the stuffier *Inlander* and the more adventuresome *Outlander* that his favorite students, the Three Graces, had founded. He also wrote dozens of poems for his next collection at his rental home across the Huron River from the campus.[10] Among these was the darker but also oft-quoted poem that ends as it opens:

> *I have been one acquainted with the night...*
> *And further still at an unearthly height,*
> *One luminary clock against the sky*
> *Proclaimed the time was neither wrong nor right.*
> *I have been one acquainted with the night.*

In the fall of 1926, Frost returned to Amherst College. He was appointed a tenured professor of English at full pay for ten weeks a year in residence, with no teaching responsibilities. At Amherst, Frost labored for the next twelve years to continue the grand experiment he and Burton had envisioned, creating many more poems, inspiring students to write, and campaigning for his poetry and ideas across the nation. Frost later secured similar arrangements at Harvard and Dartmouth, and then, once again, at his Amherst College home. Such non-teaching positions were the exceptions that proved the rule, but the Frost-Burton model did establish a precedent that enabled other poets and creative writers to find positions teaching classes, seminars, and workshops.

Whether Frost would "influence the thought of nations" remained an open question.

THEN: KENNEDY AND FROST AT MICHIGAN AND AMHERST, 1960–63

On October 13, 1960, in the third of four prime-time televised presidential debates, Richard Nixon challenged the more youthful-looking Kennedy as too strident a warmonger. With the Soviet Union's growing threat after Sputnik and the Cold War heating up, the vice president noted that in the twentieth

---

10   This is the house Henry Ford bought and moved to Greenfield Village in 1937.

century only three presidents, all Democrats, had carried the nation into war.

After the debate, Senator Kennedy flew into Willow Run Airport, near Ypsilanti, Michigan. Arriving late that night, he rode in a silent motorcade to Ann Arbor to sleep at the University of Michigan Union. When a huge throng outside clamored for him, the candidate couldn't resist emerging at 2 a.m. to speak from the front steps of the Union. Kennedy challenged the thousands of students:

> How many of you who are going to be doctors are willing to spend your days in Ghana? Technicians or engineers: how many of you are willing to work in the Foreign Service and spend your lives traveling around the world? On your willingness to do that, not merely to serve one year or two years in the service, but on your willingness to contribute part of your life to this country, I think will depend the answer whether a free society can compete. I think it can. And I think Americans are willing to contribute. But the effort must be far greater than we've ever made in the past.

His challenge received universal applause, soon followed by a petition signed by 1,000 Michigan students volunteering to serve. It was not surprising when JFK made his formal call for a Peace Corps two weeks later. The concept helped to establish his standing as a proponent of peace through action, as well as a Cold War proponent of military strength sufficient to contain the Soviet dictatorship and its Warsaw Pact puppets behind their Iron Curtain, including the Berlin Wall, where JFK would later stand before 450,000 for a memorable defense of freedom and democracy.

Early the next morning, I joined a crowd of thousands outside the old railroad terminal. We gathered to witness Jack Kennedy speak from the platform at the back of the caboose before he set off on a whistle-stop tour across our key swing state. Amidst all the cheering, it was hard to hear him conclude his stump speech with his rallying cry from Frost: "*But I have promises to keep/And miles to go before I sleep!"*

In the spring of 1962, Michigan students invited Frost to return for one last poetry reading. Once again, he filled Hill Auditorium. Frost exited stage left, only to return a few weeks later to receive an honorary degree before tens of thousands of well-wishers at Michigan Stadium. His citation declared, "As a public personage and a statesman by virtue solely of the exercise of poetic genius…Robert Frost [is] our nation's poet laureate. Setting aside the negative force of Shelley's dictum that poets are the unacknowledged legislators of the world, the university happily acknowledges the public offices of this some-time poet-in-residence and frequent and most welcome guest in the degree now conferred upon him, *Doctor of Laws.*"

Frost died on January 29, 1963 at age eighty-eight. For his public memorial service on February 17 in Johnson Chapel at Amherst, seven hundred guests led by Chief Justice Earl Warren celebrated the poet and his poetry. Now, the task of building the Robert Frost Memorial Library on the north side of the main quadrangle remained as his final honor.

President Kennedy appeared on October 26 for a convocation and formal groundbreaking for the new Frost library. After introductory remarks calling on the College and its students to put their learning "to the service of the Great Republic," Kennedy focused on the subject that brought him to honor the poet: the extent to which poetry and the other creative arts influence the exercise of national power and enrich American life and democracy. "In America, our heroes have customarily run to men of large accomplishments. But today this college and country honors a man whose contribution was not to our size but to our spirit, not to our political beliefs but to our insight, not to our self-esteem, but to our self-comprehension. In honoring Robert Frost, we therefore can pay honor to the deepest sources of our national strength."

He then stated his major premise:

> [Those] who create power make an indispensable contribution
> to the nation's greatness, but [those] who question power make

a contribution just as indispensable, especially when disinterested, for they determine whether we use power or power uses us.

The president proceeded to explore why the life and work of Robert Frost exemplified such independent questioning:

> At bottom, he held a deep faith in the spirit of man, and it's hardly an accident that Robert Frost coupled poetry and power, for he saw poetry as the means of saving power from itself.

The president then "deepened," as Frost so often had advised, this premise: "When power corrupts, poetry cleanses. For art establishes the basic human truths which must serve as the touchstone of our judgment."

"The artist," the president continued, "however faithful to his personal vision of reality, …has, as Frost said, a lover's quarrel with the world. In pursuing his perceptions of reality, he must often sail against the currents of his time. The artist's fidelity has strengthened the fiber of our national life…

The president summed up his view of poetry and power: "In serving his vision of the truth, the artist best serves his nation."

Kennedy then turned to the role of art in American life and spirit:

> …the nation which disdains the mission of art invites the fate of Robert Frost's hired man, the fate of having nothing to look backward to with pride and nothing to look forward to with hope.

And offered his alternative vision:

> …I look forward to an America which commands respect throughout the world not only for its strength but for its civilization as well.

Then concluded by honoring Frost with his personal eulogy: "Robert Frost was often skeptical about projects for human improvement, yet I do not think he would disdain this hope. As he wrote during the uncertain days of the Second War:

Take human nature altogether since time began,
And it must be a little more in favor of man,
Say a fraction of one per cent at the very least,
[Or] Our hold on the planet wouldn't have so increased.

Because of Mr. Frost's life and work…our hold on this planet has increased."

Robert Frost had realized the hope he shared with Michigan's President Burton. The poet had become that "rarest type of personality," a creative artist who saw "visions and dream[ed] dreams, who…actually produc[ed] the results which influence[d] the thought of nations."

THEN: WITNESS AT THE WHITE HOUSE, 1993-1997

In January 1993, one of my many former mentees, Gene Sperling, called me to join him on the staff of President Clinton's newly established National Economic Council (NEC). In March, I escaped the "sixteen-hours per day, seven days a week" schedule to visit my daughter Kate in Boston. An Amherst alumna, she was taking pre-med courses in Boston in pursuit of a neuroscience career. We explored the JFK Presidential Library and Museum. At the end of the exhibit with President Kennedy's most memorable speeches, we stopped to see and hear his eulogy for Frost. As we entered the gift shop at the end of the tour, she saw a large, thirty-by-twenty-inch black-and-white poster of the president sitting relaxed in an easy chair, suit coat unbuttoned, right elbow crooked, fingers extending to his temple. "JOHN F. KENNEDY" appeared in big bold letters below. Above the photo, six lines of fine print appeared. We had to walk right up to the poster to read "J. F. K. Amherst College, October 26, 1963" and the key quote on the role of "those who question power…For they determine whether we use power or power uses us."

I bought the poster and had it framed. For the next four and half years, it hung on the wall of my large office in the Old Executive Office Building. The image of JFK became the focal point for every person upon first entering the room. Without exception, each was drawn to this poster and then couldn't resist moving close up to read the fine print. The reactions ranged from shakes of the head with a nervous laugh of self-recognition from the bigger egos to nods with a wry smile from those who had a broader perspective. But even the biggest know-it-alls couldn't help lowering their voices and having second thoughts whenever I nodded toward the poster rather than argue a point.

One morning four years later, I took offense when the NEC principals decided to reject proposing a self-financing Lifelong Learning Trust Fund for all. They chose instead to expand a series of separate and incremental spending outlays and tax incentives to help pay tuition and related expenses. Seething at what I considered a self-inflicted loss of a signature legacy for the president and all Americans for generations to come, I returned to my office. I walked up close to the poster and pondered President Kennedy's reminder. And I realized I had become so certain about my grander proposal that I no longer cared to listen to those who raised questions, suggested limits, or proposed alternatives. That evening, I told NEC Director Sperling why it was time for me to go back home to Ann Arbor. At his request, I agreed to stay through the summer to help with what became the 1997 Balanced Budget Act. Later, I would look back, perhaps with too much pride, at a good run. But that fall, I returned home to my family duties and looked forward with hope to new opportunities.

TODAY

On the centennial of President Kennedy's birth and of Amherst College first hiring Robert Frost, it's an appropriate time to take stock of the continuing import of Frost's legacy and of President Kennedy's last major address honoring the poet.

First, with the possible exception of Maya Angelou I doubt there is an

American poet since Robert Frost who has so "influence[d] the thought of nations." But many other creative artists—novelists, filmmakers, screenwriters, playwrights, directors, singer-songwriters—surely have. Yet poetry is far from dead. Its brevity may once again be appreciated as the soul of wit, whether told at a high-pitched slant like Emily Dickinson or with the just as penetrating "pangs," as Frost liked to call his gentler twists of deeper meaning. After all, *Hamilton* is a fantastic American musical in verse. And from the tens of thousands of youth who say their poems or sing their rap at poetry slams, who's to say that another poet, playwright, or singer-songwriter won't grow to create new poems with more influence on the thought of nations than Frost, Shakespeare, or, according to the Nobel Prize Committee for Literature, Dylan?

Second, I can report with increased confidence on another matter that brought Frost and Burton together in common cause in 1921. They shared a revolutionary vision "for keeping the creative and the erudite together in education where they belong; and [where the creative can also] make its demand on the young student." A funny thing happened about this creative demand *on* students over the past two generations. It has grown instead into a rising demand *from* students to create, "to write, write, write" as Frost so often encouraged, to learn by doing. And this student demand has spread to other departments and colleges from architecture to engineering, from music to the sciences, from business to medicine. The academics may still rule most faculty roosts, but the artists, creators, inventors and discoverers now cut a wide swath on most campuses. Ironically, in the canon of the academics who teach literature, Robert Frost is the American poet most read, studied, and analyzed.

Third, since JFK, no president has combined poetry and prose so well and spoken his prose with such poetic resonance. Reagan, a former actor, and Obama, an ex-teacher and preacher, occasionally soared higher, but never with the same crisp analysis, sharp wit, and care for words, both told at a slant and spoken with such a pang, as Kennedy.

In his inaugural address, Kennedy offered parallel admonitions on national security and foreign policy, two principles that all his predecessors and successors since World War II eventually learned while in office.

First, with respect to our allies, "Divided there is little we can do [, and] we dare not meet a powerful challenge at odds and split asunder." Rather than denigrate our democratic allies, now numbering in the billions, who have *elected* to live in freedom and democracy since World War II, we must civilly resolve our differences.

Second, with respect to the adversaries of democracy and liberty, "Let us never negotiate out of fear. But let us never fear to negotiate," particularly from a position of military, economic and, yes, moral strength. Rather than appease the autocrats who rule Russia and China, we must never "tempt them with [such] weakness." Through strength, surely, we can forge "a beachhead of cooperation" between the autocrats and our democratic allies to defend all of us against the common threats of terrorist attack and degradation of the global environment.

Presidents have made the mistake of ignoring these twin pillars of our bipartisan national security and foreign policy. Notably, Kennedy did so in his first year of confrontation with Khrushchev, and George W. Bush and Barack Obama each did so early in his dealings with Putin.

In saying "The Gift Outright" at JFK's Inauguration, Frost proclaimed the blessings of and duties owed to this land of ours, "Such as she was, such as she *would* become, *has* become, and for this occasion…such as she *will* become." President Kennedy's words in his final address honoring Robert Frost, still speak truth to power:

> When power leads man towards arrogance, poetry reminds him of his limitations. When power narrows the areas of man's concern, poetry reminds him of the richness and diversity of his existence. When power corrupts, poetry cleanses.

And deeds can speak louder than words, for as Robert Frost noted in accepting his first fellowship at Michigan, it's "always…about" creating "definite deeds to be growing," including in the highest office in our land. We turn to the words of Frost and Kennedy to rekindle our resolve to act, and not to leave our nation to the fate of Frost's hired hand that JFK warned of in his eulogy for the poet,

"the fate of having nothing to look backward to with pride and nothing to look forward to with hope."

1. Robert Frost, photo by Yousuf Karsh.
   Copyright by Yousuf Karsh; with permission of the Robert Frost Estate.

2. JFK presenting the Congressional Gold Medal to Robert Frost for his contribution to American letters, March 26, 1962.
AP photo with permission and with permission of the Robert Frost Estate.

3. *Amherst Student*, October 26, 1963. Courtesy of the Amherst College Archives and Special Collections, Amherst College Library.

CONVOCATION   SPECIAL

Amherst Student

ESTABLISHED IN 1868

VOL. XCIII, NO. 11   AMHERST, MASS., SATURDAY, OCTOBER 26, 1963   TEN CENTS

KENNEDY GIVEN HONORARY LLD, ENVISIONS A FUTURE AMERICA

President Hails Artist As Vital to Nation

by Dave Kirp

Saturday, Oct. 26—Addressing a special convocation of Amherst College, President John F. Kennedy today called for "an America which will reward achievement in art as well as achievement in business."

Twenty seven hundred people jammed the Cage to hear the President, and to witness the awarding of Honorary Doctors of Law degrees to the President and to poet Archibald MacLeish. Fifteen hundred more students and alumni filled the Alumni Gymnasium and Kirby Theater to watch the ceremonies on television.

The President praised Amherst for the recognition of its obligation to serve not only private interest but the public interest as well. "What good is a private college unless it serves a great national purpose?" he said.

"The problems we face are staggering," the President went on. We need the service of every educated man."

President John F. Kennedy addresses standing-room-only crowd at Convocation in Cage. John J. McCoy '16, Trustee Chairman, listens at right.
—*Photos by DeLeon*

Kennedy called Robert Frost, "one of the great figures of our time, an artist and an American." His efforts prove that there are contributions to be made to the spirit of the

For text of Kennedy address, see page 5.

land as well as to our size. The real source of our strength," said Kennedy, "is our spirit."

The President went on to stress the role of art in establishing the basic human truths. Art is he said, "the last champion of the independent mind." Our nation has fallen short of its highest potential, and it is the task of the artist, ever true to himself, to point out where we have gone wrong.

Convocation—'The Birth of Memory'

President Calvin H. Plimpton introduced both Kennedy and MacLeish. He spoke of the gathering as "really the birth of memory . . . We too will tell our grandchild of this day . . ." Plimpton also stressed that the college in serving the public in-

Amherst Men Break Library Ground
J.F.K. Praises Frost for Toughness

by Ned Lyle

Saturday, Oct. 26—Shortly after one o'clock today, with the sun out and the heavy morning mist gone, ground was broken for the Robert Frost Library by President Plimpton and six Amherst men whose classes ranged from '16 to '64. President Plimpton and six Amherst men whose classes ranged from '16 to '64. President Kennedy gave a brief address at the twenty-minute ceremony, but preferred to leave the spadework to the other seven.

The official groundbreakers thus were John J. McCoy '16 (Chairman of the Board of Trustees), C. Scott Porter '19 (Dean of the College), Leonard P. Moore '19 (President of the Alumni Society), Newton F. McKeon '26 (College Librarian), Harry

Plimpton wields first shovel in Frost Library ground-breaking.

Smiling President mixes with spectators on way to ceremony.

Plimpton Calls Day A "Lustrous" Event, And Memory's Birth

In his speech at the Convocation ceremony this morning, President Plimpton attempted to locate the significance of today's events.

He began by citing President Abraham Lincoln's Gettysburg Address as an example of how wrongly speakers have estimated the significance of important assemblies in the past. Lincoln declared that speeches delivered at Gettysburg would soon fade from memory, but that the sacrifice which had been made there would never be forgotten.

Turning to the Amherst Convoca-

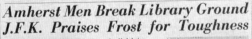

4. JFK's helicopter at Amherst College.
   Courtesy of the Amherst College Archives and Special Collections, Amherst College Library.

5. Amherst President Calvin Plimpton, JFK, and J. Alfred Guest.
   Courtesy of the Amherst College Archives and Special Collections, Amherst College Library.
   Photo by Pat DeLeon.

6. Civil rights vigil during Kennedy's visit.
   Courtesy of the Amherst College Archives and Special Collections, Amherst College Library.

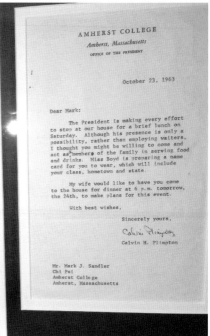

AMHERST COLLEGE
Amherst, Massachusetts
OFFICE OF THE PRESIDENT

October 23, 1963

Dear Mark:

The President is making every effort to stop at our house for a brief lunch on Saturday. Although his presence is only a possibility, rather than employing waiters, I thought you might be willing to come and act as members of the family in serving food and drinks. Miss Boyd is preparing a name card for you to wear, which will include your class, hometown and state.

My wife would like to have you come to the house for dinner at 6 p.m. tomorrow, the 24th, to make plans for this event.

With best wishes,

Sincerely yours,

Calvin Plimpton

Calvin H. Plimpton

Mr. Mark J. Sandler
Chi Psi
Amherst College
Amherst, Massachusetts

7. JFK on the dais before his speech.
   Courtesy of the Amherst College Archives and Special Collections, Amherst College Library.

8. JFK and Archibald MacLeish.
   Courtesy of the Amherst College Archives and Special Collections, Amherst College Library. Photo by Pat DeLeon.

9. Amherst President Plimpton and JFK in open car.
   Courtesy of the Amherst College Archives and Special Collections, Amherst College Library.

10. JFK and President Plimpton; Mark Sandler's framed invitation.
    Courtesy of the Amherst College Archives and Special Collections, Amherst College Library.

11. JFK delivering "The Last Speech."
    Courtesy of the Amherst College Archives and Special Collections, Amherst College Library.

12. Robert Frost at the podium, "Saying" his poems.
    Courtesy of University of Arizona Libraries, Stewart L. Udall papers, az 372, box 372; with permission of the Robert Frost Estate.

13. Robert Frost with Premier Khrushchev.
    Courtesy of University of Arizona Libraries, Stewart L. Udall papers, az 372, box 105; with permission of the Robert Frost Estate.

14. Ted Nelson on the job in Turkey.
    Courtesy of Ted Nelson's personal collection. Photo by Deborah Clancy.

15. Ted Nelson at home in Flint.
Courtesy of Northern Light
Productions, *JFK: The Last Speech*.

16. Steve Downs with the Peace Corps
in India.
Courtesy of Steve Downs' personal
collection and Northern Light
Productions, *JFK: The Last Speech*.

17. Steve Downs in Albany.
Courtesy of Northern Light
Productions, *JFK: The Last Speech*.

18. The Palumbo wedding.
    Courtesy of Gene Palumbo's personal
    collection. Photo by Ellen Calmus.

19. Gene Palumbo with students in
    El Salvador.
    Courtesy of Northern Light
    Productions, *JFK: The Last Speech*.

20. George Wanlass with young art
    student.
    Courtesy of Northern Light
    Productions, *JFK: The Last Speech*.

12

A LOVER'S QUARREL

The events of October 26, 1963 celebrated Robert Frost's life and work. Appreciating that celebration, like appreciating Frost's poetry, demands that readers follow Frost's admonition to "go deeper." In this chapter, Jay Parini—the poet's acclaimed biographer—David Stringer—a secondary school English teacher—and Brad Collins—an art historian, take us deeper into Frost's work, the challenge of teaching poetry, and the impact of the Enlightenment on visual art. Each essay illustrates a facet of the interplay of art and culture.

Robert Frost and the Nature of New England

Jay Parini

I'VE BEEN THINKING about Robert Frost and his poetry for half a century and wrote a biography of him in 1999, a book that was twenty-five years in the making. Frost has haunted me my whole life. I've lived in his footsteps, teaching at Dartmouth for a while, then (mostly) at Middlebury. I often take walks in the woods behind his cabin in Ripton, Vermont, and his language fills my head and heart. When I look out from the steps of the cabin at the hills behind, I often say to myself the lines from "Out, Out—": "Five mountains ranges one behind the other / Under the sunset far into Vermont."

Ralph Waldo Emerson said, "Nature is the symbol of spirit," and I think part of Frost's achievement was to find the correspondences between the spiritual and physical world. His nature is spiritual in its depth, with its symbolic resonances. Whatever season he writes about, it seems like a season of the soul; there is a perfect Frost poem for almost anytime of year. "Two Tramps in Mud-Time," for example, is the perfect poem for spring, as when he writes:

You know how it is with an April day
When the sun is out and the wind is still,
You're one month on in the middle of May.
But if you so much as dare to speak,
A cloud comes over the sunlit arch,

A wind comes off a frozen peak,
And you're two months back in the middle of March.

Frost was deeply Emersonian, and he came by this affiliation honestly: his mother—Belle Moody Frost—was a devout Swedenborgian, and Emanuel Swedenborg himself was the eighteenth century Swedish scientist and philosopher who studied and revealed the correspondences between spirit and nature. He looked for instances in nature that could allow for an entry into a larger whole, as in the figure of speech called synecdoche, where the part stands in for the whole. Not surprisingly, quite early in his career, Frost came to regard synecdoche as essential to his craft. "I started calling myself a synecdochist when other poets starting calling themselves imagists or vorticists," he said.

Synecdoche allows one part of something to stand in for a larger or more general concept, so that one natural image leads us toward the whole of nature. And it's important to make the connection here between synecdoche and metaphor, as they remain so closely related. A metaphor is often a symbol, of course, and symbolic thought involves synecdoche: you allow the part to imply or gesture toward something beyond it, to lead us into a wider arena of thought and feeling.

Needless to say, poetic thought is metaphorical thinking. The poet names something, and it implies other things; comparisons are made, however explicit or inexplicit. In "Education by Poetry," which I take to be Frost's most complete essay on poetics, he writes: "Poetry begins in trivial metaphors, pretty metaphors, 'grace' metaphors, and goes on to the profoundest thinking that we have. Poetry provides the one permissible way of saying one thing and meaning another. People say, 'Why don't you say what you mean?' We never do that, do we, being all of us too much poets? We like to talk in parables and in hints and in indirections—whether from diffidence or some other instinct."

It is, I would suggest, these "hints and indirections" that lie at the heart of Frost's poetry. He says one thing, meaning another. He leads us one way while asking us to understand that another way exists, that there is a tension, a troubling double-consciousness that will never let one thing rest alone, that is always leading us astray or, ideally, saving us.

Frost continues: "I have wanted in late years to go further and further into making metaphor the whole of thinking." He notes that scientific and mathematical thought all depend heavily on metaphors; in this, he bridges the gap—he always did—between poetry and science. He was, at heart, a naturalist, and his examination of the natural world as an early ecologist, was profound and particular.

When I came to Middlebury, in the early eighties, I got to know Reginald Cook, who had taught American literature for decades and was a good friend of Frost. They often took long hikes together in the Green Mountains. Once they began a hike on the Long Trail, on Bread Loaf Mountain, and they had not managed to get very far when Frost yelled ahead: "Hey, stop. Come here!" He led Cook to a tree where he found a peculiar green mold growing at the base of the trunk. Frost studied it for a while, but was unable to identify the mold. He cut off a slice, put the sample into his handkerchief, then insisted on heading straight to the college library, where he knew there was a good book about molds. The point is that he wanted this kind of *particular* knowledge.

In fact, Frost had a more detailed sense of the natural world than almost any other major poet, including Wordsworth. He named particular trees, plants, and shrubs. He understood the disposition of pastureland and town. In "Directive," for example—one of his most ambitious and intellectually rich poems—he demonstrated a remarkable grasp of geological formations.

This knowledge came from reading as well as close observation. Frost always read deeply in science, with a particular interest in geology and botany. But he also discovered a good deal of what he knew about the natural world from his hikes, his habitual walking in the woods. Like Emerson, he may well have felt free in the woods, and young. Whether on the farms in Derry or Laconia, or walking in the lush countryside near Amherst College, where he taught for many decades, or trooping over Bread Loaf Mountain in Vermont, he was always looking as well as measuring himself against the natural world.

His poems, quite often, feature a man walking out in the woods by himself. "The Wood-Pile," for instance, might be taken as the archetype of such a "walking out" poem, where a man walks into a swamp and discovers a cord of wood, which someone had put up and left to decay for unknown reasons. He contemplates the "slow, smokeless burning of decay" that seems inevitably part of the natural process. Reading Frost, one discovers the pattern repeated again and again: the solitary walker who confronts the nature of nature in New England firsthand and comes to understand something about the world, of nature and of spirit, by firsthand observation.

In his seminal essay, "The Poet," Emerson wrote that "the world is a temple whose walls are covered with emblems, pictures and commandments of the Deity—in this, that there is no fact in nature which does not carry the whole sense of nature; and the distinctions which we make in events and in affairs, of low and high, honest and base, disappear when nature is used as a symbol."

Once again, we enter the realm of synecdoche: the poet reads the natural world, gleans images, intuits their connection to large realities. Emerson wrote: "As the limestone of the continent consists of infinite masses of the shells of animalcules, so language is made up of images, or tropes, which now…have long cease to remind us of their poetic origin. But the poet names the thing because he sees it, or comes one step nearer to it than any other."

One might look at a poem by Frost that seems almost purposefully designed to illumine the nature of synecdoche in actual operation. Here is "Fragmentary Blue," a brief lyric:

Why make so much of fragmentary blue
In here and there a bird, or butterfly,
Or flower, or wearing-stone, or open eye,
When heaven presents in sheets the solid hue?

Since earth is earth, perhaps, not heaven (as yet)
Though some savants make earth include the sky;

And blue so far above us come so high
It only gives our wish for blue a whet.

The poem invites us to think in a synecdochal fashion. Why make a great deal of fuss over blue in bits and pieces—in a bluebird or perhaps a butterfly or some blue flower, a cornflower or heal-all, perhaps, by the side of the road? Why startle at the blue in a sapphire that someone might wear on a necklace? Why tremble before the alluring azure shimmer of an eye? Why get excited by these fragments when the sky itself unreels sheets and sheets of the stuff: cerulean blue heaped upon blue?

Now comes the particular Frost-ian turn, and one that separates him from Emerson. It comes in that second stanza, in the opening lines: "Since earth is earth, perhaps, not heaven (as yet) / Though some savants make earth include the sky." Earth is earth. This echoes the famous line in "Birches"—"Earth's the right place for love." The boy in "Birches" was actually in no mood to climb that tree right up to heaven; he didn't want to be swept away, not yet; he was still one of the living. Frost put breaks on the transcendentalist wish to fly away, to feel the currents of Universal Being circulate through his veins. But "wait a moment," says Frost, "this is not *yet* heaven."

Frost's mother may have been a devout Swedenborgian; he came by the transcendentalist impulse honestly. But his father, Will Prescott Frost, was no transcendentalist—not by a long shot. He was a tough newspaper man, a religious skeptic, an ironist to the core. And so Frost—as poet, if not as human being—felt the tug from above and below. He notes in "Fragmentary Blue" that the sky is "so high" that it "only gives our wish for blue a whet." That is, we are tempted to fly off into the heavens, as in "Birches," but it's so high, so far from earth. As it were, the living must trod the earth. "Earth's the right place for love. / I don't know where it's likely to go better."

Frost was always a poet of subtle transformations, seeing the cycles of nature as inevitably wearing but also provocative. While we live on earth, this is the right place for love, and we are never quite in the Garden of Eden. *That* is for heaven. We inhabit a fallen world: in this, Frost hardly veered from the standard Christian idea of original sin. Think of that lovely brief lyric: "Nothing Gold Can Stay":

> Nature's first green is gold,
> Her hardest hue to hold.
> Her early leaf's a flower;
> But only so an hour.
> Then leaf subsides to leaf.
> So Eden sank to grief,
> So dawn goes down to day.
> Nothing gold can stay.

This is a poem about the cycles of nature, and it has a lot to say about the role that nature plays in the life of the spirit. Nature gives us gold in spring, in the flower of an early leaf: it's a point of acute and particular observation. Frost—that walker in the woods—knows whereof he speaks. The reader, too, will be struck by the stunning clarity and surprise of this line, where Frost says "gold," not "yellow." Gold is more symbolic than yellow, with its connotations of heavenly reward. There is the "gold standard" in economics. The stock market may crumble; but the price of gold remains fairly steady. Whatever else happens, an ounce of gold is worth roughly what a fairly expensive man's suit will cost. It's reliable. Yet nature won't hang onto this value; the gold fades in an hour.

Of course this term itself is extremely loose: "only so an hour" is a synecdochal ter; it means a short while. Soon the process of transformation occurs, as "leaf subsides to leaf." This becomes symbolic, too, associated with Eden, which "sank to grief" when Adam and Eve allowed themselves to partake of the Tree of the Knowledge of Good and Evil. You must not want to know so much; but poets want to know. The poet is always the serpent in the garden, whispering in the ear of the reader, tempting curious Adams and curious Eves. Time slips by, as dawn "goes down" to day. Has anyone before Frost ever used that verbal sequence in this context? Does one "go down" from dawn to day?

Daylight is full knowledge. It is the wide perspective of the poet of full consciousness. One could celebrate this knowledge, but Frost framed the poem with the image of gold once again. Nothing gold can stay—not on this earth, not in our time.

Frost often cycled through the tingling transformation of seasons, reading the changes as metaphors with a deeply spiritual eye. Not surprisingly, many of his poems begin in spring, always a favorite season of poets. The first poem in *West-Running Brook* is "Spring Pools," Frost's ultimate statement on this season that so appealed to him, as it wavers between the deathly aura of winter and summer's fullness. It's the season of resurrection, too: the Easter season. Here is the poem, one of Frost's best:

> These pools that, though in forest, still reflect
> The total sky almost without defect,
> And like the flowers beside them, chill and shiver,
> Will like the flowers beside them soon be gone,
> And yet not out by any brook or river,
> But up by roots to bring dark foliage on.
>
> The trees that have it in their pent-up buds
> To darken nature and be summer woods—
> Let them think twice before they use their powers
> To blot out and drink up and sweep away
> These flowery waters and these watery flowers
> From snow that melted only yesterday.

The pool is a natural symbol for mind, often invoked by poets from Milton and Wordsworth to Seamus Heaney and Mary Oliver. But it's a complex idea, the mirror of the mind, one that has roots in Platonic philosophy. Richard Rorty, one of our shrewdest of recent philosophers, traces the lineage of this idea in *Philosophy and the Mirror Nature* (1979). It's a problematic symbol, as Rorty noted, but one that seems impossible to get around. In Frost's poem, the pools in the forest reflect a perfect, a "total sky." The idea of a total sky is intriguing: it anticipates the sheets of reeling blue sky in "Fragmentary Blue." It's also an image of heaven, a changeless world, beyond mutability.

But we're still on earth in this poem. Nothing gold can stay here, and nothing blue can stay either. The trees' invisible roots will mop up these reflecting pools; the process of "birth, and copulation, and death," a phrase from T. S. Eliot, goes on and on; the sucking up of the pools by the trees is itself synecdochal; it represents the dark side of transformation, as the water is sucked away. Dryness or bareness come about—on the ground, shadowed by the "dark foliage" of the leaves, which represent a new version of the pools. This is transmogrification: the magical transformation of one substance or form into another.

Now Frost is never afraid to anthropomorphize, and so we hear about these "pent-up buds" that have in their mysterious powers to "darken nature and be summer woods." Pent-up? Everything in nature is pent-up, yearning to become something else. Every moment in the life of any human being leans into the moment that breaks just ahead. But Frost ended with a wry warning, asking the trees to "think twice" before they perform an act of alchemy, turning "flowery waters" and "watery flowers" into dark foliage. The transformation, to a degree, involves loss: loss of brilliance, loss of image, loss of the mind's reflective powers. Only yesterday the snow melted, and now we're moving rapidly toward summer. But as we know from Shakespeare's "Sonnet 18," even "summer's lease hath all too short a date."

Now the problem of summer's short lease is dealt with handily by Frost in "Hyla Brook," one of his most intriguing early poems, from *Mountain Interval*. The poet considers other ways that water—always a symbol of life—is lost or transmogrified. This poem, like so many of Frost's poems, is really about writing, about the loss of imaginative powers. The brook represents the creative spirit, and by June it has "run out of song and speed." You go looking for this brook too long after June and you will find it either sucked up and transformed into jewel-weed, with its "weak foliage," or gone underground. Frost, as a naturalist, knew that brooks do not just disappear; they go underground. Again, there are literal and metaphorical layers here, all working together quite brilliantly. The dry bed of the brook becomes "a faded paper sheet," the sheet the poet works on, that shows a lack of energy, refusing to yield a poem. But perhaps the poem goes merely underground, into the unconscious, to resurface at a later date. The song cannot be stopped, only diverted. Life—in this poem—is perpetual motion, translation, reinvention.

Frost wrote so many good summer poems that it's hard to know where to begin when thinking about them. I love "The Oven Bird," an affecting lyric about this "singer everyone has heard / Loud, a mid-summer and a mid-wood bird." In many ways, Frost was a mid-summer and a mid-wood singer at heart. But even here he recalls "that other fall we name the fall." The question Frost asked again and again in poems, openly and covertly, is "what to make of a diminished thing."

And so we come to autumn—any poet's prime season, perhaps, as alluring as spring as a source of metaphors. Frost's version of Keats' magnificent "Ode to Autumn" is "After Apple-Picking," which lies at the center of *North of Boston*. The synecdochal work here is that of picking apples, putting them away for later use; it represents the work of picking poems from the tree of inspiration, choosing just the best ones to "Cherish in hand, lift down, and not let fall." These apples are the fruits of summer, the fruits of creativity at its peak. One must carefully harvest them, treasure them. But it seems exhausting work: the summery world offers so much to pick: "There were ten thousand thousand fruit to touch."

Frost once again noted that he's on the ladder *toward* heaven, that it's sticking through the treetops, gesturing toward heaven still, but there is no sense in which the poet is ready to climb all the way up into the sky. The boy in "Birches" doesn't want to do that, nor does our faithful apple-picker. But "After Apple-Picking" is mysterious in its gnarled plotline. The poet can't rub the strangeness from his sight; he's in a stupor, a dream. "Magnified apples appear and disappear / Stem end and blossom end / And every fleck of russet showing clear." The speaker is drunk on the harvest, confused, ready to die of exhaustion. Or just go to sleep, "This sleep of mine, whatever sleep it is."

He may go into hibernation now as "Essence of winter sleep is on the night."

Every season gestures to the season before it, but also points toward the season to come. And so winter is coming on.

Frost wrote vividly about winter too. It's hard to imagine better poems of this season than "An Old Man's Winter Night," "Dust of Snow," "Stopping by Woods on a Snowy Evening," "Looking for a Sunset Bird in Winter," or "Desert Places." This is, of course, the season of death and forgetting. It's the season of doom and darkness. But it's also the cradle of spring. Soon the underground streams will gather force, the snow will melt, the spirit yield to the "watery flowers" and the "flowery waters."

I would note here the little poem "A Patch of Old Snow." Frost writes:

There's a patch of old snow in a corner
That I should have guessed
Was a blow-away paper the rain
Had brought to rest.

It is speckled with grime as if
The small print overspread it,
The news of a day I've forgotten—
If I ever read it.

Poetry is "news that stays news," said Ezra Pound. But this patch of old snow is not poetry. It's speckled with grime like newsprint. One quickly forgets the previous season, which hangs on in remnants, fragments, bits and pieces of blown paper.

Frost celebrated the recovery of life in poem after poem, such as "A Hillside Thaw," where he talks about "The hillside on a day the sun lets go / Ten million silver lizards out of snow!" Here as elsewhere Frost meditates on natural cycles, walks into the woods and finds emblems of spirit. He looks for spirit in nature, and nature in spirit. He teased and questioned. He interrogated images.

He remains, however, a solitary figure. "Men work alone," he writes in "The Strong Are Saying Nothing," "their lots plowed far apart." He plows his own poetry and imaginative lot, stands, observes the passing seasons, finds synecdochal images in those seasons. And refuses to yield to final answers, or lift off into the heavenly skies. "There may be little or much beyond the grave," he says, "But the strong are saying nothing until they see."

"All Revelation" remains one of my favorite (although lesser known) poems by Frost: a perfect coda to the idea of nature as symbol of spirit, and another example of synecdoche at work, what Frost wonderfully called "skirting the hem of nature's garment." It goes—

Eyes seeking the response of eyes
Bring out the stars, bring out the flowers,
Thus concentrating earth and skies
So none need be afraid of size.
All revelation has been ours.

Frost was, and remains, America's great poet of nature, especially the nature of New England. He was one of our most singular and striking voices. The complexity of his thought, coupled with the granular weight of his language, draw us back to his poetry again and again. It's easy to underestimate Frost, as the lines themselves are both fetching and, as poetic language, quite simple. His simplicity is deceptive, and as one follows this poet through the woods, looking and listening beside him, watching the many transformations he described so well, one is lifted by him into the realms of spirit. He was, I think, a spiritual master, and one of the most gifted teachers who ever lived and wrote.

Poetry, Power, and High School English

David Stringer, '64

I WAS A FIRST-YEAR TEACHER of creative writing in Ann Arbor, Michigan, when I first experienced the intersection of poetry, power, and high school English. On a lovely spring day, large lawnmowers were at work outside our third-floor windows. My students tore their eyes away from whatever I was doing, and one of them shouted, "They are killing the flowers!" Dandelions, yes, but flowers. This being the '60s, they dashed outside to throw their bodies on the lawn in front of the machines—before the eyes of half the school and, soon, my principal. It was a humbling experience, especially for me.

A second intersection followed several years later. After a snowfall, a student had taken it upon himself to trace the word "FUCK" in large letters on the soccer field, again in view of much of the school. The principal instructed his vice-principal to "do something." The vice-principal, with great creativity, transformed the offending word to "BOOK." One of my students memorialized the transformation in a poem titled, "The Four-Letter Word Talkin' Blues." He described a guy who traveled the country with a can of spray paint making similar transformations to graffiti from shore to shore. Eventually, the two words exchanged meanings. The poem provided several examples, and concluded with an arrest and the words, "Fuck him." I wish I still had the poem.

I made a career out of teaching English to high school students in Ann Arbor. Most of my students went on to become adults. When I closed the door to my classroom, we became a place with our own culture. I never knew for sure if I was the only one who felt that way. My approach to teaching poetry had nothing to do with the tedious stereotypes of the high school classroom: memorizing "figures of speech," counting syllables, learning the names of famous poets, and doing what is called "scanning" a poem. Neither did I want to see the reading of poetry to be an exercise in solving a puzzle for "deep hidden meanings," which we abbreviated DHMs. No, I wanted to find ways to show my students that poems could speak to them, grounding them in real human experience and at the same time expanding their worlds.

In eleventh grade American literature, we spent an hour on "The Road Not Taken." My plan was to imitate Frost, to teach by misdirection. After reading the poem aloud a couple of times, we quickly moved to exploring the way our choices, sometimes unknowingly, can make a huge difference in life. Where you sit in this classroom, and who sits next to you, might lead to your choice of a marriage partner. Where you go to college—Michigan or Michigan State?—might lead to your choice of career. What you had for breakfast before your ACT exam might lead to what college decides to admit you. After wallowing in that pseudo-philosophy for a while, we turned back to the poem. Frost made it clear that the two roads were worn "about the same, / And both that morning equally lay." The difference is not in one road or the alternative, but in the different, and hidden, futures each one offered. What "had made all the difference" was the speaker's mindset, his insistence on venturing on "the one less traveled by." The difference is within *him* (or her, by which I meant *you*). Once I hammered that point at them for a while, I'd ask them to write about what they looked for in the road of their choice and what that showed about their character. I wanted them to see and feel that they were a part of history and a part of ongoing humanity.

A part of history? For many high school kids, their sense of the future extended to 3 p.m., to Friday night, or maybe to summer. The past had a similarly short scope. I tried to teach poetry as a way to get beyond that, a way to confront some essential truths:

— We die: Including friends and loved ones. "Spring and Fall: To a Young Child," "Janet Waking," "Because I Could Not Stop For Death," "We Real Cool."

— Love endures: "Valediction: Forbidding Mourning," "Those Winter Sundays."

— We live in a world of horrors—so? "Dover Beach," "The World Is Too Much with Us."

— We live in a beautiful world: "The Red Wheelbarrow," "Fern Hill."

— We are part of something immeasurably large: "The Book of Job," "It Is a Beauteous Evening."

— We are confronted with difficult choices: "Traveling Through the Dark," "To Be, or Not to Be."

— Character matters: "Invictus," "The Road Not Taken."

— It is good to question your values and assumptions, to be uncomfortable: "The Book of Job," "The Tyger."

Read the suggested poems, or perhaps your own favorites, to see how far the language of my list falls short of the power of each poem's voice. Each poem has concrete specificity embodied in a voice, and that voice is a large part of the "meaning" of the poem, by which I mean its power.

High school students have difficulty with a poem's "meaning." They often mistake the meaning with a lame generalization, like mine above. Far too often, I've heard a student begin a sentence with, "What this poem is trying to say is…"

Trying, alas, but handicapped by being a poet, the author could not say it directly or clearly.

No, the voice a poem creates brings it to life. That life-force, created by rhythms, line-breaks, and the music of its sounds, *is* the poem's meaning. Blake's "The Tyger" would not be the same without the chant-like voice "Tyger Tyger, burning bright"; nor would Thomas's "Fern Hill" sing its meaning without its musical language, "My wishes raced through the house high hay"; nor would Stafford's "Traveling Through the Dark" exercise its subtle power without its off-rhymes: road/dead, killing/belly, engine/listen; nor would Brooks' "We Real Cool" work its music without the syncopation created by line and stanza breaks ("We / Thin gin. We / Jazz June. We / Die soon.").

I would occasionally make this point by trashing a poem, by changing the language of a poem to destroy its magic. "It is a beauteous evening, calm—free also." Or, "I took the one less traveled by / And it was a really big deal." Or, "We real cool. / We left school." We then compared the trashed version with the original. Students enjoyed this exercise, especially the trashing. The relationship between voice and meaning became clearer, and though I did not use the word "power" in our discussions, I believe the point was felt if not made explicitly. "Power" is a word with connotations that, for most teenagers (and politicians), do not apply readily to poetry.

What does this have to do with leveraging social and political power? A lot, and perhaps not much. To my knowledge, none of my students has become president, but that's not entirely my fault. I do recall, however, one girl whose ambition was to become president of Bangladesh. Poetry shows us alternatives to a focus on wealth and power. In a sense, it presents an antidote ("Ozymandias"). Humility has its own power. We can exercise that power through the choices we make, choosing who gets our vote, yes, but also where we shop, what we buy, where we spend our time, how we speak to other people, how we communicate in ways other than speaking. Poetry in the classroom offers a springboard to the exercise of power, preferable to saving the dandelions or upsetting the principal. Language matters.

Let me offer an example. I taught William Carlos Williams' "The Red Wheelbarrow" by presenting the poem on the blackboard, one stanza at a time, skipping the first stanza. I asked the class what the poet noticed. We examined "glazed with rain / water" and how placing the wheelbarrow "beside the white / chickens" is different from describing the chickens as beside the wheelbarrow. Then I would reveal the opening stanza, "so much depends / upon." Suddenly the poem, they would say, is "about the economics of farming." If it's important, the students felt, it must be about money, not beauty. We had more to discuss.

When I introduced my high school seniors to modern poetry, Robert Frost played a direct part in my teaching. I used the language of Frost's "The Oven Bird" to introduce three major modern themes: "that other fall we name the fall," "in singing not to sing," and "what to make of a diminished thing." We discussed, and I illustrated, the view of the world as fallen, not only in the biblical sense but also with post-World War I disillusionment. I showed how the moderns found different ways to "sing," going beyond the regular rhymes and meters of most earlier poetry. And "what to make of a diminished thing" pointed away from moralizing, grandiosity, and romantic flights, directly to the red wheelbarrow.

So what, exactly, depends upon that red wheelbarrow?

The Cultural Implications of Post-1970 Art
The End of the Enlightenment?

Bradford R. Collins, '64

"I think of art as a Distant Early Warning system that can always be relied on to tell the old culture what is beginning to happen to it."
—Marshal McLuhan

AT OUR FIFTIETH class reunion in 2014, I spoke about the profound changes in the visual arts that have occurred since we graduated and what those changes tell us about shifts in Western culture. This subject bears directly on the central issue of President Kennedy's convocation address at the groundbreaking ceremony for the Robert Frost Library in 1963. In his speech, Kennedy compared Frost's skepticism about "projects for human improvement" with his own more sanguine view. Using a classical rhetorical device, anaphora, Kennedy made a series of projections on the future of America and the world, each of which began with the phrase, "I look forward to..." Kennedy expressed more than a personal conviction; he articulated the fundamental Enlightenment optimism that characterized the modern era up to that point. Although the eighteenth century carries the label of "the Enlightenment," that timeframe more accurately extends into the modern era, when the hopeful convictions about "man" and "his future" that developed in the eighteenth century became widely integrated into our collective thinking.

When Kennedy spoke at Amherst, this optimism was about to be tested by the seismic events of the 1960s, beginning with the assassination of the president himself. Those events raised serious doubt about the Enlightenment project and its prospects. The arts, particularly the visual arts, reflected the growing doubt. Those changes in the arts and their implications can be properly understood only in the larger context of the relationship between the Enlightenment and modern art. Given the space allotted me, this will necessarily involve my painting with a broad brush, but one can often see more from a wide perspective than from focusing on details and specifics. The panoramic view of Western art since the mid-1960s suggests a crisis of cultural values with potentially epochal dimensions; Kennedy's projections and the feelings they stirred in us in 1963 may now belong to another time.

The Enlightenment was the culmination of efforts begun by Renaissance Humanists, who turned away from medieval dogma and sought to better understand nature and mankind through reason and empiricism. In political and economic thought, the changes that began slowly took on increased volume and velocity from the late seventeenth century to the end of the eighteenth. The growing number of so-called *philosophes*, or practical philosophers, and their supporters did not agree on all matters, but what emerged from their debates was a new worldview concerning humans and their institutions. The consensus held that humans were rational and essentially good, which meant that they could be allowed their freedom. The most revolutionary element of the new worldview was the claim that the ultimate purpose of the individual life was not service to God or the State but to oneself. It naturally followed that the purpose of government was to serve its subjects. The result of this conceptual revolution was the pair of political revolutions that inaugurated the Modern era, the American in 1776 and the French in 1789.

These Enlightenment ideas about humanity developed in a synergistic relationship with the Scientific Revolution. In fact, the socio-political optimism of Enlightenment thinkers was ultimately grounded in the Scientific Revolution of the sixteenth and seventeenth centuries. As the growth of science demonstrated, nature operates by laws that are amenable to human understanding. What really excited the *philosophes* was the corollary: through understanding nature, humans can learn to control it for our collective betterment. In short, through the power of reason, humans can arrive at truths that will enable us to improve the quality of our lives. The result was twofold: first, the Industrial Revolution and somewhat later, the new human social sciences, such as psychology and sociology. The essence of this new worldview can be encapsulated in a single word: progress, the idea that human history will henceforth be the story of the gradual improvement in human existence, producing, in the words of Immanuel Kant, "Mankind's final coming of Age."

In the United States, the Enlightenment faith of our Founding Fathers in "life, liberty, and the pursuit of happiness" was strengthened over the next two centuries by the steady progress of industry and science. Even the horrors of the Civil War, the Great Depression of the 1930s, and the two world wars did little to shake Americans' fundamental optimism about human progress. As a result, there is little in American art before about 1970 to contradict it. Our landscape and figure paintings from the nineteenth to the mid-twentieth century constantly affirm the goodness of both nature and humanity. Much of our national art also celebrates scientific advancement and human ingenuity. Winslow Homer's *The Life Line* (1884) provides a nice example. Homer depicted a woman being rescued from a sinking ship via a newly developed device called a breeches buoy, a kind of zip line set up from ship to shore that can be automatically adjusted to changes in the former's movements. Homer covered the face of the male rescuer with the woman's scarf in order not to detract from the true hero of the piece, the breeches buoy, and its implications concerning the ability of humans to solve their problems.

In Europe, however, the artistic response to the Enlightenment was initially quite different, reflecting the events following the French Revolution, the Reign of Terror and the subsequent Napoleonic Wars. The impact of these events on early Enlightenment artists is most clearly seen in the work of the great Spanish Romantic, Francisco Goya. A member of a circle of Enlightenment advocates in Madrid at the end of the eighteenth century, Goya created a series of eighty aquatints and etchings published for public consumption in 1799 as *Los Caprichos*. His survey of the various superstitions and follies of contemporary Spanish society illustrated the monsters produced when Reason sleeps. Although Goya's hopes for awakening Reason survived the horrors of the Peninsular War (1807-14), they were completely quashed when Ferdinand VII became king in 1814. Ferdinand immediately revoked the constitution and reinstituted the Inquisition, one of Goya's chief targets in *Los Caprichos*. Goya most fully expressed his complete disillusionment with Enlightenment optimism in the utterly pessimistic scenes of the "Black Paintings" as they came to be called that he produced on the walls of his house in the early 1820s.

Elsewhere in Europe, doubts about Enlightenment assumptions were best expressed in the popular theme of the storm-tossed boat, a metaphor for the uncertainty of our individual and collective future. The most famous examples are probably Théodore Géricault's *The Raft of the Medusa* (1818-19) and J. M. W. Turner's *The Slave Ship* (1840). The latter painting was inspired by an actual incident in which the opportunistic captain of a slave ship headed into a typhoon threw his diseased and dying cargo overboard in hopes of collecting insurance, since only slaves lost at sea because of a storm qualified for reimbursement. The work not only contradicted the Enlightenment conviction that humans are basically good, but also the notion that nature was reasonable and benign.

By mid-century, skeptical voices had been largely quieted as a result of progressive developments, which included not only the steady abolishment of slavery from country to country but also, and more importantly, advances in science and industry as featured in the newly fashionable world's fairs. The most conspicuous of these developments was undoubtedly the rapid growth of railways. Before the invention of the airplane in the early twentieth century, the railroad was the foremost symbol for progress, both industrial and social. Trains were featured in countless paintings of the mid- to late century, both in the U.S. and Europe, including a series by Claude Monet in 1877 dedicated to the railway yard at the Gare Saint-Lazare in Paris.

The fullest artistic expression of Enlightenment faith, however, was in the period of modern art that historians refer to as the Modernist era or the Age of the *Avant-Garde*, which dates from roughly 1880 to 1970. A military term for the elite guard who lead the way for the regular troops, *avant-garde* was first applied to artists by Henri de Saint-Simon, a utopian socialist, in his 1825 book *Opinions Littéraires, philosophiques et industrielles*. In a conversation between an industrialist, an economist, and an artist, the latter declares that "We, the artists, will serve as the *avant-garde*. [...] When we wish to spread new ideas amongst men...we inscribe those ideas on marble or canvas."

A number of mid-century French artists, Gustave Courbet most notably, embraced the idea of the artist as political activist. The failure of the Workers Revolution of 1848 undermined both the prospect of socialism and the *avant-garde* idea of the activist artist for the following generation. Thus, Edouard Manet and the Impressionists took an apolitical approach to their work.

When *avant-gardism* was re-embraced by some of those grouped under the label of Post-Impressionism—a catchall term for those who came through Impressionism and went their separate ways—the idea took on new meaning. Most importantly, it referred to artistic advancement, to the idea that art was evolving in a particular direction or "the mainstream." The *avant-garde* were those who led the way, who took the next step in that development. It was this new idea, and the corollary that if an artist wanted to be taken seriously by critics and historians he should produce something "advanced," which drove the mind-boggling changes in modern art in the ensuing years.

In the work of many of these artists, the idea of artistic advancement was tied to and combined with the idea of promoting social progress. But unlike Courbet and the original *avant-garde*, the new breed sought to promote their own social agendas. Georges Seurat and his iconic painting, *Sunday Afternoon on the Island of the Grande Jatte* (1884-86) provide the classic example. Seurat called himself a Neo-Impressionist, by which he meant that his work offered a new and improved version of what Monet and company were producing in terms of both method and function. Whereas the Impressionists produced quick, immediate records of the world as seen, Seurat approached his painting more scientifically, both in the use of color complements intended to combine in the eye for a heightened approximation of natural light and in terms of emotional expression. Seurat posited that upward moving lines—like the shoreline in *The Grande Jatte*—in combination with colors that are bright and warm—elicit a happy emotional response in the viewer. And instead of merely pleasing his audience, Seurat meant to inspire them with a vision of a more evolved and civilized society. The key to the painting is the contrast between the restrained behavior of the people, particularly the little girl in white at center, and the unrestrained play of the unruly dogs in black at the bottom. In effect, Seurat was showing us the next step in the human evolutionary process that began with monkeys, which is why he included one in the painting.

Another Post-Impressionist, Paul Cezanne, also wanted to produce an improved version of Impressionism, although his was a purely artistic endeavor without social or political thrust. In contrast to Monet's purely phenomenological approach to nature, Cezanne wanted to record the fact of its stability and solidity as well. That he did so in an increasingly abstract style in his late paintings of Mont Sainte-Victoire inspired Pablo Picasso and Georges Braque to develop the first non-representational art form in their Analytical Cubist works of 1911-12. These paintings in turn inspired a whole generation of European artists to either take liberties with representational forms, like the Italian Futurists, or abandon them completely, as in the case of Piet Mondrian or the Russian Constructivists. Unlike the Cubists, the Italian Futurists and the Russian Constructivists had clearly defined Utopian goals. On the basis of the aesthetic principles he developed in his art, Mondrian wished to redesign "everything that exists." He held a naïve belief that environment alone determines psychology, and that harmonious surroundings would produce harmonious people and societies. Constructivists such as Naum Gabo, on the other hand, believed that art was "contagious." Their engineered art would produce the constructive geniuses who would help create the new Communist Utopia.

Seurat's work instigated the rationalist, anti-intuitive strain of Modernist art that reached its apogee before World War II in the work of Mondrian and the Russians, but it also contributed importantly to the counter-strain that emphasized emotion and intuition. Seurat's use of color for expressive purpose was the starting point for Vincent van Gogh's preoccupation with color. During the last year of his life, van Gogh came to use color expressionistically, not to characterize his subjects but to record the purely personal feelings he brought to them. Van Gogh's work touched off the expressionist wave of *avant-garde* art that swept Europe in the years before World War I in Fauvism, The Bridge, and The Blue Rider movements, most famously. In the years between the two wars, this current was continued by the Dadaist and culminated in Surrealism, which sought the complete liberation of the id.

Surrealist art came in two forms, the regressive representational style of Salvador Dali and the freely expressive automatist brand practiced by most members of the group, such as Joan Miro and André Masson. It was out of this latter side of the movement that American Abstract Expressionism emerged in the post-war period. Jackson Pollock, Willem de Kooning and their colleagues were the first Americans to be recognized as leaders of the *avant-garde*, thereby shifting the center of the art world from Paris to New York. Consciously steered by the critic Clement Greenberg and his followers, Abstract Expressionism "naturally" evolved into Post-Painterly Abstraction at the end of the 1950s and then to Minimalist painting and sculpture in the 1960s. The decade witnessed other developments as well, of course—the Neo-Dada productions of Jasper Johns and Robert Rauschenberg that opened the way for Pop Art, most notably—but according to the reigning Greenbergians, these were merely "fads," historical cul-de-sacs with no relation to the "mainstream" development of Modernist art, which meant that they could be ignored.

But it was Minimalism, not Neo-Dada or Pop that turned out to be the dead end, the movement that marked the end of Modernism. The decade of the 1970s was quickly dubbed the Post-Minimalist era. A profusion of different kinds of art emerged in that decade in *reaction to* Minimalism, often using its formal means but for radically different ends. In the seventies, we saw the first signs of the pluralism that now characterizes contemporary art.

Instead of movements and all that they imply about historical development, we now have tendencies and groupings. Indeed, most of these are more for the art historian's convenience than an indication of collective aims. The YBAs, for example, have little in common except for the fact that they are all young, British, and artists!

The new radical pluralism was the first indication that the art world had lost faith in the *avant-garde* concept and its corollary, an artistic mainstream, which had driven production for nearly a century. Although the term *avant-garde* is still in use, it now simply refers to something new or different, not to something historically "advanced" or better.

What collapsed, in fact, was the Enlightenment idea of historical progress. The events of the 1960s and early 1970s had put historical progress, the meta-narrative that had underpinned *avant-gardism*, in doubt. The assassinations of John F. Kennedy, Robert Kennedy and Martin Luther King Jr., the Vietnam War, the failure of May 1968 and other student-led initiatives on the continent, and most importantly the growing awareness that the Industrial Revolution had led to profound ecological disturbances threatening the viability of life on the planet, collectively rendered the idea of progress dubious. The utter failure of world leaders to deal effectively with the existential crisis of climate change and a host of social problems has only confirmed and deepened those doubts.

Evidence of this new skepticism appears everywhere in the art produced after the collapse of Modernism—the era now referred to simply as Post-Modernist. The most noticeable feature is the near disappearance of images of the ideal, the very basis of human art through the ages! To be sure, one can still find beauty, especially in photography, but much of this is either manipulated and thus offered as mere *imagery*, or exceptional moments stolen from an otherwise defective world. More importantly, since Diane Arbus and Lee Friedlander emerged in the late 1960s, most art photography has been devoted to images of social chaos, human degradation, or physical imperfection, as in the work of Raghubir Singh, Nan Goldin, and Rineke Dijkstra, respectively.

The "artist activist" has not disappeared. An internet search of the term will turn up the names of dozens of artists dedicated to the prospect of human betterment. The super-realist sculpture of Duane Hanson, the installations of Ai Weiwie, and the graffiti of Banksy, all document our current imperfections with the hope that we might reform them.

But "telling truth to power," to rephrase Kennedy, is only meaningful if those being addressed are responsive. The current consensus is that these artistic voices, however admirable their intentions, are being heard only by the proverbial choir: that Hanson has had no more effect on American culture than Ai Weiwei has had on the Chinese government or Banksy on those responsible for the Palestinian situation. Which is to say that contemporary art seems to offer no match for our current problems.

The vast majority of the recent depictions of human imperfection are offered simply as true, without expectations. This testimony comes in two main varieties. The first—found in the work of John Currin, Charles Ray, Lisa Yuskavage, and Rachel Harrison—is presented for our amusement, as farce, scenes from the human comedy. Such work falls under the rubric of "endgame," a term borrowed from chess to describe the point in the contest when defeat is clear but one still has a few moves left. Strategically, these are artists making the best of a bad situation. Jeff Koons's highly crafted kitsch and Sigmar Polke's decorative approach to the chaotic flood of contemporary imagery might also belong under this broad umbrella. The second variety includes the work of Philip Guston, Lucian Freud, Mike Kelly, Kiki Smith, Eric Fischl, David Salle, Georg Baselitz, and Paul McCarthy. Their work, to varying degrees, is dispiriting and/or depressing. In the work of these artists, and the photographers mentioned above, the Utopian optimism of the Enlightenment has given way to dystopian fears.

Whether the skeptical and pessimistic currents of post-1970 visual art toll the end of the Enlightenment or just the latest crisis of Enlightenment faith will depend on the larger culture. Can we marshal our reason, decency, and common sense to pull out of our current cultural tailspin? Kennedy and the *philosophes* are holding their collective breath.

13

LIFTING THE HUMAN SPIRIT

As the Eisenhower era ended, a new kind of politician stepped onto the stage. Although John F. Kennedy respected the aging leaders who had guided the Allies through the dark days of World War II, he represented a new generation. In this chapter, Chancellor Nick Zeppos of Vanderbilt University, noted actor and artist Robert Redford, and distinguished Rabbi Peter Rubinstein offer a fascinating spectrum of views on Kennedy's vision, his optimism, and his aspirations.

When a President Dared to Go to Amherst

Nicholas Zeppos

ONE DAY IN late October 1963, a sitting American president dared to do something that, today, would set off a political firestorm: John F. Kennedy visited an elite college. And if the optics of that weren't controversial enough in our current age, when most presidents contort to prove they are regular folk, consider why Kennedy went to Amherst in the first place: To eulogize a poet.

A poet!

A president today might as well pay tribute to polo. Or arugula. Or France. Democrat or Republican, we don't much like it when our presidents fancy anything fancy.

Maybe the same rules didn't apply in 1963. Maybe President Kennedy, who famously *was* an elite, felt no compunction about visiting a school mainly populated by his fellow white, wealthy males. Perhaps "elite" was not yet an epithet and pointed questions about who pulled the levers of power in America had not yet risen to the level of national debate. Maybe Americans in the early 1960s *expected* their presidents to be snobs. Or, it might just be that the president, settling into the latter half of his first term, simply felt confident that he could endure whatever brickbats befell him for making the trip. In any case, one of the many reasons Kennedy's visit to Amherst is still notable almost six decades later is because a president today would be hard-pressed to pull it off.

Even if his visit was not as audacious as it appears to our contemporary eyes, his speech certainly was. Set aside, for the moment, Kennedy's eloquent tribute to Robert Frost, and his ringing articulation of the role of the artist in a healthy democracy. Instead, consider what he led with in his opening paragraphs. On that day in October, the president of the United States choppered in and held Amherst, and the nation, to account.

"What good," Kennedy asks, a mere two minutes into his fourteen-minute speech, "is a private college or university unless it is serving a great national purpose?" Then, in short order, he exhorts students to put their talent and privilege to work for "The Great Republic;" calls out both public and private universities for their disproportionate admission of the wealthy; handily encapsulates America's income and opportunity gaps; and, for good measure, squeezes in nods to segregation and geopolitics. No doubt he bookended it all with that dazzling Kennedy smile.

This is a remarkable thing, because the president didn't have to do any of it. He could have easily gotten away with serving up bromides. He could have used his charisma and Arthur Schlesinger Jr.'s prose to make the day a pleasant but forgettable photo-op that simply validated the self-satisfaction of his fellow elites and the rest of the 10,000 Americans swarming the campus that day. Instead, he set the context for a tribute to a Yankee poet with a dark streak by first declaring that the problems America faced were "staggering." He contrasted our national aspirations with our actual progress and pointed out that the American project was incomplete because the American promise had not been kept for everyone.

This frankness at the outset is one reason I admire the Amherst speech so much. His "moonshot speech" a year earlier leaned toward the technocratic and echoed with Manifest Destiny; his speech in West Berlin the previous June can be regarded as Cold War posturing. Both were gorgeously written, stirringly delivered, and, arguably, necessary. But those speeches were concerned with America as a conquering or deterrent force in the world; both faced defiantly outward. The Amherst speech, start to finish, asked America to look inward—to reflect upon its darkness as well as its light; to both acknowledge its shortcomings and fully comprehend its potential for greatness.

In hindsight we ask, couldn't he have done even more? Couldn't he have given a whole speech about any one of the issues he raised? And of course the answer is yes. America's racial injustice alone warranted more condemnation and remedy from the biggest of bully pulpits. (The civil rights protesters keeping vigil outside the theater where Kennedy spoke knew this, too.) And we know now that the president's actions were not always consistent with his rhetoric. But the fact remains that Kennedy didn't have to go to Amherst and make his audience uncomfortable, and it is worth noting that he did.

I don't think it is a coincidence that he chose a college campus as the place to do this. America's colleges and universities are gatekeepers for the American Dream. They are—or should be—forums for testing ideas, airing uncomfortable truths and taking stock of ourselves as a nation. Today, as in Kennedy's time, America's colleges and universities play a vital role in delivering on the American promise.

In fact, if we are tempted to gloss over the speech's early paragraphs to get to the more famous and uplifting prose about Frost, it might be because the president's assertions do not stop us in our tracks. They are probably too familiar to do so. Fifty-five years later, our story is in many ways the same.

We still face unacceptable gaps in equity. Wealth inequality has risen for decades and is, today, a raw nerve in the body politic in a way it was not during Kennedy's era. Racism, systemic and otherwise, remains entrenched. Certain unalienable rights are still denied to too many Americans, who are told to wait at the back of the line for opportunity. This is another reason the Amherst speech resonates. The president's call to action could have come this morning.

At least as much as in Kennedy's day, we need more college graduates to put their talents to use for the common good. Our nation faces serious, mounting challenges, yet much of the student ambition I see is aimed not at addressing national concerns, but at inventing some dazzling new technology or at securing immortality by having something named for themselves. A lopsided number of students want to be creators rather than servants. Our nation needs both. So I tell students that, yes, some of them will go on to start something new, but more of them must commit to stewarding something bigger than themselves, to making it better and then handing it off to someone else. That's how organizations, communities, and democracies survive.

Also, now as then, we must make college more accessible. The percentage of college graduates in the U.S. population has stagnated. To be sure, we've come a long way from the mostly male, white, and wealthy student bodies that defined institutions like Amherst in the middle of the last century. At Vanderbilt, 45 percent of our 2017 freshman class was made up of students of color. Fifteen percent of our students come from families whose income is below the federal poverty level. We've replaced student loans with grants and scholarships, enabling more students to afford college without burdensome debt. Universities around the country have made similar progress.

But we all must throw open our doors even wider, and that means striving for diversity of all kinds. As meeting students from both Syria and Monkey's Eyebrow, Kentucky, recently reminded me, the world never ceases to amaze with the breadth and variety of its people. Our universities must include more of it—not only to make opportunity more widely available, but also to prepare students for basic citizenship in a society that contains multitudes.

Universities can also serve the American project by helping to restore civil discourse and compromise, two indispensable ingredients of democracy that seem threatened with extinction. Our politics have degenerated into a shouting match. Left and right, blue and red, are crouched in their ideological bunkers. We have all been carved into reductive demographics by pollsters and journalists, and into marketable bits and bytes by social media. Legislatively, we are at a virtual standstill, with Democrats and Republicans clinched like two exhausted boxers trading lame body punches in a bout where the bell never rings. All the while, our era's own "staggering problems" fester. Anxiety and alienation grow, and, with them, desperation and intolerance. This is not an America that President Kennedy, no stranger to partisanship and bareknuckle politics, would recognize.

Colleges and universities can be a powerful antidote to this breakdown in dialogue. They are, by definition and history, places for the exchange of ideas and incubators of solutions. They are uniquely situated to bring Americans of all backgrounds together and teach us how to get along. They remind us that we are, in a democracy, obligated to coexist with ideas that make us uncomfortable and to cooperate with people we disagree with.

We see this playing out on campuses all over the country as students on both the left and right passionately question what free speech and open discourse mean. And while we'd be better served by less scuffling for the cameras and more of the reasonable discourse that actually characterizes dialogue at universities most of the time, I'm encouraged that this debate is raging. A university campus, where ideas are routinely and rigorously challenged, is just the place for it, and historically *has* been the place for it. I believe this is why Kennedy tweaked the noses of the students of Amherst that day.

Our colleges and universities must be among the fiercest protectors of First Amendment rights. They must resist censorship from all sides. They must not cede the public square to the loudest shouters. They must ensure that the centuries-long American conversation continues. The protesters at Amherst did not shut down the event or shout down the president; yet they injected their voices into the debate.

Of course, the Amherst speech was not all grim data and stern call to duty. Not quite halfway through, after giving Amherst students one last poke in the conscience by hoping aloud that they'd be worthy of their "long inheritance," the president finally turns his attention to the ostensible man of the hour, Robert Frost. And it is here that the speech famously achieves lift-off.

With all due respect to the singularity of art, and of poetry in particular, I believe the bracing truths President Kennedy articulates so eloquently in the rest of his remarks can apply to higher education as well. At its best, education, too, can "cleanse." It, too, is concerned with "the basic human truth, which must serve as the touchstone of our judgment." Education, like art, "strengthens the fiber of our national life," and, by countering ignorance and arrogance, and by cultivating empathy and understanding and self-awareness, it helps protect us from our darker angels. And education, like art, should be concerned with the long game—not with what is popular or politically expedient, but with what has proven over time to be true. In this way, education, like art, serves our nation, because the American project is ongoing, a bequest to future generations and a dream that must constantly be dreamed anew if it is going to serve all of us—and if it is going to endure.

Finally, President Kennedy delivers the famous fusillade of sentences that close out his speech—and blossom in the breast of the listener—like fireworks. It is here that he rhythmically and repeatedly sounds the aspirational phrase, "I look forward to an America." These lines are as inspiring as any he ever spoke. Implicit in them is the assertion that to realize his vision we must solve the problems he described in the first part of his speech. It was true then, and it is true now: Until we address the issues raised on that day in October by the president who dared to visit an elite college and speak hard truths to its students, and until we learn how to talk to one another other again, and work across our differences to meet our common challenges, then, indeed, in the words of the president, "the presuppositions upon which our democracy is based are bound to be fallible."

I, too, look forward to an America like the one President Kennedy envisioned. I wager it is that vision that motivates many of us in higher education to come to work every day; America's universities are in the American Dream business. But if we do not heed Kennedy's call across the decades and finish the work before us on America's campuses and in the rest of our greatest institutions, it might be that the best we can hope for is not an America that is a better, brighter version of itself, but an America that simply still exists.

Society's Questioner[1]

Robert Redford

DO WE USE POWER? Or does power use us?

I first became acquainted with JFK's speech honoring Robert Frost while writing my own speech on the importance of art in society. One passage of his speech still leaps out at me. He describes Frost and the artist's role as questioner of our society by saying, "The men who create power make an indispensable contribution to the Nation's greatness, but the men who question power make a contribution just as [in]dispensable, especially when that questioning is disinterested, for they determine whether we use power or power uses us."

When we use power, how do we do so?

I first experienced power used well in third grade. I was in math class drawing pictures under my desk again. My teacher caught me and demanded I tell the class what was so interesting that I couldn't be bothered to pay attention. I was ordered to show and explain my drawing. It was a closed-loop commentary on violence: cowboys firing bullets at Indians, Indians shooting arrows back, and B-51 bombers dropping their payloads on the cowboys.

Then something unexpected happened. The other students got engaged in my drawing and its story. I hadn't intended to create a tiny artistic challenge to the dominant virtuous-cowboys-killing-savage-heathens story of

---

1   Copyright Robert Redford, reprinted with permission.

the day; I was simply trying to entertain myself with pictures. But it struck a chord in my audience.

That's when my teacher made a choice for which I'm still grateful. She could have chosen to humiliate and make an example of me. Instead, she offered me a trade: I was to have fifteen minutes each Wednesday to teach the class by telling the stories of my drawings. In exchange, for the other 235 minutes of class time each week, I had to pay attention to the lesson.

My teacher was in the position of power that day. The easy choice would have been to denigrate the drawing, and the student, and to rule the classroom with fear. Instead, she allowed creativity to flourish and welcomed a different approach.

To this day, I appreciate how she used her power. I have benefited from a life in art ever since.

Art benefits the world. Kennedy knew that. When he says, "I see little of more importance to the future of our country and our civilization than full recognition of the place of the artist," I agree with him wholeheartedly. Many politicians, many presidents, would not. When our leaders talk about creating jobs, it's unlikely they have "poet" or "playwright" in mind. When they speak about American ingenuity, it's usually about entrepreneurs and inventors, not artists.

Yet artists are as essential as inventors or entrepreneurs. And there is no more important role the artist plays than questioner of our society—not because she is a scold, but because she is an idealist, demanding that we hold ourselves to the model of who we can be, not who we are. Kennedy says in the speech, "If sometimes our great artists have been the most critical of our society, it is because their sensitivity and their concern for justice, which must motivate any true artist, makes him aware that our Nation falls short of its highest potential."

I wonder what Kennedy would think of our nation, and how our political leaders use power, right now. He might offer the same Woodrow Wilson quote he cites in the speech: "What good is a political party unless it is serving a great national purpose?"

You will often hear people give a reductive challenge about a piece of art: "What's the point of that painting?" I'd like to ask in return, "What's the point of a politician?" Art has a thousand objectives: to inspire, challenge, provoke, soothe, calm, anger, unite. Our politicians frequently have one: to hang on to power at all cost. It keeps our nation frozen in a state of seemingly benign suspended animation. We Americans shrug at the intractability of it all, resigning ourselves to a sort of barely tolerable political atrophy. In Kennedy's decade, we put a man on the moon and passed the Civil Rights Act. Now we struggle to pass a bill or schedule a hearing to confirm a Supreme Court justice.

Yet, dismissing stalemated government as business-as-usual is foolish and dangerous. It fosters a political climate ripe for a more sinister stranglehold on power, one in which the great problems of our time (climate change, inequality, religious intolerance, and extremism) can't be tackled, and dissent of any kind, be it journalistic or artistic, is not tolerated.

But our union has always been threatened. Our fragile experiment roars on.

As a nation, we tend to step back from the brink before tyranny takes hold.

Kennedy called himself an idealist without illusions. I count myself in that same camp, and in my core I believe America will continue to defend itself from stagnation and abuse of power. And I believe the artist is our best warrior in that fight. I agree with JFK when he says, "I see little of more importance to the future of our country and our civilization than full recognition of the place of the artist."

It's a measure of the man that Kennedy—even at what was the apex of America's economic might, when it might be most tempting to seek a stranglehold on power and lock America in that time and place—embraced the arts and diversity of thought.

I wish that Kennedy were here now to ask us again his immortal question. What can we do for our country?

My answer (and perhaps his): question it. Challenge it. And empower others to do the same.

The Touchstone of Our Judgment

Rabbi Peter J. Rubinstein, '64

AT THIS JUNCTURE in our nation's history, it would be well for us to reflect on the essential values upon which our beloved country was founded. And it would do us equally well to humbly reflect on the intersection of those uniquely American values that in some utopian way pervaded the culture of Amherst College during our college years, with the basic human truths and values upon which our faiths, personal moral codes and our behaviors are founded.

In the speech President Kennedy intended to deliver on November 22, 1963, the day he was assassinated, Kennedy was determined to discuss "the status of our security because this question clearly calls for the most responsible qualities of leadership and the most enlightened products of scholarship." His message rang with confidence, "words alone are not enough. The United States is a peaceful nation. And where our strength and determination are clear, our words need merely to convey conviction, not belligerence. If we are strong, our strength will speak for itself. If we are weak, words will be of no help."[2]

Unintentionally, perhaps, Kennedy echoed Benjamin Franklin who wrote to his parents in 1738, "I think vital Religion has always suffer'd, when

---

2   "JFK's never-delivered speech from Dallas," November 21, 2013, http://www.post-gazette.com/news/nation/2013/11/22/Full-text-JFK-s-never-delivered-speech-from-Dallas/stories/201311210356

Orthodoxy is more regarded than Virtue. And the Scripture assures me, that at the last Day, we shall not be examin'd what we thought, but what we did; and our Recommendation will not be that we said Lord, Lord, but that we did good to our Fellow Creatures."

Separated by more than two centuries, Franklin and Kennedy articulated one of those pervasive American values: "words need merely to convey conviction," "we will be judged by what we did." Upon reflection, I have realized the enormous impact, the prescient quality, that Kennedy's 1963 convocation address at Amherst had for me. Speaking about Robert Frost that October day of our senior year, Kennedy provided a primary leitmotif for my nascent professional and personal life when he said, "He [Frost] brought an unsparing instinct for reality to bear on the platitudes and pieties of society. His sense of the human tragedy fortified him against self-deception and easy consolation."

Kennedy's words, as well as Frost's poetry, have resonated, echoing at my core over the decades. They became part of the story of my becoming a Rabbi and how I discovered the values that now permeate my life.

Beginning at Amherst, I became fully aware that we are measured by what we do and not by what we say or intend. I came to care passionately about how each of us lives, how we treat others, how we function in the neighborhood of humanity. Good intentions and ethical platitudes provide no justification for indecent or hurtful behavior.

For me, as probably for others, my college years were the critical moment: when heart and mind collided, when theory and reality caustically rubbed against each other, when we intuitively questioned the "truths" with which our parents attempted to raise us, or when we realized we were devoid of "truths" that were sufficiently powerful and encompassing to prepare us for life's complications, existential questions and confounding ethical dilemmas.

For me, the search began with a classmate's innocent question as to what I, as a Jew, believed. My Jewish identity was impeccably strong. I knew what I was, but I had not delved into what, if anything, I believed. That question ignited a search for my faith. I ached to determine the purpose *of* my life and the meaning *in* my life. At Amherst, as an English major and pre-med, that ache led me to learn about every religion taught in the curriculum of the college's Religion Department. As I tried to formulate some level of God-idea and belief, I concluded that the theologians of those years, at the dawn of an increasingly tempestuous era, were not the "God-talkers," the preachers or the scholars, but the writers. The writers did not teach about God or faith; instead they embedded the search for God and their God-perspectives in their characters. For me, William Faulkner exemplified the most intense theological portrayals. Eventually, Paul Tillich's opus *Systematic Theology*, with his concept of "ultimate concern," provided the etymology for my search. These first elementary dabblings in my God and faith search culminated in my senior thesis *'Depth' in a Culture: A Study of Paul Tillich and William Faulkner.*

Both Tillich and Faulkner, with their authentically Christian inclinations, ironically became guides for my exploration; although they provided roadmaps, neither one could completely presume the language, interpret the imagery, or contour an explanation for a young Jew's search for meaning, belief, and faith. Immediately after college graduation, my older brother, who was then a rabbinic student, asked me what I was doing studying a Christian theologian. Believing he would provide a response to my dilemma, I popped the question: "What do Jews believe?" His answer was not an answer but a piece of advice: "If you want to know that, you need to ask my theology professor, Dr. Eugene Borowitz." And so I did, over a beer at a bar on Manhattan's West Side.

Borowitz, justifiably, asked me what was my problem. I explained that I didn't have a problem, just a question: "What do Jews believe?"

Borowitz then convinced me: "If you want to learn that, you have to study with me."

With a bit of irreverent arrogance, I told him I'd give him a year to teach me everything I needed to know about God and Jewish belief. That year has stretched into a lifetime as I continuously attempt to decipher basic human truths, refine the purpose of my life and the meaning in it.

I've come to understand that despite the shared hope for unanimity on the matter of truths that bind us, we ultimately need to accept that the human condition and our personal realities catapult each of us into a world where we zig and zag in our pursuit for "truth" as an anchor to which all humanity is tethered. Those truths evolve, and eventually our personal primary principles and values emerge.

Along my way these three "truths" have contoured my life and have become the touchstone of my judgment.

1) WE ARE BETTER WHEN WE MAKE THIS WORLD BETTER. WE ARE OUR SISTERS' AND BROTHERS' KEEPERS.

We are all responsible for the care of all people, even as we nurture our own survival; this is both the supreme purpose of our life and a great paradox.

We will not be judged by our success in times of prosperity. That success is easy. Rather we will be judged by how decently we comport ourselves in times of adversity. That decency is the challenge.

Supporting the weak and the needy is a mainstay of our national character and purpose of our existence. President Obama said during his tenure, "Large-heartedness is part of the American character." Large-heartedness should be an anchor of every caring soul. It should be fundamental to the character of each of us.

The ethical principles of the great religious traditions of the modern world all command us to accomplish everything that adds to life and does not destroy life. The ultimate test of proper behavior is whether we are adding to the health and well-being of human interchange and the wholeness of society. Many of our classmates have done this by putting back in place the broken fragments of human failure. We add to life by supporting human rights, and by pushing for help for the thirty-six million American citizens living in poverty. We add to life by supporting scientists engaged in innovative research that expands the boundaries of our knowledge. We add to life by being guardians of the environment and trustees of its natural resources, and by permitting healthy expressions of love according to human desire. And yes, we even add to life by allowing death its natural course. These are lessons which emerge from our commitment to life around the world and in this nation.

A Talmudic blessing affirms, "Blessed are you God who discerns secrets, for the mind of each is different from the other, just as the face of each is different from the other."[3] We each have a unique role to play in the unfolding drama of history.

If we will continue to be a great nation, if we will continue to be a great citizenry, then we will continue to play a great part in this world. We are brothers and sisters to all people. We need to care for them at times with our voice, our presence, our efforts, and our resources. Let it never be said that we remained on the sidelines. Otherwise we become complicit in the evils of society.

2) PIETY IS NOT THE SAME AS DECENCY.

We know that religious leaders have brought shame on their communities and constituents. Massive financial scandals, money-laundering, trafficking in human organs, and condoning sexual abuse tarnish our virtue.

Especially horrific reports of scandal and abuse within traditional portions of our communities diminish our character.

Some religious adherents of all denominational persuasions have subjugated the common good to their own personal profit and have done wrong. Piety camouflaged as self-righteousness or truculent arrogance invades our communities.

We know better!

We condemn those who defend abominable misbehavior and outrageous illegality under the cover of piety in all of its manifestations. Attendance at prayer meetings by politicians, quoting of scripture and other religious texts in public statements, speaking in the name of God by any of us is simply a brandishing of sacral self-righteousness, indicating no stake in the arena of individual or communal decency.

Religious organizations and communities of faith are at a crossroads in this country. By what will we be judged? We measure ourselves by the depth

---

3   Berakhot 58a

of our character, that is, by our decency, our courage and the embodiment of our convictions. Our religious passions must be embedded in the seriousness of our life work.

We impugn the character of our faith when a gaping abyss opens between our actions and our affirmations, a chasm separates our conduct and our creeds, a rift divides our precepts and our practice.

Refining and strengthening our character will always be irrelevant to those who despise us because of our race, religion, country of origin or gender, but it is absolutely essential to the quality of our existence, a measure of our moral aptitude. Examination of our own behavior and level of decency has the potential to catapult us forward to a reawakening of truth and confession, of affirmation and commitment and to a recalibration of our moral vision.

3) PERSONAL CHARACTER TAKES WORK.

Personal character is the prism through which each of us deliberately makes our decisions. Personal character clarifies the moral spectrum of our principles. It defines how we choose to live our life and how closely our behavior is aligned with our principles, values, and the person we want to be.

We are not born of impeccable virtue, nor are we inherently sinful. We are built of what Kant calls the "crooked timber of humanity." The legends and stories of Scripture mobilize us to do better, to be kinder, to reflect more deeply and to recognize that in David Brooks' words "We all have dappled souls."

In his wonderful book *The Road to Character*, Brooks differentiates between "résumé virtues" and "eulogy virtues." We know the difference intuitively.

Résumé virtues are the skills that we "bring to the job market" and that we proffer as our contributions to the work place and reasons for job success. But "eulogy virtues," the things that are talked about at funerals, are deeper. In Brooks' words they are the virtues that "exist at the core of your being— whether you are kind, brave, honest or faithful, what kind of relationships you formed." In Faulkner's words they are the "old verities and truths of the heart."

At some season of our life we have to measure our own character by fully accepting the "crooked timber" of our humanity.

For many of us there were times when we didn't respond to our family's needs because we singularly focused on another, possibly less important, responsibility in pursuit of success in career. After all, ego can be a seductive trap.

We all struggle with the hope that our descent into the "valley of humility" will eventually lead us to the ascent of character.

I choose to believe that we all want to behave better. Ultimately, we hope our character, values, humility, and moral constitution will shape our behavior, moving us ever closer to the person we want to be, with our principles and behavior perfectly aligned.

Robert Frost wrote, "I have been one acquainted with the night." President Kennedy commented that Frost "knew the midnight as well as the high noon, because he understood the ordeal as well as the triumph of the human spirit, he gave his age strength with which to overcome despair."

As if giving a prelude to Kennedy's assessment, William Faulkner took a measure of his own generation and claimed in his 1950 Nobel Prize acceptance speech that each human being:

> [M]ust teach himself that the basest of all things is to be afraid; and, teaching himself that, forget it forever, leaving no room in his workshop for anything but the old verities and truths of the heart, the old universal truths lacking which any story is ephemeral and doomed— love and honor and pity and pride and compassion and sacrifice...

> I believe that man will not merely endure: he will prevail. He is immortal, not because he alone among creatures has an inexhaustible voice, but because he has a soul, a spirit capable of compassion and sacrifice and endurance.[4]

That aspiration has been entrusted to us. At the end of my senior thesis, I concluded that "after all is put before our eyes, after every possible degradation

---

4   William Faulkner from his speech at the Nobel Banquet at the City Hall in Stockholm, December 10, 1950, Nobelprize.org. Nobel Media AB 2014, https://www.nobelprize.org/nobel_prizes/literature/laureates/1949/faulkner-speech.html.

is suffered there is always a gesture, that certain something which expresses the hope of the individual and declares for himself, his retention of humanity."

I still embrace that ideal, and I hope that we will each, individually, re-confirm the human truths that are the touchstone of our judgment.

We still have much to do for our world, our nation, and ourselves. It would be good for us to get on with it.

14

ASPIRATIONAL LEADERSHIP

Robert Frost's core concept of education embodied action, learning by doing. Kennedy derived his core concepts of leadership from the study of power. Before he attained the presidency, his earlier writing had focused on how individuals gained and exercised power. Both men understood the importance of putting thought into action.

The focus shifts now from Frost, Kennedy, and the impact of their words to the application of their principles today and in the future. This chapter juxtaposes essays from Pulitzer Prize-winning presidential historian Jon Meacham, former congressman and teacher-writer Mickey Edwards, and millennial political activist Steven Olikara to illustrate the realities of aspirational leadership, of moving from thought to action.

The World of Thought and the Seat of Power
The Leadership of John F. Kennedy

Jon Meacham

NO ONE COULD SAY he hadn't been clear. On Thursday, January 14, 1960, Senator John F. Kennedy, a candidate for the Democratic presidential nomination, took the occasion of a luncheon at Washington's National Press Club to lay out his vision of the office he was seeking. "The modern presidential campaign," he said, "covers every issue in and out of the platform from cranberries to creation. But the public is rarely alerted to a candidate's views about the central issue on which all the rest turn. That central issue—and the point of my comments this noon—is not the farm problem or defense or India. It is the presidency itself."

To Kennedy's mind, the Oval Office was "the vital center of action," the pivot on which all else, from party politics to foreign policy to culture itself, turned. "In the decade that lies ahead—in the challenging, revolutionary sixties—the American Presidency will demand more than ringing manifestoes issued from the rear of the battle," Kennedy told his National Press Club audience. "It will demand that the President place himself in the very thick of the fight, that he care passionately about the fate of the people he leads, that he be willing to serve them, at the risk of incurring their momentary displeasure."

His understanding of the office was rooted in that of Jackson, Lincoln, and the two Roosevelts—men who considered the presidency to be the overarching element of American life and government. "Whatever the political affiliation of our next President, whatever his views may be on all the issues and problems that rush in upon us, he must above all be the Chief Executive in every sense of the word," Kennedy said. "He must be prepared to exercise the fullest powers of his office—all that are specified and some that are not. He must master complex problems as well as receive one-page memorandums. He must originate action as well as study groups. He must reopen channels of communication between the world of thought and the seat of power."

It was the boldest of job descriptions, and it foreshadowed the style and the substance of the leadership Senator Kennedy would offer when he became President Kennedy fifty-three weeks later. To him, the life of the mind and the life of the nation were inextricably intertwined, and this connection between the vision of the artist, the poetry of history, and the values of the country was a perennial one in his all-too-brief reign. "Our national strength matters," Kennedy said at Amherst College in the tragic autumn of 1963, "but the spirit which informs and controls our strength matters just as much."

The leadership of the spirit—what Franklin Roosevelt had called "moral leadership"—was a Kennedy hallmark. He believed politics a noble profession, and he worked within the tradition of the Founders, men who understood that politics and culture were of a piece. A republic was only as good as the sum of its parts, which is why public virtue mattered so enormously. "Machiavelli, discoursing on these matters," Algernon Sidney, the seventeenth-century English theorist and politician, once wrote, "finds virtue to be so essentially necessary to the establishment and preservation of liberty, that he thinks it impossible for a corrupted people to set up a good government, or for a tyranny to be introduced if they be virtuous."

The cultivation of civic virtue was a consuming, if little-noted, Kennedy undertaking. A practical, hard-headed politician, he nevertheless heard the music of history. His appeals to endure against Soviet tyranny, or to go to the moon, or to join the Peace Corps were framed in terms of American greatness and human progress, not in the narrower confines of this legislative session or that midterm election. This is why so many of us remember him so fondly, even if some of us might have disagreed with him in real time. He spoke to our better angels, and posterity rewards those who point ahead more than it does those who clench their fist.

Such was the essence of his leadership. Two elements repay our consideration: first, his capacity to learn from his own mistakes, thus respecting the primacy of reason and of fact, and, second, his insistence on that the creative life inform our political life.

First, the practical side. On the morning of Tuesday, October 16, 1962—the beginning of the two most dangerous weeks in human history—Kennedy was briefed on the deployment of Soviet nuclear missiles in Cuba, a move by the Kremlin that put these weapons of mass destruction less than fifteen minutes away from Washington. Kennedy called his attorney general, Robert Kennedy, with the news. "Oh shit, shit, shit," RFK said. "Those sons a bitches Russians." As Mrs. Kennedy described it to Arthur Schlesinger, Jr. after her husband's assassination, "It was just Cuba, Cuba, all the time in one way or another." The thirteen-day crisis itself in October was a blur of late hours and perpetual meetings. "There was no day or night," said Mrs. Kennedy.

The context of the crisis is, as always, critical. In the heart of Europe, Berlin was in play, its fate essential and unknowable. The United States had deployed some Jupiter missiles to Turkey, seemingly shifting the balance of strategic power to American advantage. Nikita Khrushchev, the Soviet leader, wanted to redress that balance and project Soviet power closer to American shores. Cuba was the perfect choice. And Kennedy, in issuing an ultimatum in September saying that the United States could not tolerate such missiles in Cuba—JFK was under attack for appearing weak on foreign policy—was now in a bind. The options: immediate air strikes to try to take out the weapons, but no one knew how many of them the U.S. could actually hit or whether the Soviets would immediately strike back. There could be an invasion. There could be a naval blockade. Or there could be diplomacy. No option was good; all risked escalation, either purposely or by miscalculation. The whole crisis was the result of a miscalculation: Moscow had wanted to install the weapons as a largely symbolic show of influence, not so much as a provocative military maneuver. Khrushchev routinely inflated Soviet strength on the grounds that "America recognizes only strength."

Kennedy, a young man with an abiding interest in history, was skeptical of the advice he received both from the military and from the CIA. The author of two books—*Why England Slept*, about appeasement, and *Profiles in Courage*—he was a man of the urgent present intrigued by the past. Perhaps above all he valued experience, and he enjoyed seeing how reality tracked—or failed to—with the assumptions of those outside the arena.

And he knew how to learn. The resolution of the Missile Crisis was rooted in the disastrous Bay of Pigs invasion of Cuba in 1961. After the botched attack just a few months after his inauguration, Kennedy was horrified by his failure to see the flaws in the planning. "How could I have been so stupid?" he asked himself and others in the aftermath. Fifteen hundred men had been sent to the beaches; later estimates suggested it would have taken a whole division—15,000 men—to conduct a successful amphibious operation of this scope. To a CIA officer he admitted, "In a parliamentary system I would resign."

To make sense of things, he turned to one of the only men who could possibly know what he was enduring. Kennedy had been dismissive of Dwight Eisenhower during the 1960 campaign, but suddenly found him a source of insight. After lunch in the presidential cabin at Camp David after the Bay of Pigs, the two men took a walk.

Eisenhower asked a crucial question. "Mr. President, before you approved this plan, did you have everybody in front of you debating the thing so you got the pros and cons yourself and then made the decision, or did you see these people one at a time?"

Kennedy's answer was not reassuring. "Well, I did have a meeting...I just approved a plan that had been recommended by the CIA and by the Joint Chiefs of Staff. I just took their advice." He would never do that again.

A cool realist in the tradition of Jefferson, Jackson, Lincoln, and FDR, Kennedy knew, as he put it, that "every President must endure a gap between what he would like and what is possible." In looking back to the past, Kennedy hoped the realism of his predecessors would make his own pragmatism seem statesmanlike rather than opportunistic.

These lessons guided him hour by hour through the Missile Crisis. In a review of a book about military strategy written just a few months before the 1960 presidential election, Kennedy had quoted Basil Liddell Hart: "Keep strong, if possible. In any case, keep cool. Have unlimited patience. Never corner an opponent, and always assist him to save face. Put yourself in his shoes—so as to see things through his eyes. Avoid self-righteousness like the devil—nothing is so self-blinding."

Such was the man who managed the Missile Crisis. The stakes could not have been higher. Possible casualty estimates range from 70 million to 100 million Americans. JFK believed the existence of the nation was in the balance.

He was governing in a new world, but one in which the analogies and experience of the past were constant forces. As Kennedy said in a speech to the American people on October 22, 1962, "The 1930's taught us a clear lesson: aggressive conduct, if allowed to go unchecked and unchallenged, ultimately leads to war. This nation is opposed to war. We are also true to our word. Our unswerving objective, therefore, must be to prevent the use of these missiles against this or any other country, and to secure their withdrawal or elimination from the Western Hemisphere." There was, therefore, only a single goal: the removal of the missiles. But how to get there?

In Moscow, Khrushchev understood that the old and the new were intersecting: the ancient impulse of great nations to expand their influence and encircle their enemies was at work in a world in which any scuffle or skirmish could end, quickly, in Armageddon. Of course, America would be obsessed with Cuba, Khrushchev thought. "The U.S. couldn't accept the idea of a socialist Cuba, right off the coast of the United States, serving as a revolutionary example to the rest of Latin America. Likewise, we prefer to have socialist countries for neighbors because that is expedient for us."[1]

At first the main options were air attack, invasion, or blockade. On Friday,

---

1   Michael Dobbs, quoting from Khrushev's memoirs in *One Minute to Midnight: Kennedy, Khrushchev, and Castro on the Brink of Nuclear War*, (New York: Vintage Books, 2009), 33.

October 19, Kennedy met with the joint chiefs. Musing about the complexities of the Cold War, the president said that an attack on Cuba might lead to a Soviet attack on Berlin. "Which leaves me with only one alternative, which is to fire nuclear weapons—which is a hell of an alternative."

General Curtis LeMay dismissed the president's concerns. Without an attack on Cuba—not a blockade, but a real attack—the Soviets would see America as fatally weak. "It will lead right into war," LeMay said. "This is almost as bad as the appeasement at Munich."

Kennedy was horrified. When LeMay said that the president was in quite a fix, Kennedy asked him to repeat himself. "What did you say?"

"You're in a pretty bad fix."

"Well, you're in there with me," Kennedy said. "Personally."

Afterward, to an aide, Kennedy observed: "These brass hats have one great advantage in their favor. If we listen to them and do what they want us to do, none of us will be alive later to tell them that they were wrong."

In the debate over air strikes, invasion, and blockade, President Kennedy resisted being seduced by any one faction of his advisers. He knew that each came to the table with preconceptions and interests of their own. Only the two Kennedys—the President and the attorney general—had the ability to see the whole. "We are very, very close to war," JFK told aides amid the crisis. "And there is not room in the White House shelter for all of us." At one point the American military went to DefCon 3, which was two levels short of nuclear war. This level of readiness meant that the nation's nuclear arsenal could be deployed—both missiles and bombers—within fifteen minutes of a presidential order.

In the end, it was a deal—the exchange of missiles in Cuba for missiles in Turkey—that ended the crisis peacefully. Bobby Kennedy served as a useful back-channel. Khrushchev turned out to be a rational actor: he was interested in temporal power, not epic destruction. And President Kennedy, by thinking practically and putting himself in his foe's shoes, had managed to bring things to a calm finish.

The politicians understood one another. Afterward, JFK remarked: "One of the ironic things…is that Mr. Khrushchev and I occupy approximately the same political positions inside our governments. He would like to prevent a nuclear war but is under severe pressure from his hard-line crowd, which interprets every move in that direction as appeasement. I've got similar problems…The hard-lines in the Soviet Union and the United States feed on one another."

Kennedy felt so elated at the conclusion to the crisis that he joked that it was a good night to go to the theater. He might as well get himself shot, he was implying, for he would never again achieve such heights. Like most if not all presidents, Kennedy was obsessed with fame and presidential reputation. "Would Lincoln have been as great a president if he'd lived?" Kennedy had once asked the scholar David Herbert Donald. No, Professor Donald said: Reconstruction would have likely undermined Lincoln's historical standing. Jacqueline Kennedy remembered "Jack saying after the Cuban Missile Crisis, when it all turned [out] so fantastically, he said, 'Well, if anyone's ever going to shoot me, this would be the day they should do it.'…Because he saw then that he would be—you know, he said, it will never top this."

That was the pragmatic Kennedy. His other great gift—that of connecting politics and culture—was on display at Amherst College in the autumn of 1963. The invitation had come from John J. McCloy, the diplomat and banker whom John Kenneth Galbraith and Richard Rovere believed to be the mythic "chairman emeritus" of the American "Establishment," which Henry Kissinger—himself a high-ranking officer in the ethos of power—once defined as "an aristocracy dedicated to the service of this nation on behalf of principles beyond partisanship." A former assistant secretary of war, high commissioner for Germany, and president of the World Bank, McCloy had been educated at Amherst College, a small, elite liberal-arts institution in rural Massachusetts. In the fall of 1963, McCloy's alma mater was breaking ground for a new library to be named in honor of the late poet Robert Frost. President Kennedy, an admirer of Frost's—he had arranged to have the poet read at his inauguration in 1961—happily accepted McCloy's invitation to speak at the ceremony.

It was the kind of occasion that Kennedy loved. Asking Frost to the inaugural had flowed from this vision, as had the White House dinner the president had hosted in the spring of 1962 for all the living recipients of the Nobel Prize from the Western Hemisphere. "I think the pursuit of knowledge, the pursuit of peace, are very basic drives and pressures in this life of ours," Kennedy had told guests at the Nobel evening, "and this dinner is an attempt, in a sense, to recognize those great efforts, to encourage young Americans and young people in this hemisphere to develop the same drive and deep desire for knowledge and peace."

At Amherst, Kennedy began by speaking explicitly of the place he had come to. "Many years ago, Woodrow Wilson said, what good is a political party unless it is serving a great national purpose?" the president asked. "And what good is a private college or university unless it is serving a great national purpose?" He reminded his listeners—estimated at perhaps 10,000—that their luck in life came at a price: service to others. "The library being constructed today, this college, itself—all of this, of course, was not done merely to give this school's graduates an advantage, an economic advantage, in the life struggle. It does do that. But in return for that, in return for the great opportunity which society gives the graduates of this and related schools, it seems to me incumbent upon this and other schools' graduates to recognize their responsibility to the public interest." He then paraphrased Winston Churchill, who had said, at Harvard University in 1943, "The price of greatness is responsibility." Kennedy made the point this way: "Privilege is here, and with privilege goes responsibility."

He then brought Frost to the fore. "This day devoted to the memory of Robert Frost offers an opportunity for reflection...for Robert Frost was one of the granite figures of our time in America," Kennedy said. "He was supremely two things: an artist and an American. A nation reveals itself not only by the men it produces but also by the men it honors, the men it remembers."

To make his point about Frost's particular place in the national culture, Kennedy set up an apposite illustration. "In America," he said, "our heroes have customarily run to men of large accomplishments." In the initial draft, he belabored the point a bit, listing such typical categories of greatness: "statesmen, explorers, generals, magnates, inventors, men of notable courage in war, men of notable enterprise in peace." This ornamentation was struck through in the final speech; he gave his audience credit to know what he meant simply with the phrase "large accomplishments."

Pivoting, he went on: "The men who create power make an indispensable contribution to the nation's greatness, but the men who question power make a contribution just as indispensable, especially when that questioning is disinterested, for they determine whether we use power or power uses us."

Kennedy was swimming in deep waters here. Describing Frost's "special significance"—Kennedy had inserted the phrase instead of "greatness," thus emphasizing what Frost meant to those beyond him and his own reputation—the president, himself something of an optimistic fatalist, said: "He brought an unsparing instinct for reality to bear on the platitudes and pieties of society. His sense of the human tragedy fortified him against self-deception and easy consolation. 'I have been,' he wrote, 'one acquainted with the night.' And because he knew the midnight as well as the high noon, because he understood the ordeal as well as the triumph of the human spirit, he gave his age strength with which to overcome despair."

Kennedy's words were unique, for he was a unique president in recognizing the role letters should play in the life of the Republic. He chose to make the journey to Amherst, and to say these words there, quite deliberately. "The heart of the Presidency," he remarked elsewhere, is "informed, prudent, and resolute choice." That he spent a portion—a not insignificant portion—of his time musing aloud about poetry and power was his way of giving that heart the fullest expression he could. He led practically, and he led spiritually. We can ask for no more than that.

In his National Press Club speech in the first weeks of 1960, Kennedy evoked Lincoln. The presidency, JFK said, must be endowed with "extraordinary strength and vision. We must act in the image of Abraham Lincoln summoning his wartime cabinet to a meeting on the Emancipation Proclamation. That cabinet had been carefully chosen to please and reflect many elements in the country. But 'I have gathered you together,' Lincoln said, 'to hear what I have written down. I do not wish your advice about the main matter—that I have determined for myself.'"

A bit later, Lincoln was ready to sign the Proclamation, Kennedy recalled, but only "after several hours of exhausting handshaking that had left his arm weak." Lincoln remarked, "If my name goes down in history, it will be for this act. My whole soul is in it. If my hand trembles when I sign this proclamation, all who examine the document hereafter will say: 'He hesitated.'"

Kennedy told the rest of the story: "But Lincoln's hand did not tremble. He did not hesitate. He did not equivocate. For he was the President of the United States." Kennedy's voice never trembled, either. That's one reason we hear it still.

The Personal Presidency: John F. Kennedy's Legacy

Mickey Edwards

PRESIDENTS OF THE UNITED STATES are most often judged—by the public, by scholars, by journalists, and thus by history—by the number and magnitude of their "achievements." For the most part, those achievements that earn the highest accolades, and reward the achievers with membership in the leadership pantheon, are quantifiable and at least figuratively solid to the touch. Abraham Lincoln drove a stake through the heart of slavery and saved the Union. Theodore Roosevelt and his cousin, Franklin, created a system of top-down populism: government by elites in the name of, and attentive to, the struggling masses, putting "for the people" at the forefront of their administrations. Ronald Reagan restored the American spirit and partially reshaped the dynamic between citizen and government. Those achievements took time, persistence, solidity of purpose. But what about John Kennedy? He had no time. His days in the presidency were tragically few. What did he leave us? What, if anything, is JFK's legacy?

In some ways, Kennedy's legacy is much the same as the legacy of a teacher. The best teachers are the ones you remember half a century after you left their classrooms. The ones who set your brain, your heart, your gut on fire with the richness of possibility. But there's more than that, because that alone is insufficient to elevate John Kennedy to the heights to which ordinary citizens have raised him, historian objectivity notwithstanding. What really entitles Kennedy's fans (that's the right word) to their high opinion of him?

For starters, Kennedy personalized the presidency. Not all presidents or presidential candidates were cool and distant—Andrew Jackson's inaugural briefly transformed the White House into something resembling a grand bazaar and social hall; Harry Truman strolled the streets in god-awful loud Hawaiian shirts; Mamie Eisenhower's bangs were as commented on as Jackie Kennedy's looks and style—but candidates for the nation's highest office either pretended detachment or reluctance (openly pursuing the office was thought unseemly) or focused their campaigning on visits with the party bosses and wealthy contributors who controlled the delegates to national party conventions.

In 1960, when Kennedy launched his campaign, thirty-four of the fifty states had not yet adopted nominating primaries, and most of those who held primaries considered them merely statements of voter preference; they had nothing to do with who the state's convention delegates would vote for when it counted. Forced by his Catholicism to somehow demonstrate his electability (the United States had never elected a Catholic president) he threw himself full force into the West Virginia primary, a critical factor being the overwhelmingly Protestant makeup of the state. The Kennedy campaign poured money, supplies, and volunteers into the state, but he also did something different: using what subsequently became known as a political "coffee klatch," he met with West Virginians in their living rooms, using his good looks, intelligence, and wit to win them over. Ordinary citizens chatted with him one on one, shook his hand, asked him questions. Kennedy's opponent was fellow Senator Hubert Humphrey, but by letting West Virginians get to know him on a personal basis, JFK won his first major political victory outside of his home state of Massachusetts, defeating Humphrey by more than twenty points. He had proven himself and demonstrated to skeptical party leaders that he could win the support of non-Catholic voters.

When the stiff and formal Richard Nixon, whom Kennedy defeated that year, finally became president, he tried to show that he, too, was a man of the people, leading to politically disastrous pictures of him strolling a beach in wing-tipped dress shoes. Political observers reflected on Texas Governor George W. Bush's defeat of Vice President Al Gore, forty years after Kennedy's West Virginia victory, as being in part a result of voters seeing Bush as the one with whom they'd prefer to have a beer. John Kennedy had brought the presidency a significant step closer to the man and woman on the street and had given them a concept of a president to whom they could relate.

In other areas, however, the Kennedy model, despite its elevating spirit, did not stick so well.

In 1963, when Amherst College invited the president to speak at a convocation honoring the memory of Robert Frost, one would have understood it to be not only an advantageous choice (after all, what school would not benefit from the prestige of having a president on campus) but also a proper choice: one could easily believe that John Kennedy was personally familiar with Frost's poetry and probably that of a good many other poets, too. He was clearly, as his Amherst speech, reproduced elsewhere in this volume, made clear, a literary man. He had written a first-rate senior thesis at Harvard ("Why England Slept," which later became a best-selling book). Even though his friend and assistant Ted Sorensen and Georgetown Professor Jules Davids did a good deal of the actual research and writing, it was Kennedy who conceived of and oversaw the publication of *Profiles in Courage*, a book that celebrated examples of political leaders willing to put their careers at risk to do what they thought was right.

It was an unfortunate fact of history, therefore, that the Soviet Union had launched an aggressive and potentially threatening space program during the Eisenhower and Kennedy presidencies. Kennedy met the challenge by establishing America's own space agency and proclaiming the conquest and exploration of space a national priority. That decision led to some of this country's most exciting and important achievements. But to meet the new challenge, Kennedy recognized that the United States would have to simultaneously beef up its production of mathematicians, engineers, and scientists. The end result was a changed focus for America's colleges and universities, away from the liberal arts, away from the humanities, away from civics and literature and critical thinking, away from the very qualities which Kennedy singled out for their importance in his Amherst speech. That decision—necessary and wise at the time—has had the unfortunate effect of an education system that produces fewer John Kennedys and, in the process, subtly changed the qualities Americans insist upon in national leaders. Our move from the soft sciences to the hard sciences has had effects Kennedy might find dispiriting.

Kennedy's Amherst speech celebrated the arts, the great animating spirit of novels and poetry and painting and sculpting, those cultural animators of what is most human in us. But that was not its only message. This was, after all, the man who in the short time of his presidency launched the Peace Corps and repeatedly promoted the qualities of outreach and growth, of inclusion and peaceful co-existence. America's strength was mobilized to promote international development and opportunity.

To be clear, there was a calculating strategic dimension to all of this—the United States and the Soviet Union were competing for the loyalties, or at least the friendship, of other nations. In Asia, China was doing the same thing. Some worried that communism was on the march and there was truth to the fear that it had significant appeal in nations where life was difficult. One of the less praiseworthy results of the Kennedy presidency was the extent to which the president's "best and brightest" advisors, largely academics who had not served in elective office, bought into the fear and pushed for what became a disastrous involvement in Vietnam. No presidency is without its failures; this was Kennedy's. And it, too, is a contributor to his legacy.

In trying to assess a singular presidency, there are complexities. Clearly the Kennedy presidency had its grand moments and its less successful undertakings. But those few years did shed some light on the qualities one should seek when selecting a man or woman to exercise the immense power resident in the presidency of the United States. Here we turn to the Cuban Missile Crisis.

The missile crisis is a historical footnote today but at the time it was a moment when the fate of nations and the lives of millions hung in the balance. Having discovered proof that the Soviet Union had placed missiles in Cuba, where they could easily reach the United States, only ninety miles away,

Kennedy's top advisors (those "best and brightest" whose advice on Vietnam was so disastrous) urged the president to fire away, blasting the Soviet missiles on their launch pads. It was one of those times when we are reminded that disastrous results can flow from a president of unsteady temperament and injudicious evaluation. Kennedy's greatest moment came not from his "bold" attack on a powerful enemy but from his steadiness. A naval blockade, warnings, and negotiation (the U.S. quietly withdrew some of its own missiles from Europe) led to the U.S.S.R. packing up its missiles and taking them home. It was a critical test for Kennedy; he was young, relatively inexperienced, and, in the eyes of Soviet leaders, likely to be easily bullied. It was vital, for the moment and for his presidency, for him to demonstrate that he, and therefore the United States, would not be pushed around while he was in the White House. It was a moment when John F. Kennedy had to demonstrate strength and resolve. He did, but by doing it in his own way, he showed what we really need in a president: a person of calm, steady temperament; a person who is thoughtful in seeking and weighing alternatives; a person sufficiently at home in his own skin to stand up to bullies abroad and unwise advice at home. That—setting a model for the kind of person we need in a moment of crisis—is Kennedy's greatest legacy.

One final note. It is usual when thinking of John F. Kennedy to focus on how briefly his candle burned. That's a false reading. As a Republican, I'm aware of how Barry Goldwater's disastrous candidacy in 1964 nonetheless motivated millions and created an army of young men and women who dominated Republican Party politics for nearly three decades. John Kennedy did that for Democrats and for liberals and for many more Americans who cherished his manner even if they disagreed with his policies. More than half a century after John F. Kennedy's death, there are still large numbers of Americans whose public careers were launched by their having fallen in love with a young warrior who died too soon but left behind a framework for judging those who would deign to lead.

My Dream for America
A New Generation of Leadership

Steven Olikara

IT HAS BEEN said that President John F. Kennedy "made America young again." In 1961, Kennedy was indeed the youngest elected President in U.S. history at the age of forty-three. His vigorous campaign inspired countless young people to get involved in politics and enter public service careers. Marking a new chapter in America, Kennedy's inaugural address noted, "the torch has been passed to a new generation of Americans—born in this century, tempered by war, disciplined by a hard and bitter peace, proud of our ancient heritage—and unwilling to witness or permit the slow undoing of those human rights to which this nation has always been committed."

I first learned about Kennedy on a children's presidential placemat while growing up in Wisconsin. Scanning across the list of gray-and-white-haired presidents, you see one young, beaming, and vibrant face. Kennedy has always been a symbol of a hopeful, future-looking America in my life.

In May of 2017, JFK would have turned 100. I had the honor of participating in the JFK100 commemorations at the Smithsonian Museum of American History and at the Kennedy Presidential Library where I serve on the New Frontier Award Committee, charged with honoring promising young public servants under the age of forty. During these events, we saw the juxtaposed images of a young president and fast-changing America, invigorated by new leadership.

What was most important about Kennedy's youth was not how young President Kennedy was or how young his supporters were, but how young his ideas were.

His ideas were "young" in two senses: their novelty brought hope to the American people and relied on particularly young people to succeed. They also remain young today, replenished by a new generation serving their country, dreaming big, and acting with courage. Our image of JFK, frozen in time after his assassination, remains youthful, and so do his ideas.

I founded and serve as president of the Millennial Action Project (MAP), the largest nonpartisan organization of young lawmakers in the U.S. MAP focuses on empowering the millennial generation to reinvigorate core American ideas of service, future-looking vision, and courage in public service. These traits are sorely needed in today's cynical political environment. We believe that these ideas exist beyond party, race, class, gender, and other identities. They exist in the souls of true leaders.

My hope in this brief passage is to illustrate these ideas in the Kennedy-era and how they apply to the challenges that my generation is taking on today.

The first young idea I want to highlight is President Kennedy's call to service, captured in, "Ask not what your country can do for you, ask what you can do for your country." That call was probably best embodied in his creation of the Peace Corps. On March 1, 1961, Kennedy signed an executive order establishing the Peace Corps (authorized by Congress that September), in which young volunteers would serve as citizen ambassadors for America's highest ideals in some of the poorest parts of the world, engaging in social and economic development projects.

I had my first encounter with the Peace Corps while I was in college, working on a safe-water access project abroad in Tanzania. In the villages outside of Morogoro, our team, a public-private partnership between USAID and Coca-Cola, worked to provide water, sanitation, and hygiene infrastructure for poor, rural school children.

I remember driving hours in constant, excruciating heat to the rural villages. Arriving at one village, I spotted a young woman who looked as if she might have been American. Eager to discover why she travelled so far into this remote area, I introduced myself and asked, "Are you from America?" She replied proudly, "Yes, I'm a Peace Corps volunteer." She explained her projects promoting the social development of the region. Her passion and skills had completely integrated her into the community. In that moment, in one of the most rural parts of Tanzania, I remember thinking, "This is America at its finest."

On that trip, I discovered many examples of the Kennedy-era service legacy that extended even deeper into some communities than I expected. For example, I met a number of young Africans named "Kennedy." It turned out that many parents in Africa named their children after either Jack or Bobby Kennedy, inspired by their vision for service, peace, and human rights.

The long-term scale of the Peace Corps has been massive. Since 1961, over 225,000 Peace Corps volunteers—primarily young people in their twenties—have served abroad in over 141 countries.

When I talk to former Governors, Senators, and other public servants who served in the seventies, eighties, and nineties, I often ask them what got them involved in politics. The most common answer I hear is, "President Kennedy asked me to serve, and I was inspired to answer that call." For many of them, their first experience in public service was as a Peace Corps volunteer.

This idea of calling on Americans to serve their country and the world was young when President Kennedy delivered it during his inaugural address; I think it must remain replenished by young people today if our democracy is going to thrive for the next generation.

The second "young" ideal Kennedy espoused in his leadership was an optimistic, future-looking vision. He inspired our nation to dream big, to elevate our vision, and imagine what we can do together in common cause with one another. That spirit is perhaps best captured through the Apollo Project.

On September 12, 1962, delivering a speech with over 35,000 people gathered at Rice University in Houston, Kennedy said, "We choose to go to the moon in this decade and do the other things, not because they are easy, but because they are hard."

There's a fascinating archival recording of President Kennedy having a discussion with the NASA administrator at the time, James E. Webb. In many words, Administrator Webb was saying, "Are you crazy? Are you nuts?" He explained the extraordinary complexity of launching a man into orbit on a short timeline, much less into deep space. And we hear President Kennedy on these recordings emphasizing over and over again that second place is not good enough. He believed we had to marshal our resources and our best talent to be the first to reach the moon.

Kennedy made the Apollo Program a priority not just for NASA but also for the nation. A generation of young people entered science and engineering fields to contribute to this effort. On July 20, 1969, when the Apollo 11 astronauts, Neil Armstrong and Buzz Aldrin, walked on the lunar surface (and Michael Collins remained in orbit), the average age of the mission control team in Houston was just twenty-six. That means the future NASA staff were teenagers when they first heard President Kennedy's call for space exploration.

Today, the space race remains replenished by young people, albeit in different forms. Look no further than Mission Control today at SpaceX, the Elon Musk-led space company (founded when Musk was just thirty years old), that is revolutionizing space exploration technology. Their ultimate goal is to bring humans to Mars. SpaceX is powered by a new generation of engineers, largely in their twenties and thirties, who are pushing America and the world to the next frontier. In 2018, SpaceX launched the world's most powerful operational rocket, Falcon Heavy, from the Kennedy Space Center's Pad 39A, the same pad that launched the historic Apollo space flights.

These notions of public service and future-looking vision, exemplified by the Peace Corps and space missions, were young in the 1960s and must remain a core part of young leaders today who are taking up the reins of government.

I believe the essential challenge we are confronted with is how we pass the proverbial torch to a new generation of leaders in this early century. This is the question that the Millennial Action Project is trying to answer: Can our generation govern with renewed energy, service, and optimism for the future?

Many people respond to this question skeptically. "In this political environment?" they ask. Sometimes when I talk about our organization and our goals to bridge the partisan divide and inspire people to work together, they remark, "Oh that's cute, I'm glad someone's working on that." But I believe in what then-Senator Obama said in 2004, that we are not just a collection red states or blue states—we are the United States. I think that ethos is deep in the millennial generation coming of age right now.

At a time when our politics is so small and cynical, I worry that people are turning away from politics, especially young people. Recent data are troubling: the majority of young people today don't believe that the political system will solve the problems that we face. Less than a third of millennials see public service as an appealing career track.

However, I believe Kennedy would be energized by the major challenges we face, and we must be too. I am hopeful because I have already seen the commitment to service and vision on the ground in our work. For example, we have worked with millennial Republican members of Congress who have become champions of mitigating climate change, one of the most difficult and divisive issues. A young congressman named Carlos Curbelo, the co-chair of the millennial-led Congressional Future Caucus and winner of the John F. Kennedy New Frontier Award, has helped to bridge the divide on this issue and successfully led bipartisan efforts to expand energy innovation programs and protect federal climate research. Such progress is possible because of the generational shift in leadership. As Bobby Kennedy once said, young people "have the least ties to the past and the greatest stake in the future."

Let me share one more example, this one of courage in public service. One of the reasons for our dysfunctional political system is the practice of gerrymandering, the way we allow entrenched, partisan incumbents to draw congressional and legislative districts and to choose their voters instead of voters choosing their representatives.

In the Millennial Action Project, we have young legislators, Democrats and Republicans, coming together for nonpartisan redistricting to end gerrymandering. In Ohio, our Republican co-chair, governing in a Republican-dominated state, leads the effort on fairer redistricting. I once asked him at a conference, "Why are you leading this effort? Aren't you disadvantaging your own party?" He replied, "I want to be a member of a party that wins elections because we have better ideas, better candidates, work harder and win the honest way. I don't want to win elections by rigging the game."

That's why I'm hopeful. I get to see this type of leadership on the ground every single day. Young leaders can and will bridge the divide on student debt, education, making entrepreneurship more accessible, democracy reform, and other important issues.

When I sense people thinking that the challenges are too big, I think about President Kennedy. I believe President Kennedy would want to face these challenges head on and move our country to action. He would want to unleash the innovation of this younger generation, marshalling the public and private sectors to work together to solve climate change, alleviate poverty, to make education more affordable.

I believe Kennedy's emphasis on passing the torch is deeply rooted in the American experience. The real genius of the Founding Fathers was to build a political system that is capable of evolving. They made a bet in 1776 on the younger generations of the future changing American politics. That remains a smart bet today.

Indeed, real political change over the course of American history has been driven by young leaders like President Kennedy. Thomas Jefferson lived to be eighty-three years old, but he wrote the Declaration of Independence when he was only thirty-three. James Madison lived to be eighty-five years old, but he was first elected to Congress when he was twenty-nine. He wrote our nation's constitution when he was thirty-six. Many of the Founding Fathers in 1776 were under the age of forty—we see them as being old because they were wearing powdered wigs and we've marbleized them over time.

I decided to leave a stable job, leave a life of relative convenience, and jump into founding the Millennial Action Project with all of my heart and all of my energy during a routine run by the Jefferson and Dr. Martin Luther King Memorials. I was standing in front of the Dr. King Memorial when I realized that it was a man in his twenties and thirties who had spoken the engraved words in front of me. Indeed, Dr. King led the Montgomery Bus Boycott when he was only twenty-six and delivered his "I Have A Dream" speech when he was thirty-four.

The real story of American democracy and American self-government is young leaders driving political transformation—making America more inclusive, more focused on the future. If a generation of twenty-somethings and thirty-somethings invented American democracy, why can't a generation of twenty-somethings and thirty-somethings reinvent American democracy today?

I hope our generation remembers what President Kennedy said on November 29, 1962: "I am certain that after the dust of centuries has passed over our cities, we, too, will be remembered not for victories or defeats in battle or in politics, but for our contribution to the human spirit."

15

"A COLLEGE SUCH AS THIS"

Throughout this book, contributing writers have directly or indirectly implied a close relationship between the arts and a liberal arts education. Journalist Fareed Zakaria, and two of our classmates— Mark Sandler and Joe Stiglitz—discuss the nature and importance of liberal arts education. Is it reasonable to expand our understanding of "art" as Frost and Kennedy used the word to embrace "the liberal arts"? You, the reader, will have to decide. After all, that's what it's all about.

Our final chapter introduces a new voice, Dakota Foster, Amherst 2018. Her essay, originally presented as part of "Poetry and Politics: A Celebration of the Life and Legacy of President John F. Kennedy," stands as an example of leadership in the next generation.

What Is the Earthly Use of a Liberal Arts Education?

Fareed Zakaria[1]

YOU ARE GRADUATING at an interesting moment in history—when the liberal arts are, honestly, not very cool. You all know what you're supposed to be doing these days—study computer science, code at night, start a company, and take it public. Or, if you want to branch out, you could major in mechanical engineering. What you're not supposed to do is get a liberal arts education.

This is not really a joke anymore. The governors of Texas, Florida and North Carolina have announced that they do not intend to spend taxpayer money subsidizing the liberal arts. Florida Governor Rick Scott asks, "Is it a vital interest of the state to have more anthropologists? I don't think so." Even President Obama recently urged students to keep in mind that a technical training could be more valuable than a degree in art history. Majors like English, once very popular and highly respected, are in steep decline.

THE VALUE OF A LIBERAL ARTS EDUCATION

But it is important to have a healthy sense of the value of a liberal education. But first, a point of clarification. A liberal education has nothing to do with "liberal" in the left-right sense. Nor does it ignore the sciences. From the time of the Greeks, physics and biology and mathematics have been as

---

1   These remarks are adapted from Mr. Zakaria's commencement speech at Sarah
     Lawrence College on May 23, 2014. Reprinted with permission.

integral to it as history and literature. For my own part, I have kept alive my interest in math and science to this day.

A liberal education—as best defined by Cardinal Newman in 1854—is a "broad exposure to the outlines of knowledge" for its own sake, rather than to acquire skills to practice a trade or do a job. There were critics even then, the nineteenth century, who asked, Newman tells us, "To what then does it lead? Where does it end? How does it profit?" Or as the president of Yale, the late Bart Giamatti asked in one of his beautiful lectures, "what is the earthly use of a liberal education?"

I could point out that a degree in art history or anthropology often requires the serious study of several languages and cultures, an ability to work in foreign countries, an eye for aesthetics, and a commitment to hard work—all of which might be useful in any number of professions in today's globalized age. And I might point out to Governor Scott that it could be in the vital interests of his state in particular to have on hand some anthropologists to tell Floridians a few things about the other 99.5 percent of humanity.

But for me, the most important earthly use of a liberal education is that it teaches you how to write. In my first year in college, I took an English composition course. My teacher, an elderly Englishman with a sharp wit and an even sharper red pencil, was tough. I realized that coming from India, I was pretty good at taking tests, at regurgitating stuff I had memorized, but not so good at expressing my own ideas. Over the course of that semester, I found myself beginning to make the connection between thought and word.

I know I'm supposed to say that a liberal education teaches you to think, but thinking and writing are inextricably intertwined. The columnist, Walter Lippmann, when asked his thoughts on a particular topic is said to have replied, "I don't know what I think on that one. I haven't written about it yet."

There is, in modern philosophy, a great debate as to which comes first—thought or language. I have nothing to say about it. All I know is that when I begin to write, I realize that my "thoughts" are usually a jumble of half-baked, incoherent impulses strung together with gaping logical holes between them. It is the act of writing that forces me to think through them and sort them out. Whether you are a novelist, a businessman, a marketing consultant or a historian, writing forces you to make choices and brings clarity and order to your ideas.

If you think this has no earthly use, ask Jeff Bezos, the founder of Amazon. Bezos insists that his senior executives write memos—often as long as six printed pages—and begins senior management meetings with a period of quiet time—sometimes as long as thirty minutes—while everyone reads the memos and makes notes on them. Whatever you will do in life, the ability to write clearly, cleanly and—I would add—quickly will prove to be an invaluable skill. And it is, in many ways, the central teaching of a liberal education.

HOW TO SPEAK YOUR MIND

The second great advantage of a liberal education is that it teaches you how to speak and speak your mind. One of the other contrasts that struck me between school in India and college in America was that an important part of my grade was talking. My professors were going to judge me on the process of thinking through the subject matter and presenting my analysis and conclusions—out loud. The seminar, which is in many ways at the heart of a liberal education—and at the heart of this college—teaches you to read, analyze, dissect, and above all to express yourself. And this emphasis on being articulate is reinforced in the many extra-curricular activities that surround every liberal arts college—theater, debate, political unions, student government, protest groups. You have to get peoples' attention and convince them of your cause.

Speaking clearly and concisely is a big advantage in life. You have surely noticed that whenever someone from Britain talks in a class, he gets five extra points just for the accent. In fact, British education—and British life—has long emphasized and taught public speaking through a grand tradition of poetry recitation and elocution, debate and declamation. It makes a difference—but the accent does help too.

The final strength of a liberal education is that it teaches you how to learn. I now realize that the most valuable thing I picked up in college and graduate school was not a specific set of facts or a piece of knowledge but rather how to acquire knowledge. I learned how to read an essay closely, find new sources, search for data so as to prove or disprove a hypothesis, and figure out whether an author was trustworthy. I learned how to read a book fast and still get its essence. And most of all, I learned that learning was a pleasure, a great adventure of exploration.

Whatever job you take, I guarantee that the specific stuff you have learned at college—whatever it is—will prove mostly irrelevant or quickly irrelevant. Even if you learned to code but did it a few years ago, before the world of apps, you would have to learn anew. And given the pace of change that is transforming industries and professions these days, you will need that skill of learning and retooling all the time.

These are a liberal education's strengths and they will help you as you move through your working life. Of course, if you want professional success, you will have to put in the hours, be disciplined, work well with others, and get lucky. But that would be true for anyone, even engineers.

I kid, of course. Remember, I grew up in India. Some of my best friends are engineers. And honestly, I have enormous admiration for engineers and technologists and doctors and accountants. But what we must all recognize is that education is not a zero-sum game. Technical skills don't have to be praised at the expense of humanities. Computer science is not better than art history. Society needs both—often in combination. If you don't believe me, believe Steve Jobs who said, "It is in Apple's DNA that technology alone is not enough. It's technology married with liberal arts—married to the humanities that yields us the result that makes our hearts sing."

That marriage—between technology and the liberal arts—is now visible everywhere. Twenty years ago, tech companies might have been industrial product manufacturers. Today they have to be at the cutting edge of design, marketing, and social networking. Many other companies also focus much of their attention on these fields, since manufacturing is increasingly commoditized and the value-add is in the brand, how it is imagined, presented, sold and sustained. And then there is America's most influential industry, which exports its products around the world, entertainment, which is driven at its core by stories, pictures, and drawings.

A GOOD LIFE, NOT JUST A GOOD JOB

You will notice that so far I have spoken about ways that a liberal education can get you a job or be valuable in your career. That's important, but it is not its only virtue. You need not just a good job but also a good life.

Reading a great novel, exploring a country's history, looking at great art and architecture, making the connection between math and music—all these are ways to enrich and ennoble your life. In the decades to come, when you become a partner and then a parent, make friends, read a book, listen to music, watch a movie, see a play, lead a conversation, those experiences will be shaped and deepened by your years here.

A liberal education makes you a good citizen. The word liberal comes from the Latin liber, which means "free." At its essence, a liberal education is an education to free the mind from dogma, from controls, from constraints. It is an exercise in freedom. That is why America's founding fathers believed so passionately in its importance. Benjamin Franklin—the most practical of all the founders, and a great entrepreneur and inventor in his own right—proposed a program of study for the University of Pennsylvania that is essentially a liberal arts education. Thomas Jefferson's epitaph does not mention that he was president of the United States. It proudly notes that he founded the University of Virginia, another quintessential liberal arts college.

But there is a calling even higher than citizenship. Ultimately, a liberal education is about being human. More than 2,000 years ago, the great Roman philosopher, lawyer, and politician, Cicero explained why it was important that we study for its own sake—not to acquire a skill or trade—but as an end unto itself. We do it, he said, because that is what makes us human: It is in our nature that "we are all drawn to the pursuit of knowledge." It is what separates us from animals. Ever since we rose out of the mud, we have been on a quest to unravel the mysteries of the universe and to search for truth and beauty.

So, as you go out into the world, don't let anyone make you feel stupid or indulgent in having pursued your passion and studied the liberal arts. You are heirs to one of the greatest traditions in human history, one that has uncovered the clockwork of the stars, created works of unimaginable beauty, and organized societies of amazing productivity. In continuing this tradition, you are strengthening the greatest experiment in social organization: democracy. And above all, you are feeding the most basic urge of the human spirit—to know.

Liberal Arts:
The Acquisition of Languages[2]

Mark J. Sandler, '64

WHEN I ASK young people the purpose of an education, most of them say that it is critical to getting a good job. While true, the answer barely hints at the real power of education and its defining role in the quality of life. *Education is the acquisition of languages.*

I don't mean just literal languages such as English, Spanish, or Mandarin. I like to broaden the definition of language to include the languages of *music, botany, astronomy, poetry, physics* and *art*, to name a few. Each has its own vocabulary and interpretation of the world.

The more languages you acquire, the richer your life will be. Languages are like arrows in your quiver. You can draw on them at will to see the same life experiences from a multitude of perspectives. The richness of each experience varies from person to person.

Here are several examples of this point. The massive ancient ruin of Stonehenge sits majestically alone on the Salisbury Plain in England. Huge stone rectangles are arrayed mostly in a very large circle, some on top of each other.

I visited Stonehenge some years ago with my father and my father-in-law, an architect. When we crested the hill that provided our first glimpse of Stonehenge, my father, who had never heard of it, asked what we knew about it.

---

2   Excerpted from *Living! (Almost) everything you need to know.* Mark J. Sandler. Book Baby. New York, 2015

At that moment his total experience was of seeing lots of huge stones in a field. I shared what little I knew of the history of Stonehenge, of its age, and of the theory that the ancient Druids might have built it. When we arrived at the site, our English guide added the languages of *physics* and *astronomy* to our experience. He explained that the ancients who had built it probably used simple physics—the fulcrum, pulleys, and wedges—to move the carved blocks into place after rolling them from a quarry miles away to barges on a river. Then with the language of astronomy he explained how the sun always rose between the two columns at the summer solstice and why a small headstone in the ground was the key to the planting cycle. Finally, with the language of *architecture*, my father-in-law spoke of columns, lintels and proportion. Slowly, with one language after another, a pile of stones turned into a wonder.

A day spent hiking offers a second example. From time to time I hike the Ute Trail in Aspen, Colorado. For years it was simply a hard climb to get some exercise and a beautiful view—a worthwhile but narrow experience. Then one day I hiked along with a young *geology* professor. As we walked along the path he pointed out some pinkish-white parts of the trail, which might once have been the ocean floor. He named rock formations millions of years old, perhaps amongst the oldest in the Rocky Mountains. I had never noticed any of it. The geology professor then said that he often hiked the same trail with a friend who was a *botany* professor from the same local college. He pointed out exceptional trees and rare plants that his friend had shown him. Needless to say, the hike has never been the same. The glimpses into their worlds of geology and botany had made a routine experience far richer.

And a third example. When his young son was killed in war, Israeli author David Grossman wrote:[3]

> It is about the main fact of my life now, yes, the thing that happened to my family, and I felt that I cannot write about anything else, and I tried to write about other things, but somehow they

---

3   David Grossman speaking at LIVE from the New York Public Library, October 13, 2010, https://www.nypl.org/sites/default/files/av/transcripts/ LIVEGrossmanKrauss_10-1.13Transcript.pdf.

feel irrelevant for me…I haven't found the answer to my very intimate private questions and I feel I need to put it into words; maybe it will make it more understandable or bearable for me…I find myself writing more and more poetry, which really surprises me deeply, and I feel that probably *the language of my grief is poetry*…I need something that for me is more refined and more delicate, and this is the language of poetry.

To really understand the story of Icarus, the boy who fell from the sky, first read the Greek myth. Then see Bruegel's painting "Landscape with the Fall of Icarus" at the Musée des Beaux Arts in Brussels. Then read W.H. Auden's poem about the painting. It begins, "About suffering they were never wrong / the Old Masters": *mythology, poetry,* and *art*.

Or you can lie outdoors on your back with a child on a clear, dark, night. Bring along the languages of *mythology* and *astronomy*. Talk about Orion, and the Bull and Cassiopeia. Find the Big Dipper. Long after you're gone, the once-child will look heavenward to find the North Star.

And then there is love, a rich experience in its own right. But bring along the languages of *poetry* and *music* and watch what happens.

So, if life is just a long chain of experiences, many of us are simply doomed to lumber dimly past them; others reach into their quiver of languages and see those same experiences through a kaleidoscope.

Addressing Inequality:
Education for the Information Age

Joseph E. Stiglitz, '64

TODAY'S ECONOMY IS markedly different from that when I was a student at Amherst, a little over fifty years ago. Four interrelated changes stand out: we've moved from a manufacturing economy to an economy based on services, knowledge, and innovation; it is a more globalized economy, with movement of people, goods, services, capital, and knowledge across borders beyond anything that we could have imagined; it is a more dynamic economy, with people frequently changing jobs and homes; and it is a far more unequal society. We've become more divided and more polarized, with income disparities that are far greater than they were in the period after World War II.

I became an economist largely because I was concerned about the poverty and inequality I saw both at home and abroad. I thought that greater understanding of the causes of inequality—that kind of understanding that can only come from deep research—would enable us to address this issue. I had grown up in Gary, Indiana, a city on the southern shore of Lake Michigan that exemplifies both the economic history of the country and the changes I've just described. As I was growing up, I couldn't imagine the process of deindustrialization that would afflict Gary and other steel towns like it; and even more important than deindustrialization were the productivity improvements, the result of advances in science and management, that allowed the same amount of steel to be produced with one sixth the labor force. When I was growing up, I was horrified by the levels of inequality and racial discrimination; I saw firsthand the consequences of labor strife and the failure of government to manage the business cycle, the large fluctuations in output that afflicted the country every few years, accompanied by layoffs. I saw the result in the lives of my classmates, as their families struggled to make ends meet, in a proudly rich country without an adequate system of social protection. But I could not have realized that, in some sense, this was the golden age of capitalism: as I studied inequality, it grew worse and worse. Access to new data and the enhanced ability to process large amounts of data showed that the U.S. was the advanced country with the highest level of inequality, and among the countries with the lowest level of opportunity. At least in a statistical sense, the notion of the American dream was a myth. The life prospects of a young American were more dependent on the income and education of his parents than in almost any other advanced country.

The plight of those without a college education has become particularly bleak. Life expectancies are in decline, income has not just been stagnant, but in decline—with no prospect of matters getting better. The fact that those with education have done so much better than those without education shines a strong light on the importance of education.

The other changes noted above reinforce the importance of education. Globalization has made the global marketplace more competitive, and smart, well-educated management combined with a well-educated and healthy labor force is necessary for success in this global competition. It should be obvious that as we move from manufacturing to a knowledge and innovation economy, the importance of education is again enhanced.

As individuals move more frequently from job to job (whether with the same or different employers) they will have to draw upon new and different skills and knowledge, and here again education is critical. There is evidence that those who are more educated are better able to make these transitions. When they lose a job, they will remain unemployed for a shorter period of time, and when they eventually get a new job, it will be higher paying.

Of course, the nature of the education system that makes for success in this new economy is different from that of the last century. This is partially a continuation of changes already in place as the economy moved from agriculture to manufacturing. Manufacturing required more and different education than that required by traditional agriculture. Success in manufacturing required certain "soft skills," such as showing up on time, and listening carefully to and following certain commands. In many areas, it required the ability to work together in teams. (In fact, some claim that it was precisely because manufacturers needed a well-trained urban labor force that there was such widespread support for public education.)

There are at least three critical changes in our education system as we move to a post-industrial age. First, the fact that the problems individuals confront will change drastically over a given individual's life—even if he doesn't change jobs, and even more so if he does—means that there has to be lifelong learning. Secondly, the internet means that individuals have at their disposal, at their fingertips, more information than was accessible in the best of libraries fifty years ago. What matters today is the ability to evaluate and process information. Metaphorically, education used to be thought of as stuffing young minds with as much information as one could in a few short years, hoping that it would be relevant as they reached middle age some decades later. We know that the information that we give them today will likely be irrelevant in the future, but fortunately, that is not what is at issue. What matters today is their ability to creatively and judiciously process the massive amounts of information and knowledge that are available.

Thirdly, especially in an innovative and innovation economy, what matters is creative thinking. We know well how to teach basic skills. We know there is no magic formula for teaching creativity. Perhaps the best way to do so is through apprenticeship, seeing the demonstration of creativity across a wide range of areas. We know too that a major source of creativity arises in the confrontation between different ideas—ideas from different disciplines or from different countries. Economists would say that there is much gain from intellectual arbitrage, taking ideas from one area and applying them to another; and that this arbitrage itself is a source of creativity.

All of these rationales for a greater emphasis on education are also reasons for a greater emphasis on liberal arts education, especially for those who will be leaders in the future. The world will be facing new and seemingly intractable problems, different from those we have ever faced before. There is no textbook that tells us how to address the problem of global warming, or how we should respond to the potential and threats of artificial intelligence, but, in one way or another, we will have to face these and a myriad of other problems. The best that we can do is to bring to bear all the relevant facts, with reasoning, deliberation, and creativity, hoping to come up with solutions. These are "systems" problems of enormous complexity, and hopefully, our education will have provided those attacking these problems with the creativity to come up with new approaches, and the technical skills and nuanced reasoning to ascertain the vast changes that alternative policies might bring about in our complex interdependent systems.

We too often forget the most important part of education occurs after individuals leave school. Formal schooling occupies only a short period of our lives. More important, in many senses, is what happens afterwards. But the formal part of education is pivotal: for it is there where, if our schools are doing their jobs, we learn how to learn, we acquire and cultivate our love of knowledge, and we come to appreciate disciplined thinking.

Just as our educational system as a whole will have to change in response to these seismic changes in our economy and in technology, so too will liberal arts education. In the nineteenth and earlier centuries, every well-educated person would know Greek, Latin, and the classics. By the mid-twentieth century, liberal arts education had changed dramatically, but at least at Amherst, there was a core curriculum, which reflected a common understanding of a shared knowledge about science, the social sciences, and humanities that was prerequisite to being well-educated. While in the middle of the twentieth century many liberal arts colleges still had required courses called Western Civilization, Amherst's course was even then slightly more global, as we discussed the encounters of different civilizations with each other.

What that core of knowledge should be in the twenty-first century is a matter still in debate; but surely it should include a more globalized view of the world, a better understanding of our planetary boundaries, and a greater awareness of technology and how changes in technology may be affecting us and our civilization. I would also argue that it should include a better understanding of where we as a society are going and where we have come from—an understanding of our economic, political, and social systems and those elsewhere in the world, and what the possibilities are of constructing alternatives.

Still, for all of these changes, the humanist core of a liberal arts education remains unchanged. It is the outgrowth of the Enlightenment, the view that through disciplined reasoning we can come to a better understanding of our world, of our society, and of ourselves. A belief too that we, as a society, through reasoning and deliberation, can improve our social institutions, helping them to ensure that each individual within our society lives up to its potential, and that our society as a whole lives up to what we as a society truly value. There can be social innovations, just as there can be technological innovations. These were shared beliefs when we were students at Amherst. We studied the spread of the Enlightenment ideas and ideals around the world. We saw backsliding in dark periods, like the fascism surrounding World War II, but that was history. In the optimism of the early sixties, as we fought for the civil rights for all Americans, we were pushing forward a new chapter in the spread of the Enlightenment. It was inconceivable to me that we would be where we are today. Seemingly, we have to relitigate the Enlightenment every day. Large swaths of Americans cast aspersions on science, and reportedly, a majority of one of America's two major parties even questions the value of universities—this in a world in which so much of the world's progress, and America's standing in the world, depends on the advances of science and technology. If these views prevail—which I hope and pray that they don't—we would see stagnation and a decline in our position in the world and in our standard of living. There are other countries that still embrace the Enlightenment ideals, countries that are today beginning to outpace the U.S. in the proportion of young and innovative firms.

EDUCATION AND THE CREATION
OF A MORE EQUAL SOCIETY

The previous paragraphs have explained the pivotal role of education in our modern society and how changes in technology and the economy have made education more important, but also made it imperative that there be changes in our education system.

The country has, in many respects, done well in adapting its education system. A modern economy requires more individuals with higher levels of education, more with university degrees. In the years after World War II, there was a vast expansion of our system of higher education. Indeed, the GI bill played a critical role in the country's transition from agriculture to manufacturing, providing to those who had fought in the war (which was essentially all young men and many women) as much education at the best schools that they qualified for. Under President Eisenhower, we upgraded our science education and extended our systems of higher education.

But somehow, between those years when we were at Amherst and today, the country lost its way in this and other areas. It has not even done well in providing the basic skills necessary for success in the twentieth century. It has done poorly on average—with American students performing more poorly on standardized tests than those in many other countries. Indeed the difference between students in one of the best performing states in the U.S., Massachusetts, and students from Shanghai, nominally at the same grade level, amounts to two full years of schooling when looking at the mathematics scores.[4]

But our school systems have served those at the bottom particularly poorly. Inequalities in education opportunity have contributed greatly to in-

---

4   Source: OECD PISA 2012 Country Note for the United States, accessible at https://www.oecd.org/unitedstates/PISA-2012-results-US.pdf.

equalities in income and in economic opportunity.[5] These inequalities have been growing. It is part of the reason that, as we noted earlier, the U.S. is the advanced country with the highest level of inequality and among the lowest levels of equality of opportunity.

But we have also not kept up with university education, especially when it comes to completing a four-year higher education degree. Other countries have recognized the critical role that an educated labor force has in economic success and have done more to ensure access for all.

One of the reasons for these dire outcomes is that our elementary and secondary education systems are local, and America is afflicted with increasing economic segregation. Moreover, our college and university education systems are fee based, with fees that are sufficiently high that a higher education is out of reach of many, especially in the "lower middle class." Even though America's selective colleges (like Amherst) are enormously generous, with need-blind admissions, providing full scholarships for all those who need them, less than 10 percent of the students come from the bottom half of the country: their local education system simply hasn't provided them with the skills needed to gain acceptance.

It would not be difficult to improve the overall quality of education and increase equality of opportunity. Put simply, we have to spend more. Sixty years ago, our public schools—and we—were the beneficiaries of a system of pervasive discrimination. There were very limited opportunities for women, so schools could hire highly qualified teachers and pay them a fraction of what similarly qualified men would be paid. But we can't do that anymore. Surely, if we care for our children, shouldn't we want them to have good teachers,

---

5   The richest 25 percent of school districts spend 15.6 percent more funds than the poorest 25 percent, according to the Department of Education. See https://www. ed.gov/news/media-advisories/secretary-duncan-urban-league-president-morial-spotlight-states-where-education-funding-shortchanges-low-income-minority-students. A study by Jackson, Johnson and Persico finds that every 10 percent increase in per pupil spending on their twelve years of education leads to 7 percent higher wages and a 3.2 percent decrease in annual incidence of poverty. See Jackson, C. Kirabo, Johnson, Rucker C., and Claudia Persico, "The Effects of School Spending on Educational and Economic Outcomes: Evidence from School Finance Reforms," *Quarterly Journal of Economics*, 131(1):157-218.

people who are dedicated to education, but choosing education as a well-paid profession? Higher pay would lead to greater respect, and the overall education experience would be improved.

Higher education too needs to be made affordable to everyone—without asking poor and middle income students to take on an enormous burden of debt. There are many ways of doing this—government tuition subsidies, more scholarships, or an income contingent student loan program, of the kind that has worked so successfully in Australia.

MORE THAN EDUCATION

A lack of quality education is contributing greatly to the country's problems. Those without an adequate education who have lost their jobs as the country has deindustrialized have found it difficult to find jobs elsewhere. Too many have become trapped in communities without jobs and without hope. It is this despair that helps explain in part the decline in life expectancy. It is what has given rise to the enormous increase in deaths from suicide, drug overdose, and alcoholism, what Anne Case and Angus Deaton have called "deaths of despair."[6]

Changes in education, though, may be easy compared to the other more fundamental changes that the country has to make, if we are to live up to the charge that our class received from John F. Kennedy, if our economy is to continue to be dynamic, and if there is to be even a modicum of social and economic justice. They are necessary but not sufficient. One of the reasons that education has been central to recent public policy discussions is that it is pivotal; but another reason is that it is relatively easy, requiring fewer of the deeper reforms in our economic and social systems.

We sometimes forget that markets don't exist in a vacuum; they have to be structured. They are structured by our laws and regulations. And the way our laws and regulations have structured our markets has led both to more

---

6   See Anne Case and Sir Angus Deaton, 2017, "Mortality and Morbidity in the 21st century," Brooking Papers on Economic Activity, Spring 2017; also Anne Case and Sir Angus Deaton, 2015, "Rising morbidity and mortality in midlife among white non-Hispanic Americans in the 21st century," *PNAS* 112(49): 15078-15083

inequality and to lower growth. It has resulted in firms being more short term in their thinking; in markets that are less competitive, and thus less dynamic; and in workers' bargaining power being eviscerated.

One of the big insights of modern economics is that equality and growth are *complementary*: more equal societies perform better. This was the central message of my book *The Price of Inequality*. We are paying a high price for our high level of inequality—it weakens our democracy, it hurts our economy, and it divides our society. This view has since become a mainstream view, with the International Monetary Fund making it central to the policy advice which they dispense around the world.

In this perspective, inequality is not just a moral issue—though it is that, especially when it comes to the extremes of inequality that we have been experiencing. It is also an economic and political issue.

CONCLUDING COMMENTS

We were lucky to have attended Amherst when we did, a moment of optimism and faith in the liberal arts education and in Enlightenment ideals. We were privileged, and I sense that many of us felt that, and felt that with privilege came responsibility: to make sure that others could enjoy the kind of education from which we had benefitted so much, and to contribute to a better world, each in our own way. The more than half century since has been marked by rapid economic growth—GDP today is five and a half times greater than what it was in 1960 when we entered Amherst, and GDP per capita is three times more.[7] But the country in many ways does not feel as optimistic, as happy, as well off. Almost surely, an important part of the reason for this is that we have allowed a great divide to open up. These are wounds that now have to be healed.

---

7   Source: FRED Economic data, Federal Reserve Bank of St. Louis, accessible at https://fred.stlouisfed.org/series/GDPC1#0 and https://fred.stlouisfed.org/series/A939RX0Q048SBEA#0.

Answering President Kennedy's Challenge

Dakota Foster, '18

PRESIDENT JOHN F. KENNEDY'S legacy of hope, largely reflected in his stirring speeches, lives on, as does the record of his challenges that remain unmet.

In the darkest section of his convocation speech at Amherst for the groundbreaking of the Frost Library, Kennedy quoted a poignant line from Robert Frost's poem, "Death of a Hired Man." Frost warned of, "the fate of having nothing to look backward to with pride and nothing to look forward to with hope."

In the fall of 1963, the United States had 16,000 troops in Vietnam, and neither the military nor the civilian political situation had stabilized. George Wallace had just assumed office as the governor of Alabama. Only a year before, the Soviet Union had positioned missiles ninety miles off our southern coast, precipitating the Cuban missile crisis. At this celebration of Kennedy and Frost, fifty-four years later, we should ask: "what can we look backward to with pride?" Where have we come as a country in the years since President Kennedy addressed Amherst and what is our responsibility as we look to the future?

There have been great national achievements—many of them. President Kennedy referenced women just twice in his speech, as compared to twenty times for men. In 1963, women composed a mere 32 percent of the American workforce. Today, that number stands at 47 percent. In the decades since President Kennedy delivered his address, nearly all institutions of higher education have opened their doors to women. America has witnessed women becoming CEOs of Fortune 500 companies (1972), justices on the Supreme Court (1981), and major party nominees for the office that Kennedy himself once held (2016).

In our national life, Americans have secured marriage equality. We have walked on the moon, invented personal computers, mapped the human genome, and developed treatments for cancer and HIV. Collectively, these are achievements that we can look back upon with pride. Yet, in many other ways, as we reflect on President Kennedy's exhortations delivered here all those years ago, we have failed to make progress, and in some ways, we have retreated further still.

Kennedy said, "There is inherited wealth in this country and also inherited poverty." However, the wealth disparity of the 1960s looks almost equitable compared to today's. President Kennedy often said: "A rising tide lifts all boats," but over the last fifty years, the yachts of the wealthy have continued to rise while the boats of the poor and middle class have been swept out to sea. Between 1963 and 2016, the income of America's wealthiest 10 percent almost doubled; the income of America's bottom 10 percent has been virtually stagnant. In 2016, the wealthiest 1 percent of citizens possessed almost 40 percent of the nation's overall wealth.

President Kennedy also urged his audience to "make it possible for Americans of all different races and creeds to live together in harmony" so that our "world will exist in diversity and freedom." America has yet to become a harmonious place of diversity and freedom. The United States holds 21 percent of the world's prisoners and incarcerates African-American citizens at five times the rate for white citizens. A quarter of our citizens who are killed by law enforcement are unarmed.

President Kennedy suggested that "a nation reveals itself not only by the men it produces but also by the men it honors." One must look no further than the violence in Charlottesville, Virginia, in the summer of 2017 to see that our nation has taken decades to seriously confront the question of whom we should honor.

Finally, President Kennedy challenged his listeners at Amherst to "protect the beauty of the natural environment." Our nation has not met his challenge. Since 2001, we have experienced sixteen of the seventeen hottest years on record. Earth's sea levels and temperatures are rising; its glaciers are melting at a record rate, and its lakes are acidifying. Furthermore, the land that this country has long preserved—its national parks and monuments—are under increasing threat, along with the federal agencies that are charged with protecting our environment.

When President Kennedy spoke in 1963, the clouds of change were gathering. Soon they would become darker still—weeks later President Kennedy would fall, and his brother, Robert, and Martin Luther King Jr. would follow. The recently constructed Berlin Wall would stand for decades.

Despite this, Kennedy created a sense of hope. So how do we recreate that sense of optimism today? Through unrest, conflict, and discourse, opportunities for advancement and hope are born. *We* must push toward the progress that can follow turbulent times. *We* must seize the opportunity to bring forth an America that future generations can look upon with hope. But we must do so with the understanding that inevitable and as yet unknown storms lie ahead.

It would be ill-advised to believe that unknown historical forces have propelled us into this state and that those forces will somehow move us into a period of progress. The responsibility for progress, as Kennedy implied, rests with us. Access to a liberal arts education, regardless of financial means, for the best and brightest students, developing leaders who are prepared to question, think critically, act collectively, and tackle the great issues of today and tomorrow, is critical. As President Kennedy said, those "who create power make an indispensable contribution to the nation's greatness but those who question power make a contribution just as indispensable, especially when that questioning is disinterested..."

With such leadership, our generation will be able to look backward with pride and forward with hope.

AFTERWORD
The Solace from Well-Chosen Words

Bestor Cram

IN 1960, NORMAN MAILER prophesized that "America's politics would now be also America's favorite movie."[1] Following three years of John Kennedy's presidency, motion pictures of assassination, murders, and funerals would unite the nation in astonished grief, in a manner we had not known before. What we had believed and trusted all changed. The solace and insight that words bring seemed to disappear. We were left to judge not if life had become a movie, but more profoundly what had this shared medium meant to our sense of self, our evolving national character, and the way we understood the world we lived in?

The fact was that we had been brought together less by an event than by an individual: Kennedy. And the camera had much to do with translating his charismatic eloquence.

As a documentary filmmaker, visual evidence is my stock in trade. I know, however, that this is not the silent film era. It is a time in which the sound that accompanies cinema is more than mere music or amplification of natu-

---

1   Neal Gabler. "Lights ... Camera ... Election!" *Los Angeles Times*, August 24, 2003.
http://articles.latimes.com/2003/aug/24/opinion/op-gabler24

ral elements. It is often the vehicle that enables the narrative to unveil itself. Often it is what provides structure, sets tone, and reveals emotion so linked to the experience of cinematic storytelling.

In the case of the two principal subjects of the film, *JFK: The Last Speech*, the passionate voices and carefully selected words provide the foundation for reconsidering an address that was largely lost in the tragic events closely following its October 1963 delivery at Amherst College by JFK, who was honoring Robert Frost. Historian Douglas Brinkley states:

> Kennedy thought oratory was a way to move people. And you saw that when he started out with his inaugural address and you follow these remarkable set of speeches. Honestly, you have to go back—I mean, FDR had great speeches, but they weren't these compositions of intellectual and civic engagement the way that Kennedy did.[2]

It wasn't the power of the speech alone or its notion of poetry and power that was the catalyst for the film's storyline, however. It was an article by Stewart Udall, shared by Executive Producer Neil Bicknell, that added a key dimension to the documentary—an intriguing revelation of the Frost-Kennedy relationship that captured the tension and complexity of the Cold War era. Udall's friendship with Frost and his working alliance with Kennedy made possible a unique moment of diplomatic artistry, and Frost was primed for it. As Udall wrote, Frost believed a "'noble rivalry' was the right theme for 'two nations laid out for rivalry in sports, science, art and democracy.'" Frost went to Moscow to meet one-on-one with Soviet leader Nikita Khrushchev. Udall continued:

> He underscored his point with one of his own aphorisms: "A great nation makes great poetry, and great poetry makes a great nation" Khrushchev studied Frost's face as Frost expounded his

---

2   Douglas Brinkley. Interview transcript for *JFK: The Last Speech*

argument. He intervened only once to say that the fundamental contest would be in the area of "peaceful economic competition." Otherwise, the Soviet leader took no issue with Frost and at one point he exclaimed, "You have the soul of a poet!"[3]

The trip ultimately did not provide the hoped-for success but it thus provided a backstory for Kennedy's visit to Amherst and a thread that was woven throughout *JFK: The Last Speech*.

Good documentary films transport us to another time and connect the past with the present. When life is put into the form of a movie, the ordinary can be transformed into the dramatic. But with Kennedy and Frost, there was never a sense of the mundane; rather, these were lives lived on the big stage. Good stuff for the filmmaker, yet not enough for a film that needs to shine a new light on well-known subjects. Over the course of prepping the project, which evolved out of material first shot at the Amherst '64 reunion, it became apparent that those who had benefited most from this moment in time at Amherst had stories of their own to tell. This began a process of meeting by phone dozens of graduates, most of whom could not remember much of the content of the speech delivered by the president. We were looking for subject matter that could be a measuring stick of the last fifty years and believed the recollections of Amherst students might provide fresh words about how we as a nation have grown. But remembering the past is not always easy. As Amherst '64 graduate Roger Mills writes:

> Those who were young adults in the early 1960s have to struggle to recall our views of the president in October 1963 and to separate them from the many different versions of him that emerged after November of that year.

---

3   Stewart L. Udall. "Robert Frost's Last Adventure." *New York Times*. June 11, 1972, https://archive.nytimes.com/www.nytimes.com/books/99/04/25/specials/frost-last.html?_r=1&oref=slogin

We began to ask the question, "How do we best understand the impact of a speech that was obscured by violence three and a half weeks later?" We realized that seeing people's lives today would be the best evidence of the speech's enduring inspiration. And thus was born the notion that this was both a telling of a little-known part of history coupled with the exploration of lives whose arc had been shaped at a liberal arts college and reflected a determination to fulfill the challenge of President Kennedy in taking on the responsibilities that privilege requires.

There are multiple roles the documentary filmmaker plays in assembling and editing a version of history and its reflection as part of the present: journalist, writer, researcher, technician, artist, and certainly pop psychologist all fit into the documentarian's toolkit. Initially, the process of making a documentary is taking stock of one's interests and biases, one's knowledge and preconceptions. Having graduated college in 1967, I came from a similar era with a similar awareness of Kennedy and Frost as the Amherst '64 graduates possessed, yet there was a gap. My graduating class was confronted with a war and selective service. I chose the Marine Corps, and rather than put my fate in the hands of the draft board, I became an officer serving in Vietnam from TET '68 to TET '69. Upon my return stateside, I filed for reclassification as a conscientious objector (CO), protesting a war that I learned too well was unjust and morally abhorrent. I have since made films that have dealt with this war and those who served as well as those who made the policies that would put Americans in harm's way. I developed an uneasy feeling about Kennedy, McNamara, Bundy, Johnson, Westmoreland, Taylor, Lodge, and other policy makers who lacked the courage to alter the course of our engagement in Southeast Asia. I remembered journalist Hedrick Smith's assessment of the Kennedy Administration in his thoughtful analysis of the Pentagon Papers published in July 1971 while I was an organizer for Vietnam Veterans Against the War.

The Pentagon's study of the Vietnam war concludes that President John F. Kennedy transformed the "limited-risk gamble" of the Eisenhower Administration into a "broad commitment" to prevent Communist domination of South Vietnam…the Kennedy tactics deepened the American involvement in Vietnam piecemeal, with each step minimizing public recognition that the American role was growing.

President Kennedy's response during thirty-four months in office, as the Pentagon account tells it, was to increase American advisors from the internationally accepted level of 685 to roughly 16,000, to put Americans into combat situations—resulting in a tenfold increase in American combat casualties in one year—and eventually to inject the United States into the internal South Vietnamese maneuvering that finally toppled the Diem regime.[4]

Believing our country has never really come to terms with Kennedy and Vietnam, I understood that embarking on a project that would celebrate President Kennedy was going to be a challenge for multiple reasons. Historian Douglas Brinkley expresses well the complexity in assessing JFK:

Vietnam is a difficult story, because on the one hand I think that John F. Kennedy always had doubts…JFK is thirty-four; he's a young man. This is 1951. He's going to run for the Senate. I think he understands even then that anybody, including the French in that case, but also by extension Americans, who tries to win a military victory against Ho Chi Minh's revolution is destined to fail. And I think he still has those doubts all the way through to his trip to Dallas in 1963…but here's the paradox. That same Kennedy expands American involvement substantially in Vietnam during his presidency.[5]

---

4 Neil Sheehan (Author), Hedrick Smith (Author), E.W. Kenworthy (Author), Fox Butterfield (Author). *The Pentagon Papers*. As Published by the *New York Times* Quadrangle Books; First edition (1971). New York.

5 Brinkley. Interview Transcript for *JFK: The Last Speech*.

It was my early life as a student that first brought me to regard Kennedy highly as a leader. It was my post-Vietnam war life that led me to reconsider his leadership and its impact upon who we are today. And it was this documentary that caused me to regard the president with a new appreciation of his principles and ethics that are part of an enduring legacy. The speech had been conveyed to me as a consideration of power and poetry. With this in mind, I read the president's address and then listened to the recording of it, which lasts just under fifteen minutes. I became convinced along with my production team that there was much to consider as I digested JFK's extraordinary insights into these two surprisingly related themes:

> If art is to nourish the roots of our culture, society must set the artist free to follow his vision wherever it takes him. We must never forget that art is not a form of propaganda; it is a form of truth.

> Strength takes many forms, and the most obvious forms are not always the most significant. The men who create power make an indispensable contribution to the nation's greatness, but the men who question power make a contribution just as indispensable, especially when that questioning is disinterested, for they determine whether we use power or power uses us.

Added to the strength and wisdom of the oratory came a series of fascinating personal stories shared by the Amherst '64 graduates who provided us with visual contemporary portraits. These storytellers—Steve Downs, Ted Nelson, George Wanlass, and Gene Palumbo—became friends in the filmmaking process, for each in their own style and expression inspired us personally with their commitments to being the change they saw so necessary for our world to become more holistic and expressive of our shared humanity. Each could be a subject for a longer documentary, but we are indebted to them for their participation and willingness to fulfill their role as part of a complex story.

In the end, what you leave out of a documentary is as fascinating as what you put in. The linear art form has a beginning, middle and end, and doesn't have the capacity for so many of the sidebar journeys one wishes to take. For example, as pointed out by our film's writer and co-producer Matthew Maclean, a poem we all know by Frost, "The Road Not Taken", has been misinterpreted by most of us, including the president himself when he quoted it at Amherst. From the *Paris Review*'s excerpt of David Orr's book, *The Road Not Taken: Finding America in the Poem Everyone Loves and Almost Everyone Gets Wrong*:

> Most readers consider "The Road Not Taken" to be a paean to triumphant self-assertion ("I took the one less traveled by"), but the literal meaning of the poem's own lines seems completely at odds with this interpretation. The poem's speaker tells us he "shall be telling," at some point in the future, of how he took the road less traveled by, yet he has already admitted that the two paths "equally lay / In leaves" and "the passing there / Had worn them really about the same." So the road he will later call less traveled is actually the road *equally* traveled. The two roads are interchangeable.[6]

Orr acknowledges Frost's extraordinary popularity and that he is "considered bleak, dark, complex, and manipulative; a genuine poet's poet, not a historical artifact like Longfellow or a folk balladeer like Carl Sandburg." He also points out that Frost's poetry is about challenging the reader to engage as an interpreter, concluding that "The Road Not Taken", is a poem about the "necessity of choosing that somehow, like its author, never makes a choice itself—that instead repeatedly returns us to the same enigmatic, leaf-shadowed crossroads."

---

6   David Orr. "The Most Misread Poem in America," *The Paris Review*. September 11, 2015. https://www.theparisreview.org/blog/2015/09/11/the-most-misread-poem-in-america/

The many roads we took on this documentary journey were possible because of the commitment of passionate Amherst '64 graduates, their college, and the support of The Arthur Vining Davis Foundation and American Public Television. *JFK: The Last Speech* has been a project of passion, in memory of a man who served our nation with a noble distinction that would seem essential to the office he held, and yet is so lacking in the politics of today. The disparity causes us to reflect on the stanzas of President Kennedy's address that speak to our need to be engaged citizens who find wisdom in the arts:

> The artist, however faithful to his personal vision of reality, becomes the last champion of the individual mind and sensibility against an intrusive society and an officious state…In pursuing his perceptions of reality, he must often sail against the currents of his time.

We learn from the past; it offers inspiration and guidance for how to navigate the ethical dilemmas we encounter on a daily basis. "When power corrupts, poetry cleanses," Kennedy said. And like many documentaries, this story has multiple endings. The day that Kennedy was shot, Kingston Trio singer-songwriter John Stewart wrote a song and then recorded it on the day of Kennedy's funeral. It was released the next month as the title song of the album *Song for a Friend*:

> When you sit and wonder why things have gone so wrong
> And you wish someone would tell us where our friend has gone.
> Look then in the hills when there's courage in the wind
> And in the face of freedom and those who look to him…
>
> When you sit and wonder why things have gone so wrong.
> It's then that we'll remember where our friend has gone.[7]

---

7   John Stewart. 1963. https://www.flashlyrics.com/lyrics/john-stewart/song-for-a-
      friend-06

The other ending has to be with Robert Frost, whom JFK eulogized at Amherst: "We must never forget that art is not a form of propaganda; it is a form of truth," said the president. I love to believe that cinema is part of understanding what the truth is. The act of going to the cinema is part of our own search for truth. It is also an affirmation of friendship, for we are able to see life in a movie and share that with those we hold dear. For many of us, it is Frost who was able to underscore our humanity simply and eloquently as an extension of who we are to one another.

The Pasture
I'm going out to clean the pasture spring;
I'll only stop to rake the leaves away
(And wait to watch the water clear, I may):
I sha'n't be gone long. —You come too.

I'm going out to fetch the little calf
That's standing by the mother. It's so young,
It totters when she licks it with her tongue.
I sha'n't be gone long. —You come too.[8]

---

8   "The Pasture" by Robert Frost from the book *The Poetry of Robert Frost* edited by Edward Connery Lathem. Copyright © 1939, 1967, 1969 by Henry Holt and Company. Reprinted by permission of Henry Holt and Company. All rights reserved.

APPENDIX A

Discussion Questions on Kennedy,
Frost, and Civic Engagement

1. JFK asked, **"What good is a private college or university unless it's serving a great national purpose?"**

Should we hold colleges responsible for serving a national purpose or should they be understood as serving basically private purposes, providing education for self-development and economic gain?

2. He continued, **"Unless the graduates of this College and other colleges like it who are given a running start in life—unless they are willing to put back into our society those talents, the broad sympathy, the understanding, the compassion—unless they're willing to put those qualities back into the service of the Great Republic, then obviously the presuppositions upon which our democracy are based are bound to be fallible."**

What are the "presuppositions upon which our democracy is based?"

JFK claimed graduates of "a college such as this" have a special responsibility for sustaining our democracy. Do you agree? Why or why not?

Who *is* responsible for maintaining our democratic system? Are there institutions that have corporate responsibility, for example Congress, the political parties, and educational institutions?

3. JFK said to his Amherst audience that **"privilege is here and with privilege goes responsibility."**

What is the nature of the privilege and of the responsibility to which he refers, and where did these ideas originate?

How has the reality of privilege and the obligation of responsibility influenced America's politics and economic system?

What is the distribution of privilege and the acceptance of responsibility today?

4. Kennedy stated that **"the problems this country now faces are staggering"** and that **"we need the service, in the great sense, of every educated man or woman."**

The problems he referenced were:

— finding ten million jobs in the next two and a half years.

— governing our relations with over 100 countries.

— making it possible for Americans of all different races and creeds to live together in harmony.

— making it possible for a world to exist in diversity and freedom.

How do the problems our country faces today differ from those Kennedy enumerated?

Why did Kennedy single out "educated" men and women; doesn't everyone share equally in the responsibility for addressing our problems?

5. Kennedy observed, **"The men who create power make an indispensable contribution to the nation's greatness, but the men who question power make a contribution just as indispensable, especially when that questioning is disinterested, for they determine whether we use power or power uses us."**

Is this an extraordinary assertion? Who questions the powerful today? Are the questioners disinterested? What about today's artists; are they disinterested questioners of power?

6. Kennedy observed, **"Robert Frost coupled poetry and power, for he saw poetry as the means of saving power from itself. When power leads man towards arrogance, poetry reminds him of his limitations...When power corrupts, poetry cleanses."**

What is the power of poetry as expressed here? Can you distinguish between external constraints on power and internal constraints, character for example? What role does poetry play in establishing and nurturing character?

7. Kennedy asserted that **"art establishes the basic human truths which must serve as the touchstone of our judgment."**

Do you agree with that statement? How does art accomplish that result? What basic human truths are meant here? In what sense do they serve as touchstones of our judgment?

8. Kennedy notes, **"If sometimes our great artists have been the most critical of our society, it is because their sensitivity and their concern for justice which must motivate any true artist, makes him aware that our nation falls short of its highest potential."**

Do artists as a group have greater sensitivity and concern for justice than the rest of society? Should they be given special attention in this regard?

9. Kennedy summed Robert Frost's contributions as follows: **"He brought an unsparing instinct for reality to bear on the platitudes and pieties of society. His sense of the human tragedy fortified him against self-deception and easy consolation. 'I have been,' he wrote, 'one acquainted with the night.' And because he knew the midnight as well as the high noon, because he understood the ordeal as well as the triumph of the human spirit, he gave his age strength with which to overcome despair. At bottom, he held a deep faith in the spirit of man."**

How can these contributions help cleanse politics? Why is a faith in the spirit of man a contribution to "good" politics?

10. Kennedy concluded, **"I look forward to a great future for America—a future in which our country will match its military strength with our moral restraint, its wealth with our wisdom, its power with our purpose.**

 I look forward to an America which will not be afraid of grace and beauty, which will protect the beauty of our natural environment.

 I look forward to an America which will reward achievement in the arts as we reward achievement in business or statecraft.

 I look forward to an America which will steadily raise the standards of artistic accomplishment and which will steadily enlarge cultural opportunities for all of our citizens.

 I look forward to an America which commands respect throughout the world not only for its strength but for its civilization as well. And I

look forward to a world which will be safe not only for democracy and diversity but also for personal distinction."

JFK made these statements over fifty years ago. How have we as a country measured up to his vision in each case?

11. The film and the book show that a number of graduates of the class of 1964 were moved by the words of Kennedy and Frost.

After reading the descriptions of their experiences, what was it that struck a particularly responsive chord in these young men? Why did the speech and subsequent events make an impact?

12. A number of those in Kennedy's audience responded to the themes of his address and their liberal education by joining the Peace Corps.

Why do you think this service was particularly appealing? How did their education prepare them for this opportunity or did it?

13. Steve Downs (chapter 7) and Gene Palumbo (chapter 8) focus on their pursuit of justice. These pursuits required them to question governmental policy. However, neither one is a poet or an artist.

Would Kennedy and Frost have approved?

14. George Wanlass (chapter 9) is not an artist but he appreciates art. He has promoted the arts among the young and those who lack resources.

Has he responded to Kennedy's call, and if so, how? How has the breadth of his education helped him in these pursuits? Does what he is doing serve democracy, and if so, how?

15. While Kennedy came to Amherst to praise Robert Frost, their relationship was not always smooth as Roger Mills details (chapter 1).

What were the points on which they disagreed? Do you accept Robert Benedetti's thesis (chapter 11) that they ultimately agreed on the responsibility of those with broad educations to assume leadership in a democracy?

16. Since 1964, Robert Frost's poetry may have become "less traveled by."

Why should we read Frost today? What does he offer that can inform the American spirit now? Are there aspects of his legacy that are not relevant to citizens today?

17. John Meacham in chapter 14 states that Kennedy "led practically and he led spiritually." And Mickey Edwards in chapter 14 concludes that Kennedy left behind "a framework for judging those who would deign to lead."

What are the major legacies of John Kennedy's public service? Frost suggested that we need objectives "to look forward to with pride"; did Kennedy provide us such objectives? What might they be?

18. Kennedy argued for the perspective of the outsider, the non-conformist, in his speech.

Is this faith in the diversity of perspectives a lasting heritage? How did his record as president measure up to this value?

19. Some argue that Kennedy picked the "best and brightest" for his administration.

Was the "best and brightest" approach flawed? In what ways? Give examples. If you were to teach a seminar on leadership, what aspect of leadership would

Kennedy best illustrate? Did his attraction to the arts support his leadership style? How?

20. A current high school graduate decides to accept Kennedy's challenges and Frost's philosophy of education.

What course of study should he/she consider? What experiences or early career paths should he/she explore after graduating from college?

21. The political climate during the presidency of John Kennedy was vastly different from today's.

What would the voters of today think of him? Would his "elite" background be a stumbling block? What about his personal life? Would he have been seen as "soft" on governmental critics? Would he win the youth vote?

22. At the end of his speech, Kennedy praised Frost by saying that because of his life, our hold on this planet has increased.

Could you say the same for Kennedy? He had great promise and gave inspiring speeches, but did he accomplish enough to increase our hold on the planet? Or, was it enough that he communicated promises for us to keep and inspiring phrases for us to remember?

23. One could characterize Gene Palumbo's account of his experiences in El Salvador as a parable. He recounted the social strife incurred when a society doesn't address polarization among its citizens.

Do you see parallels between his experience and current realities in politics at home and/or aboard?

24. Several authors implied that Frost and Kennedy "invented" or contrived their public images. In the 1950s, many Hollywood stars crafted a public persona; however, that was not an expected behavior for a poet or a politician.

How would you describe their public images? Does Kennedy's speech fulfill or contrast with his public persona? Does what he says of Frost fulfill or contrast with Frost's public persona?

25. In Part 2, chapters 6 through 10, members of the Amherst class of 1964 detailed the ways Frost and Kennedy impacted their lives.

Do you see common threads in their stories? Describe them. Did these narratives suggest divergent interpretations of Frost and Kennedy within the group? Did any of these classmates misunderstand Kennedy or Frost? What do their experiences have to teach others?

APPENDIX B

Peace Corps Service

Amherst Class of 1964

Douglas Bray	Turkey	1964-66
Stephen Downs	India	1964-66
Pat DeLeon	Training Center, Hawaii	1969-70
Peter Easton	Niger	1964-67
Cristopher Gray	Nigeria	1964-66
Norman Groetzinger	India	1966-68
John Keffer	Panama	1966-69
Carl Levine	Brazil	1968-70
Theodore Nelson	Turkey	1964-68
Arthur Schoepfer	Kenya	1964-66
Richard Sparks	Nigeria	1964-66
Richard Stauffer, Jr.*	(site unknown)	1964-75
Charles Stover	Niger	1964-66

*Service unverified

ABOUT THE AUTHORS

Robert R. Benedetti, Ph.D. Professor Emeritus, Department of Political Science, University of the Pacific. Formerly Executive Director, Harold S. Jacoby Center for Public Service and Civic Leadership, University of the Pacific. A '64

Neil C. Bicknell, Co-Editor, MBA, CFA. CEO of The Bicknell Group; Former CEO, U.S. Pension, V.P. Goldman Sachs & Co., V.P. PaineWebber, Inc., Village Trustee, Scarsdale, New York; Officer, U.S. Navy, 1966-69; Vice Chair, ReclaimTheAmericanDream.Org, Inc.; Executive Producer, *JFK: The Last Speech.* A '64

Jesse M. Brill, J.D. Publisher of *The Corporate Counsel* and *The Corporate Executive* newsletters, along with many other books and resources on securities law. A '64

Bestor Cram, Award-winning Independent Film Director/Producer/ Cinematographer; Founder and Creative Director of Northern Light Productions (NLP); Recent works: *Birth of a Movement* on public television, exhibits at National WWII Museum; President-elect, International Quorum of Motion Picture Producers.

Bradford R. Collins, Ph.D. Professor, School of Visual Art & Design, College of Arts and Sciences, University of South Carolina. Author of *Pop Art (Art and Ideas).* A '64

Patrick H. DeLeon, Ph.D., J.D., MPH. Distinguished Professor in Health Policy and Research, Uniformed Services University of the Health

Sciences. Formerly Chief of Staff for United States Senator Daniel Inouye. Past President of the American Psychological Association (APA). A '64

Paul R. Dimond, J.D. Former Special Assistant to the President of the United States for Economic Policy and Director of the National Economic Council. Author of *Beyond Busing* and *The Supreme Court and Judicial Choice*, as well as a historical novel, *The Belle of Two Arbors*. A '66

Stephen F. Downs, J.D. Senior Attorney, State of New York. Former Chief Attorney for the New York State Commission on Judicial Conduct. Former Executive Director, National Coalition to Protect Civil Freedoms. Peace Corps Volunteer in India 1964-66. A '64

Stephen J. Drotter, Jr., President, Drotter Human Resources, Inc. Former Senior Vice President of Corporate Human Resources at Chase Manhattan Corporation. Chairman and Co-Founder of the Leadership Pipeline Institute. Co-Author of *The Leadership Pipeline* and *The Succession Planning Handbook for the Chief Executive,* and author of *The Performance Pipeline.* A '64

Mickey Edwards, J.D. Vice President and Program Director, Rodel Fellowships in Public Leadership, The Aspen Institute. Former member of Congress, taught at the Kennedy School of Government, Harvard University and the Woodrow Wilson School of Public and International Affairs, Princeton University. Author of *Reclaiming Conservatism* and *The Parties Versus the People: How to Turn Republicans and Democrats into Americans.*

Dakota Foster, Marshall Scholar for 2018. Intern, Washington Institute for Near East Policy (2015), U.S. House of Representatives' Committee on Foreign Affairs (2016). A '18

James T. Giles, LL.B. Of Counsel, Blank Rome LLP. Former Chief Judge, United States District Court for the Eastern District of Pennsylvania, 1999 to 2005. Served on the Eastern District Court, 1979 to 2008. A '64

Thomas P. Jacobs, Jr., M.D. Professor, College of Physicians of Columbia University. Recipient of the Ewig Award for Excellence in Teaching and the Leonard Tow Award for Humanism in Medicine. Served as Medical Officer in charge of a Military Provincial Health Assistance Team in the Republic of Vietnam. A '64

Joseph P. Kennedy III, J.D. U.S. Representative from the 4th Congressional District, Massachusetts. Served in the Peace Corps: Puerto Plata, Dominican Republic, 2004 to 2006.

Robert A. Knox, Ph.D. Associate Director and Research Oceanographer Emeritus, University of California, San Diego, Scripps Institution of Oceanography. A '64

Donald P. Lombardi, MS. Founder and Chief Executive Officer of the Institute for Pediatric Innovation. Former Chief Intellectual Property Officer of Boston Children's Hospital; Adjunct Assistant Professor of Pediatrics, Tufts University School of Medicine. A '64

Douglas R. Lowy, M.D. Deputy Director of the National Cancer Institute. Awarded the 2011 Albert B. Sabin Gold Medal and the 2017 Lasker-DeBakey Clinical Medical Research Award. A '64

Biddy Martin, Ph.D. President of Amherst College and Scholar of German Studies. Former Chancellor of the University of Wisconsin-Madison and Provost at Cornell University. Member of the American Academy of Arts & Sciences.

Jon Meacham, Presidential Historian, Author of *The Soul of America: The Battle for Our Better Angels*. Visiting Professor of Political Science, Vanderbilt University. Pulitzer Prize for Biography/Autobiography 2009 for *American Lion: Andrew Jackson in the White House*. Former Executive Editor and Executive Vice President, Random House. Former Editor-in-Chief, *Newsweek*.

Mitchell R. Meisner, Ph.D., J.D. Real Estate Attorney at Honigman Miller Schwartz and Cohn LLP in Detroit. Former College Professor in Political/Social Science, International Relations, specialized in Chinese Politics. University of Chicago Woodrow Wilson Honorary Scholar and National Defense and Education Act Scholar. A '64

Roger M. Mills, Co-Editor and Author, M.D. Former Professor of Medicine, University of Florida. Former Vice President, Medical Affairs, Scios Inc. 2009 Simon Dack Award, American College of Cardiology. Author of *Nesiritide: The Rise and Fall of Scios* and *240 Beats per Minute, Life with an Unruly Heart*, with Bernard Witholt. A '64

Ted Nelson, Editor-at-Large, *East Village Magazine*, Flint, Michigan. CEO of Hollywood Awards, and Founder and former CEO of the Education for Involvement Corporation. Former Peace Corps Volunteer in Turkey and Staff Member, Washington, DC, 1964 to 1968. A '64

Steven Olikara, Founding President of the Millennial Action Project, a national, nonpartisan organization dedicated to activating millennial policymakers. Former Udall Scholar and Aspen Ideas Scholar.

Gene Palumbo, MA. Gene has worked as a freelance journalist in El Salvador since 1980. He covered the country's civil war (1980-1992). The local correspondent for the *New York Times*, he has also reported for National Public Radio, the BBC, the Canadian Broadcasting Company, *Commonwealth Magazine* and *Time Magazine*. A '64

Jay Parini, Ph.D. The D. E. Axinn Professor of English and Creative Writing at Middlebury College. Poet, Novelist, Frost Biographer, and a leader in the genre of biographical fiction. Guggenheim Fellowship (1993-1994). Winner of the Chicago Tribune-Heartland Award in 2000 for *Robert Frost: A Life.*

David L. Pearle, M.D. Cardiologist, Professor of Medicine/Director of Interventional Cardiology, University Hospital, Georgetown University. Medstar Heart & Vascular Institute. A '64

Robert Redford, Actor, Director, Producer, Environmentalist, and Philanthropist. Trustee, Natural Resources Defense Council. 2002 Academy Award for Lifetime Achievement. 2016 Presidential Medal of Freedom.

Peter J. Rubinstein, M.H.L, D.D. Director of Jewish Community and the Bronfman Center for Jewish Life, and Rabbi Emeritus of Central Synagogue, New York. Taught at Manhattanville College, Colgate University, San Jose State, and the Hebrew Union College-Jewish Institute of Religion (New York and Cincinnati). A '64

Mark J. Sandler, MBA, J.D. Former Senior Managing Director of Bear, Stearns & Co., Inc. Former Partner with Donaldson Lufkin & Jenrette. Served as Trustee of Amherst College and Northfield Mt. Hermon School. Emeritus Trustee, New Jersey SEEDS (Scholars, Educators, Excellence, Dedication, Success). A '64

Stephen E. Smith, J.D. Retired Minnesota Attorney; Former Chair and General Counsel, Enova Medical Technologies, Inc. Former General Counsel of Advanced Respiratory, Inc., Scanhealth, Inc., Exos Corporation, and Genii, Inc.; and breeder and trainer of Morgan horses. A '64

Richard E. (Rip) Sparks, Ph.D. Research Director, National Great Rivers Research and Education Center. Former Director of the Illinois Water Resources Center at the University of Illinois Urbana-Champaign. Peace Corps volunteer, Nigeria, 1964 to 1966. A '64

Paul C. Stern, Ph.D. Director, Standing Committee on the Human Dimensions of Global Climate Change, National Research Council, National Academy of Sciences. Co-Author of "The Struggle to Govern the Commons," published in *Science* in 2003, winner of the 2005 Sustainability Science Award from the Ecological Society of America. A '64

Joseph E. Stiglitz, Ph.D. University Professor, Columbia University. 2001 Nobel Memorial Prize in Economic Sciences. Former Senior Vice President and Chief Economist of the World Bank. Former Member and Chairman of the Council of Economic Advisers. A '64

Charles C. (Smokey) Stover III, MA. Former Treasurer/Senior Consultant, Innovative Development Expertise & Advisory Services; Principal Program Associate, Management Sciences for Health; CEO Northeast Psychiatric Associates; Former Public Health Commissioner, Commonwealth of Massachusetts, Peace Corps Volunteer, Niger, 1964 to 1966. A '64

David H. Stringer, MAT. Poet, Author, Ghostwriter, and Blogger. Former high school English teacher (thirty-two years) in Ann Arbor, Michigan. A '64

George R. Wanlass, MA. President, Sagwich Land and Livestock, Inc.; Art Curator for the Nora Eccles Harrison Art Museum at Utah State University. A '64

Chatland B. Whitmore, Jr., Former Marketing Manager at Norwich Eaton Pharmaceuticals. Former Manager at Proctor & Gamble Company. A '64

Jan Worth-Nelson, Co-Editor, MSW, MFA. Lecturer Emeritus, University of Michigan–Flint. Editor of *East Village Magazine*, Flint, Michigan.

Author of *Night Blind*, top ten finalist in literary fiction, *ForeWord Magazine* Book of the Year Awards, 2006. Former Peace Corps Volunteer, Kingdom of Tonga, 1976 to 1978.

Fareed R. Zakaria, Ph.D. Award-winning Journalist and Author. Contributing Editor for the Atlantic Media group. His books include*: From Wealth to Power: The Unusual Origins of America's World Role, The Future of Freedom, The Post-American World,* and *In Defense of a Liberal Education.*

Nicholas S. Zeppos, J.D. Chancellor of Vanderbilt University. Served from 2002 to 2008 as Vanderbilt's Chief Academic Officer, overseeing the university's undergraduate, graduate, and professional education programs as well as research efforts. Former Chair of the Scholars Committee on the Federal Judiciary. Former Chair of the Rules Advisory Committee of the U.S. Court of Appeals for the Sixth Circuit. Former President of the Southeastern Conference and Co-Chair of the United States Senate Task Force on Government Regulation of Higher Education.

ACKNOWLEDGMENTS

WHILE DISCUSSING "The Four Beliefs," Robert Frost said about every work of art, "You say as you go more than you even hoped you were going to be able to say, and come with surprise to an end that you foreknew only with some sort of emotion. You have believed the thing into existence."[1]

Many people joined together and believed the documentary, *JFK: The Last Speech* into existence and now many people have come together to believe this companion book into existence. Words of recognition and gratitude are in order.

Without the film, this volume would not exist. Northern Light Productions took hold of a many-pronged story and made a film of beauty and significance—especially the amazing visionary Bestor Cram, whose voice comes through in the afterword for this book; also Portland Helmich and Matthew Maclean, who became our sister and brother in telling our stories. The film editor Glenn Fukushima worked his magic behind the scenes as did many others of the NLP team to whom we extend thanks.

The supporters behind the film include Amherst College, under President Biddy Martin and Trustees Chair Cullen Murphy, whose belief and practical assistance made it come true. Also, key support came from the Arthur Vining Davis Foundations, under President Nancy Cable's leadership, and from the dozens of members of the Amherst Class of 1964 who believed with us enough to make it happen.

---

1   Robert Frost, "The Four Beliefs" in *The Collected Prose of Robert Frost*, edited by Mark Richardson, 2007, The Belknap Press of Harvard University Press.

The editors were joined by a loyal and hardworking core team of classmates in creating this book and participating in our weekly conference calls for the past year. They include Bob Benedetti, Ted Nelson, Stephen Smith, Richard (Rip) Sparks, and Charles (Smokey) Stover. Also lending support were Dick Joslin and Mark Sandler.

Our publisher, Mascot Books, is clearly a professional organization and has been a pleasure to work with from our first contact with Andy Symonds to our working relationships with Kristin Perry and Geoffrey Stone, as well as the behind the scenes support staff handling layout and editing. They have patiently accommodated our every request and provided valuable guidance.

Of course, the heart and soul of this book are the remarkable stories and scholarship contributed by our authors. A special thanks belongs to them: Joseph Kennedy III, Jay Parini, Nicholas Zeppos, Robert Redford, Jon Meacham, Mickey Edwards, Steven Olikara, Fareed Zakaria; Amherst administration and alumni—Cullen Murphy, Biddy Martin, Paul Dimond '66, and Dakota Foster '18; and our class of '64 classmates—Farzam Arbab, Robert Benedetti, Jesse Brill, Bradford Collins, Pat DeLeon, Steve Downs, Steve Drotter, James Giles, Thomas Jacobs, Robert Knox, Don Lombardi, Doug Lowy, Mitch Meisner, Roger Mills, Ted Nelson, Gene Palumbo, David Pearle, Peter Rubinstein, Mark Sandler, Steve Smith, Rip Sparks, Paul Stern, Joseph Stiglitz, Charles Stover, David Stringer, George Wanlass, and Chatland Whitmore.

Special additional thanks among this group to Rip Sparks for creating the annotated timeline—and in the process unearthing some new discoveries, and Robert Benedetti for developing the discussion questions.

Along the way many people have provided advice and assistance. Special mention is due to Paul Dimond, above and beyond his authorship contributions, Jon Hubert, Ray Suarez, and especially Judy Bicknell, who has been a full partner in this endeavor from the beginning.

In creating an anthology, making contacts with the writers is central to the task and kind assistance was provided by many, including District Director Nick Clemons in Joseph Kennedy's office; Julia Wilson in Steven Olikara's office; Attorney Barry Tyerman and his assistant Susan Johnson on behalf of

Robert Redford; Melanie Galvin in Fareed Zakaria's office; Vice Chancellor Steve Ertel; and Nikki Suzzanne Younger on behalf of Nick Zeppos; Sarah Thomas and Debarati Ghosh in Joseph Stiglitz's office; Susan Englehardt and Molly Whalen working with Biddy Martin; Mareen Johnson in Doug Lowy's office; and Chelsea Bassman in Rabbi Peter Rubinstein's office.

In assembling the photo credits and permissions, special assistance was provided by Peter Gilbert on behalf of the Robert Frost Estate; Julie Grahame on behalf of the estate of Yousuf Karsh; Jesus Chavez at the Associated Press; Shane Butler at Northern Light Production; and Roger Myers, Trent Purdy and Joseph Diaz at the University of Arizona Libraries Special Collections.

Finally an extra special thanks to our spouses—Judy, Katherine, and Ted—who supported our effort and put up with our fretting, obsession, and never-ending hope for perfection.

All of these people helped us believe this volume into existence and come to an end that we "foreknew only with some sort of emotion."

Neil Bicknell
Roger Mills
Jan Worth-Nelson